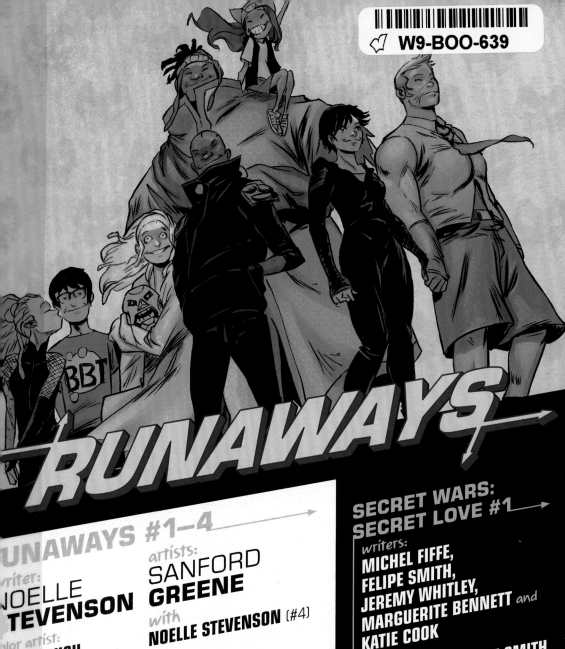

RUNAWAYS

RUNAWAYS #1–4

writer:
NOELLE STEVENSON

artists:
SANFORD GREENE
with
NOELLE STEVENSON (#4)

color artist:
JOHN RAUCH

letterer:
VC'S CLAYTON COWLES

cover art:
SANFORD GREENE & JOHN RAUCH

assistant editor: **JON MOISAN**
editor: **WIL MOSS**

SECRET WARS: SECRET LOVE #1

writers:
**MICHEL FIFFE,
FELIPE SMITH,
JEREMY WHITLEY,
MARGUERITE BENNETT** and
KATIE COOK

artists:
**MICHEL FIFFE, FELIPE SMITH
& VAL STAPLES, GURIHIRU,
KRIS ANKA** and **KATIE COOK**

cover art: **DAVID NAKAYAMA**
editor: **EMILY SHAW**
senior editor: **MARK PANICCIA**

collection editor: JENNIFER GRÜNWALD
assistant editor: SARAH BRUNSTAD
associate managing editor: ALEX STARBUCK
editor, special projects: MARK D. BEAZLEY
senior editor, special projects: JEFF YOUNGQUIST
vp, print, sales & marketing: DAVID GABRIEL
book designer: RODOLFO MURAGUCHI

editor in chief: AXEL ALONSO
chief creative officer: JOE QUESADA
publisher: DAN BUCKLEY
executive producer: ALAN FINE

RUNAWAYS: BATTLEWORLD. Contains material originally published in magazine form as RUNAWAYS #1-4 and SECRET WARS: SECRET LOVE #1. First printing 2015. ISBN# 978-0-7851-9882-6. Published by MARVEL WORLDWIDE, INC., a subsidiary of MARVEL ENTERTAINMENT, LLC. OFFICE OF PUBLICATION: 135 West 50th Street, New York, NY 10020. Copyright © 2015 MARVEL No similarity between any of the names, characters, persons, and/or institutions in this magazine with those of any living or dead person or institution is intended, and any such similarity which may exist is purely coincidental. Printed in Canada. ALAN FINE, President, Marvel Entertainment, Publishing; DAN BUCKLEY, President, TV, Publishing and Brand Management; JOE QUESADA, Chief Creative Officer; TOM BREVOORT, SVP of Publishing; DAVID BOGART, SVP of Operations & Procurement, Publishing; C.B. CEBULSKI, VP of International Development & Brand Management; DAVID GABRIEL, SVP Print, Sales & Marketing; JIM O'KEEFE, VP of Operations & Logistics; DAN CARR, Executive Director of Publishing Technology; SUSAN CRESPI, Editorial Operations Manager; ALEX MORALES, Publishing Operations Manager; STAN LEE, Chairman Emeritus. For information regarding advertising in Marvel Comics or on Marvel.com, please contact Jonathan Rheingold, VP of Custom Solutions & Ad Sales, at jrheingold@marvel.com. For Marvel subscription inquiries, please call 800-217-9158. Manufactured between 10/16/2015 and 11/23/2015 by SOLISCO PRINTERS, SCOTT, QC, CANADA.

10 9 8 7 6 5 4 3 2 1

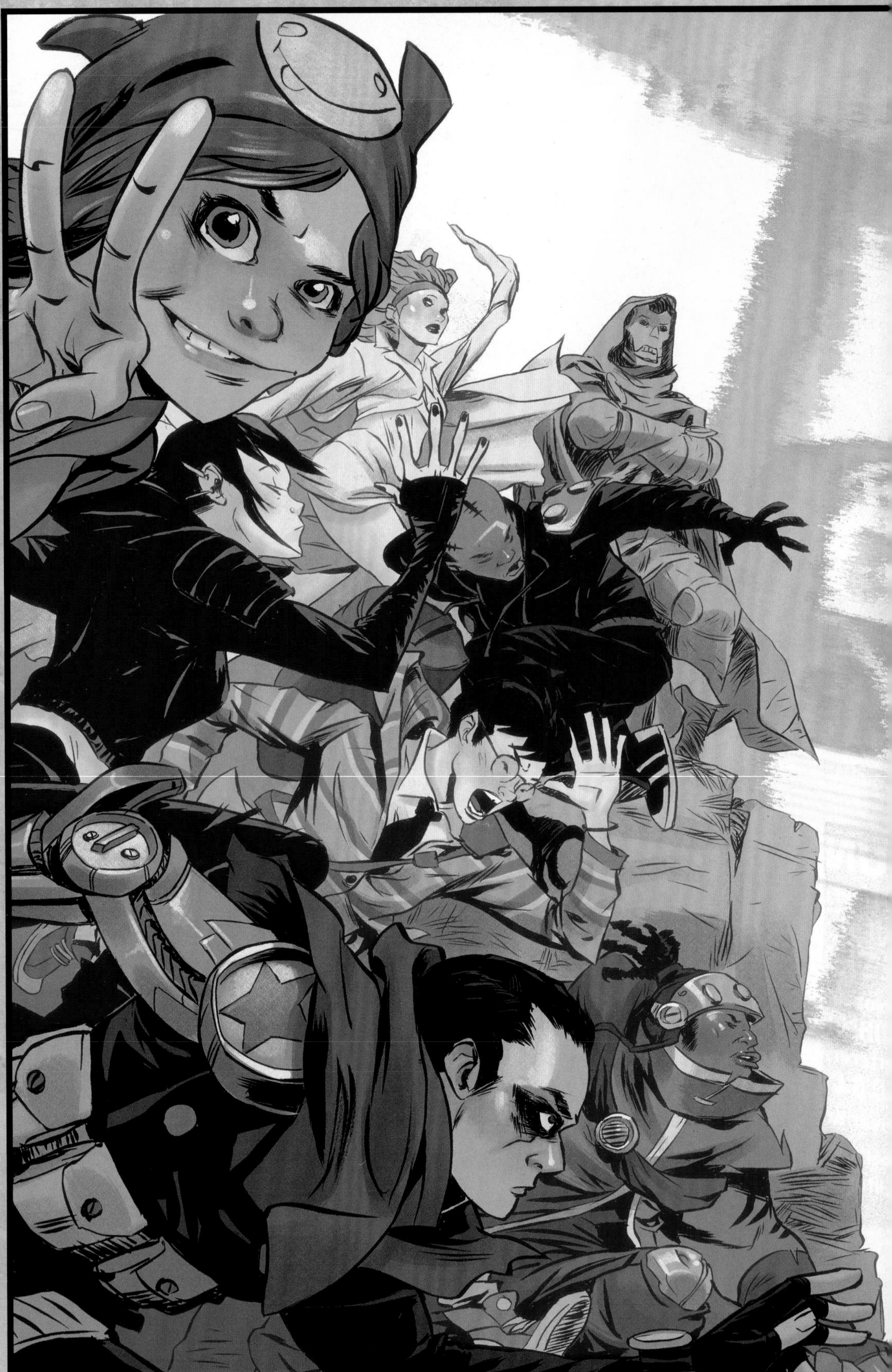

#1

SECRET WARS

THE MULTIVERSE WAS DESTROYED!

•

THE HEROES OF EARTH-616 AND EARTH-1610 WERE POWERLESS TO SAVE IT!

•

NOW, ALL THAT REMAINS...IS **BATTLEWORLD:**

A MASSIVE, PATCHWORK PLANET COMPOSED OF THE FRAGMENTS OF WORLDS THAT NO LONGER EXIST, MAINTAINED BY THE IRON WILL OF ITS GOD AND MASTER, VICTOR VON DOOM!

•

EACH REGION IS A DOMAIN UNTO ITSELF!

RUNAWAYS

◆ DOOMED YOUTH ◆

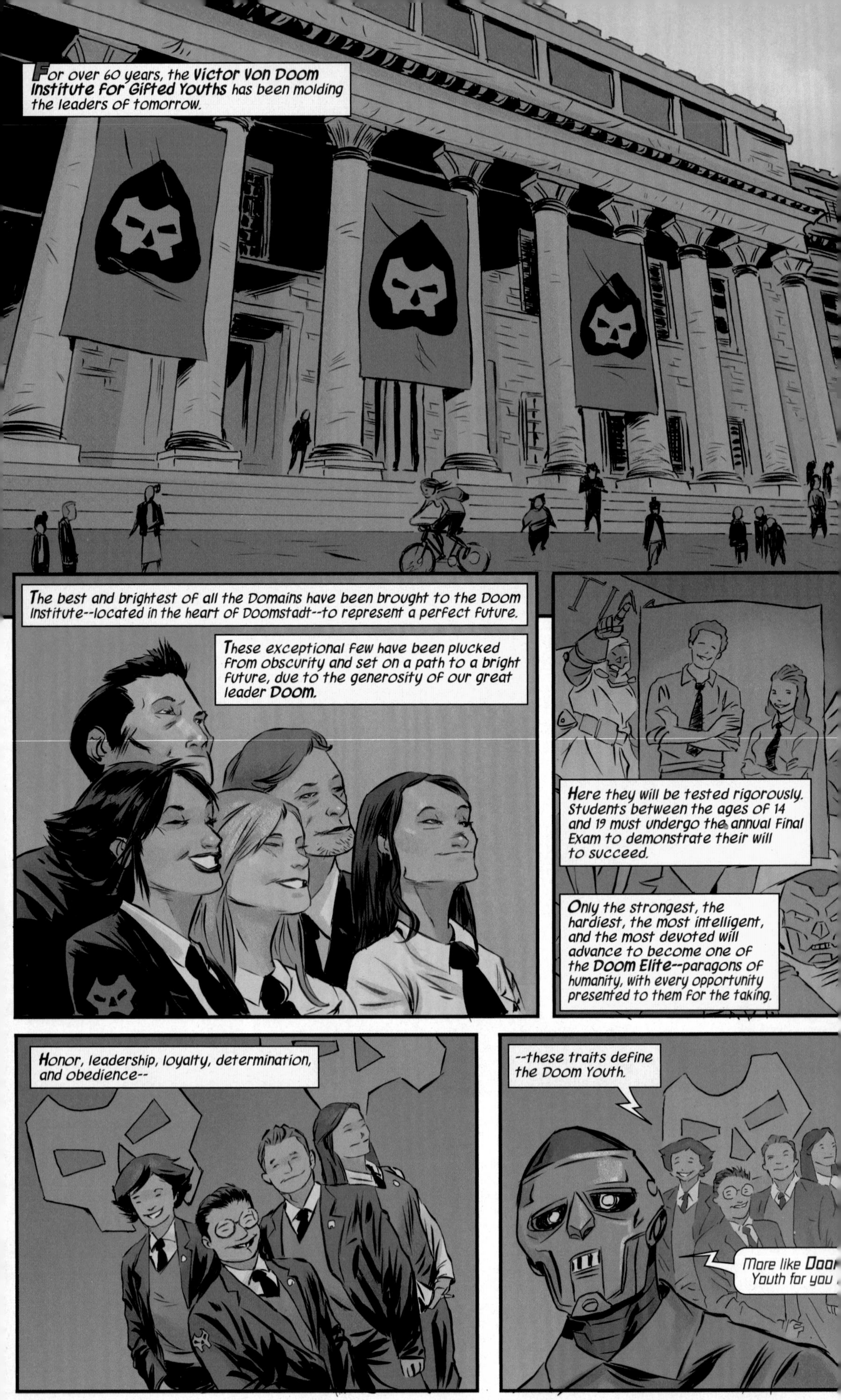
For over 60 years, the Victor Von Doom Institute for Gifted Youths has been molding the leaders of tomorrow.
The best and brightest of all the Domains have been brought to the Doom Institute--located in the heart of Doomstadt--to represent a perfect future.
These exceptional few have been plucked from obscurity and set on a path to a bright future, due to the generosity of our great leader DOOM.
Here they will be tested rigorously. Students between the ages of 14 and 19 must undergo the annual Final Exam to demonstrate their will to succeed.
Only the strongest, the hardiest, the most intelligent, and the most devoted will advance to become one of the Doom Elite--paragons of humanity, with every opportunity presented to them for the taking.
Honor, leadership, loyalty, determination, and obedience--
--these traits define the Doom Youth.
More like Doo
Youth for you

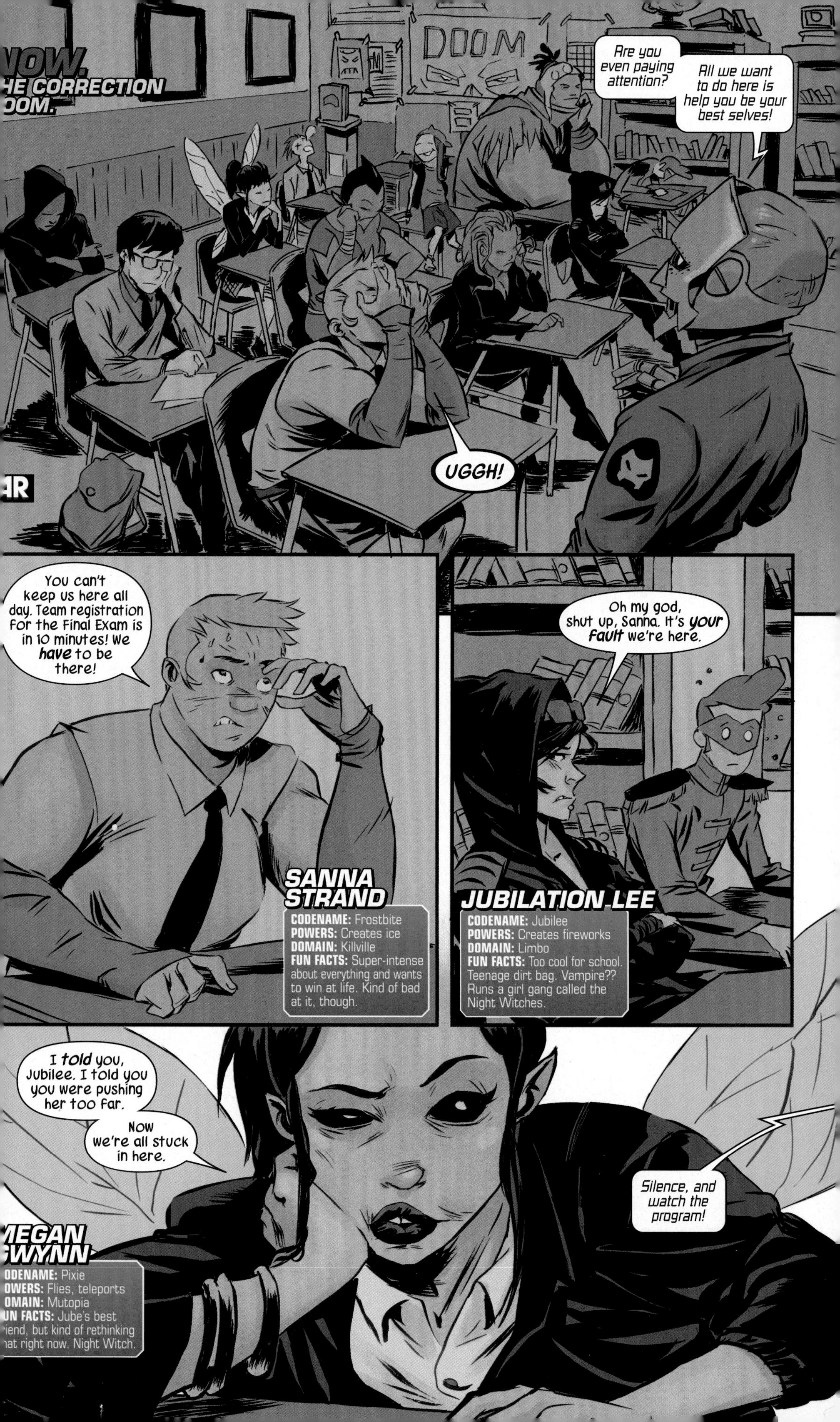
NOW.
HE CORRECTION
OOM.
DOOM
Are you even paying attention?
All we want to do here is help you be your best selves!
UGGH!
You can't keep us here all day. Team registration for the Final Exam is in 10 minutes! We *have* to be there!
SANNA STRAND
CODENAME: Frostbite
POWERS: Creates ice
DOMAIN: Killville
FUN FACTS: Super-intense about everything and wants to win at life. Kind of bad at it, though.
Oh my god, shut up, Sanna. It's *your fault* we're here.
JUBILATION LEE
CODENAME: Jubilee
POWERS: Creates fireworks
DOMAIN: Limbo
FUN FACTS: Too cool for school. Teenage dirt bag. Vampire?? Runs a girl gang called the Night Witches.
I *told* you, Jubilee. I told you you were pushing her too far.
Now we're all stuck in here.
Silence, and watch the program!
MEGAN
WYNN
ODENAME: Pixie
OWERS: Flies, teleports
OMAIN: Mutopia
UN FACTS: Jube's best
iend, but kind of rethinking
hat right now. Night Witch.

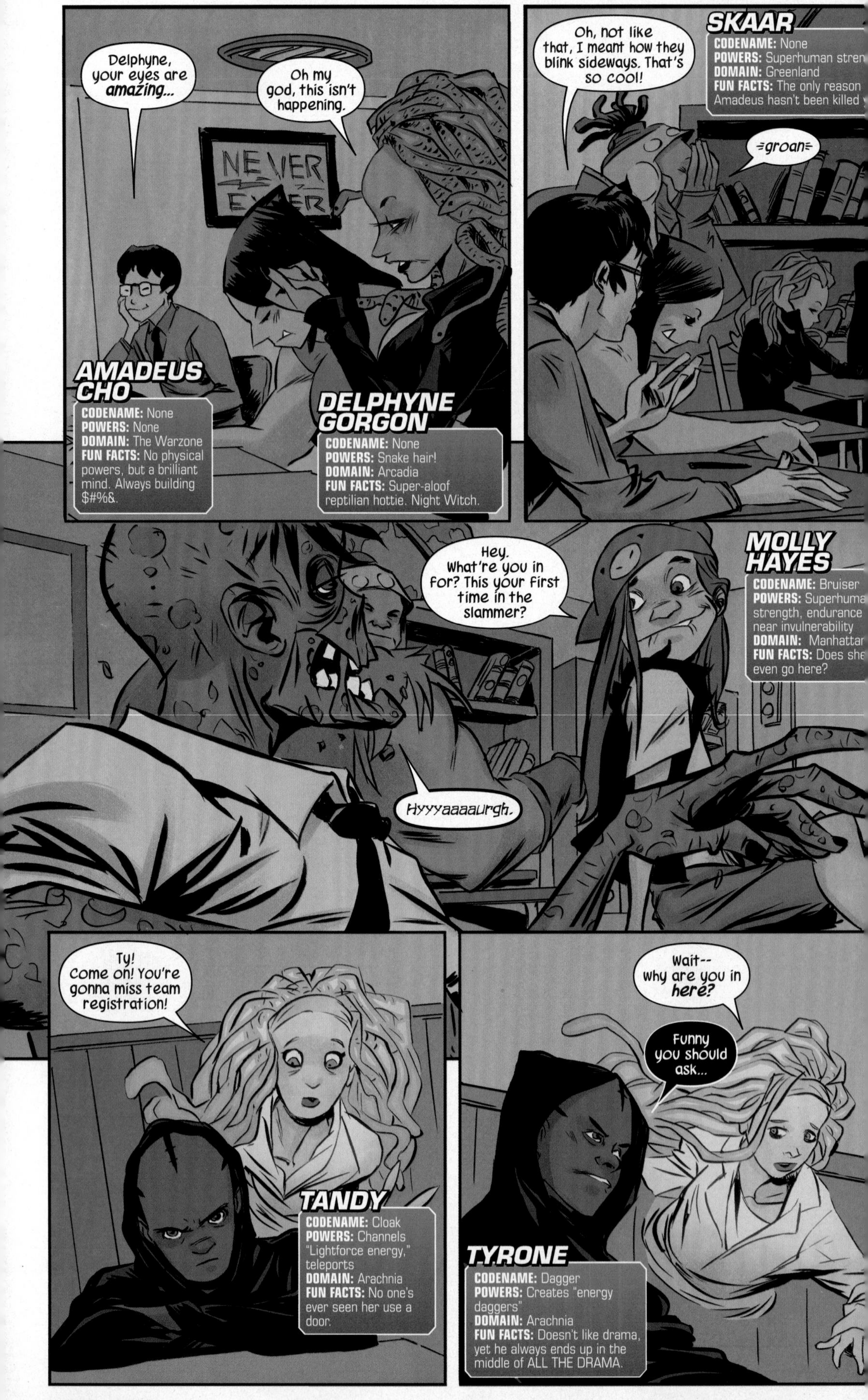

Delphyne, your eyes are *amazing...*
Oh my god, this isn't happening.
NEVER EVER
AMADEUS CHO
CODENAME: None
POWERS: None
DOMAIN: The Warzone
FUN FACTS: No physical powers, but a brilliant mind. Always building $#%&.
DELPHYNE GORGON
CODENAME: None
POWERS: Snake hair!
DOMAIN: Arcadia
FUN FACTS: Super-aloof reptilian hottie. Night Witch.
Oh, not like that, I meant how they blink sideways. That's so cool!
SKAAR
CODENAME: None
POWERS: Superhuman stren
DOMAIN: Greenland
FUN FACTS: The only reason Amadeus hasn't been killed
=groan=
Hey. What're you in for? This your first time in the slammer?
MOLLY HAYES
CODENAME: Bruiser
POWERS: Superhuma strength, endurance near invulnerability
DOMAIN: Manhattar
FUN FACTS: Does she even go here?
Hyyyaaaaurgh.
Ty! Come on! You're gonna miss team registration!
TANDY
CODENAME: Cloak
POWERS: Channels "Lightforce energy," teleports
DOMAIN: Arachnia
FUN FACTS: No one's ever seen her use a door.
Wait-- why are you in *here?*
Funny you should ask...
TYRONE
CODENAME: Dagger
POWERS: Creates "energy daggers"
DOMAIN: Arachnia
FUN FACTS: Doesn't like drama, yet he always ends up in the middle of ALL THE DRAMA.

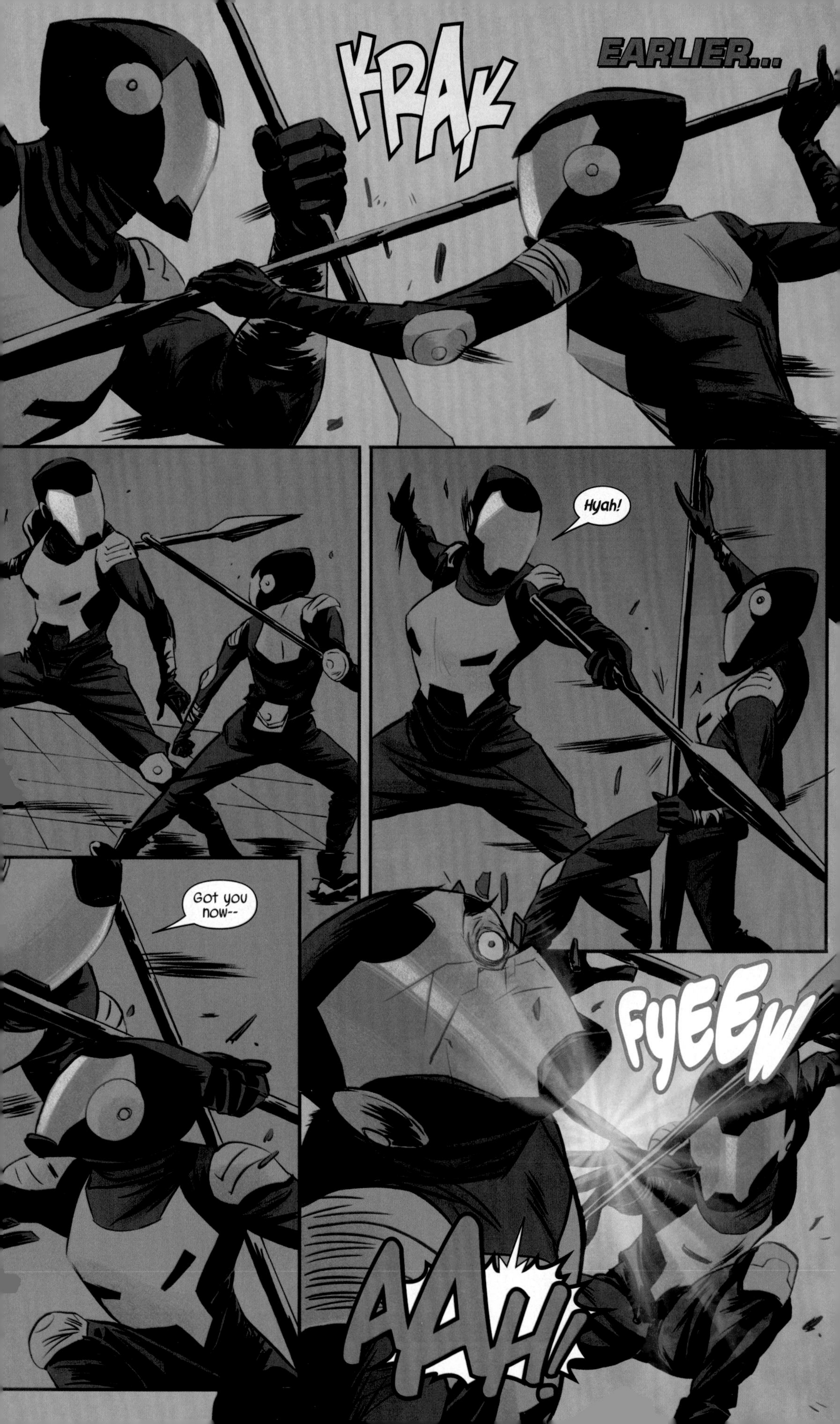
EARLIER...
KRAK
Hyah!
Got you now--
FYEEW
AAH!!

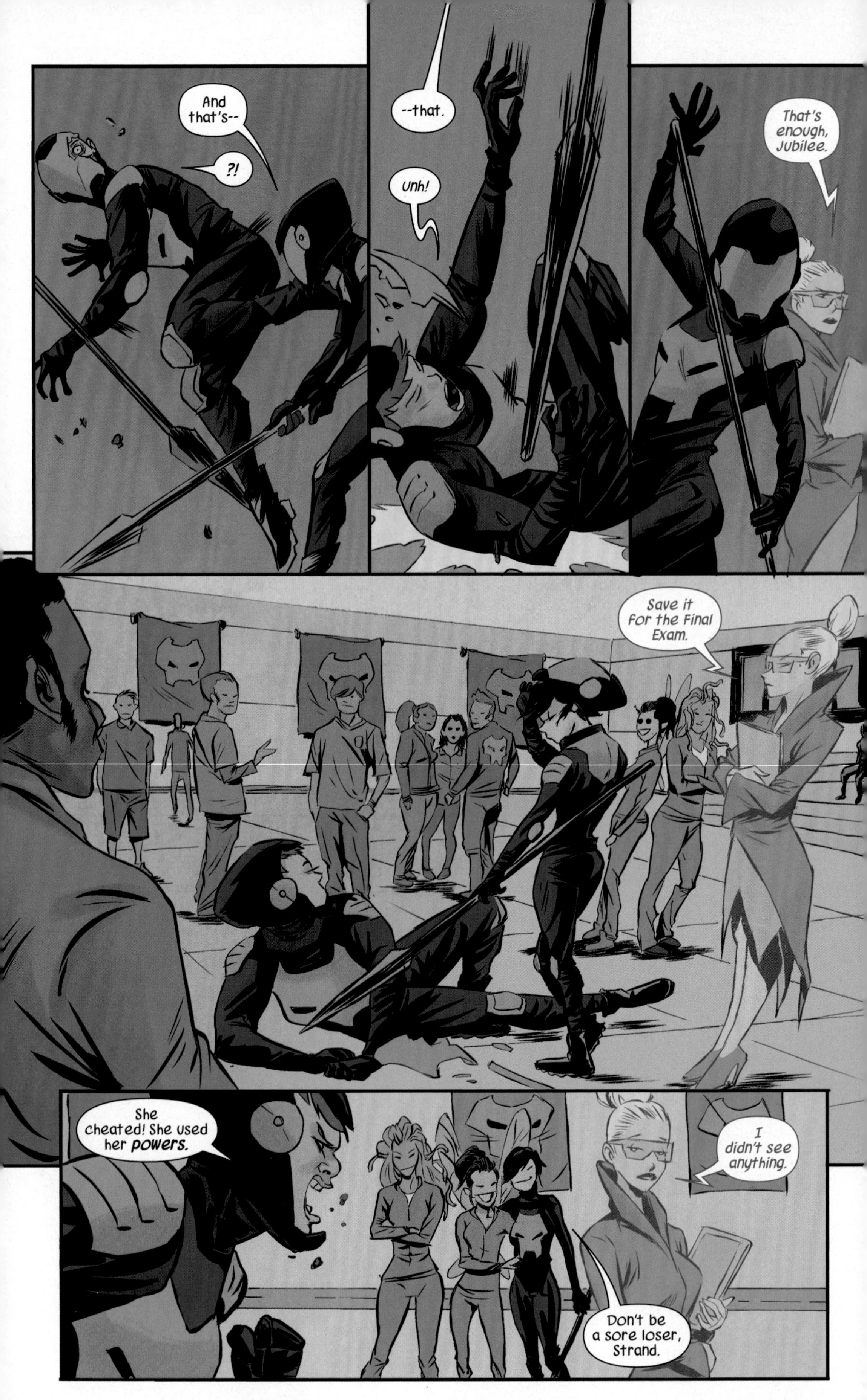

And that's--
?!
--that.
Unh!
That's enough, Jubilee.
Save it for the Final Exam.
She cheated! She used her *powers.*
I didn't see anything.
Don't be a sore loser, Strand.

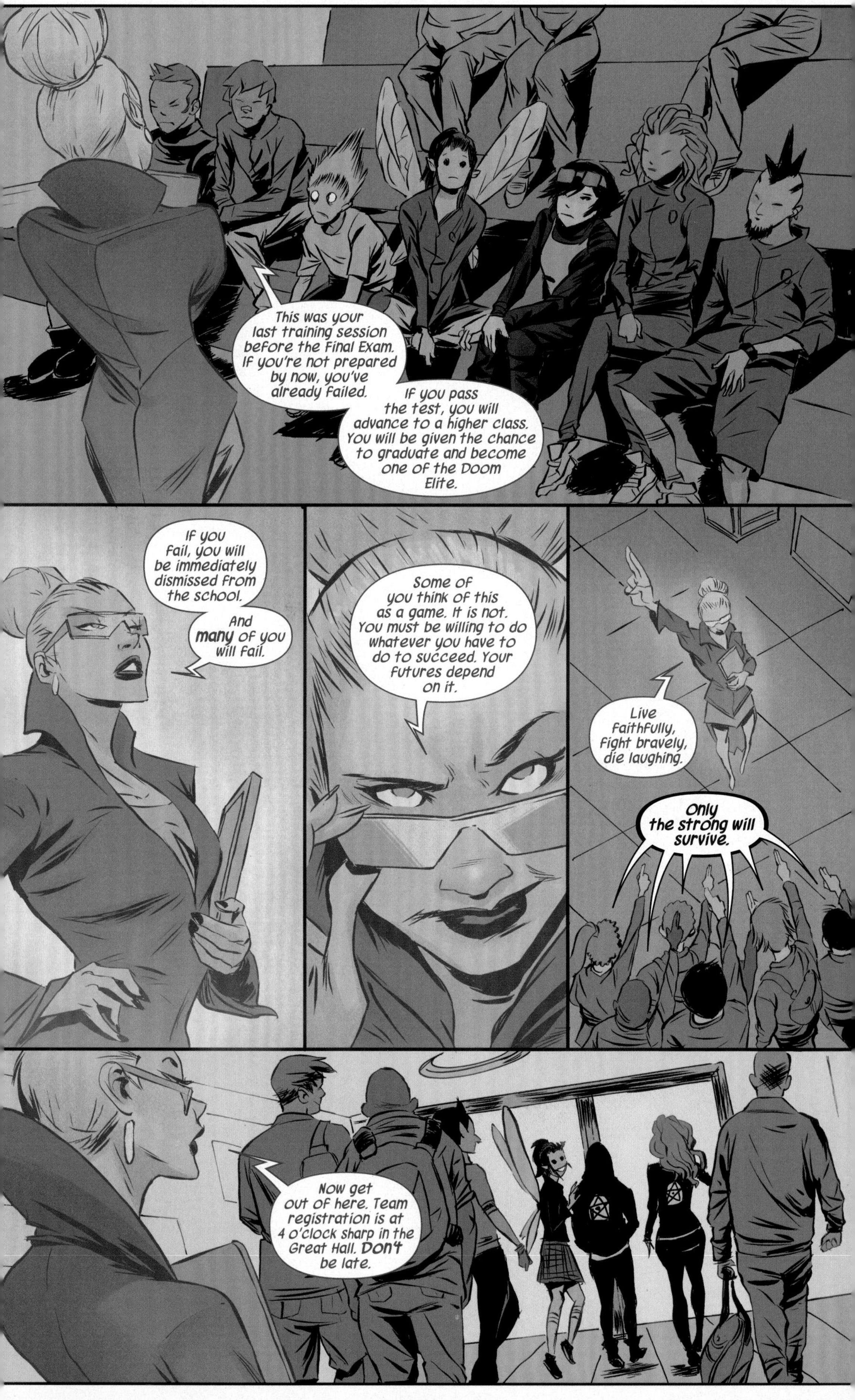
This was your last training session before the Final Exam. If you're not prepared by now, you've already failed.
If you pass the test, you will advance to a higher class. You will be given the chance to graduate and become one of the Doom Elite.
If you fail, you will be immediately dismissed from the school.
And **many** of you will fail.
Some of you think of this as a game. It is not. You must be willing to do whatever you have to do to succeed. Your futures depend on it.
Live faithfully, fight bravely, die laughing.
Only the strong will survive.
Now get out of here. Team registration is at 4 o'clock sharp in the Great Hall. **Don't** be late.

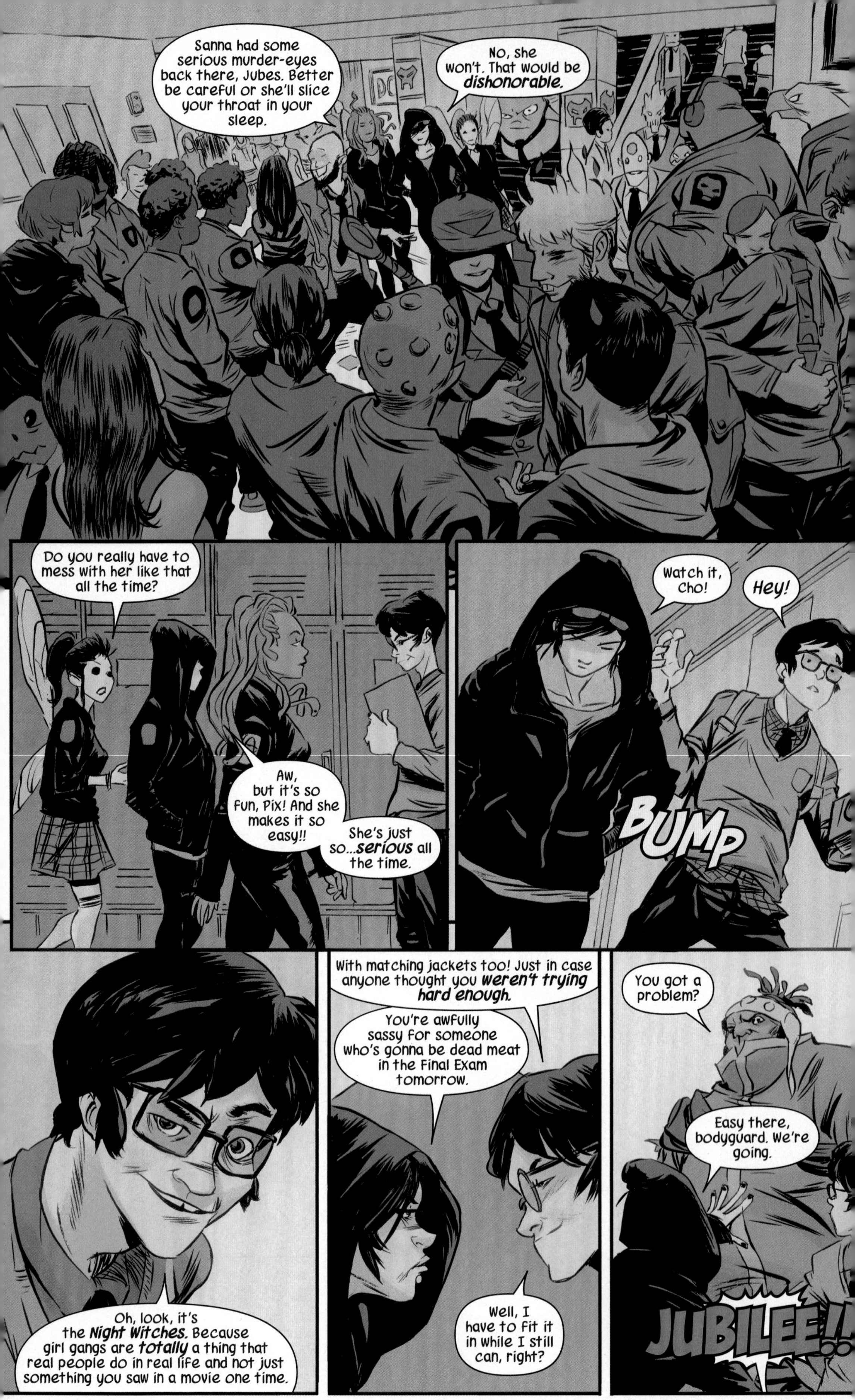
Sanna had some serious murder-eyes back there, Jubes. Better be careful or she'll slice your throat in your sleep.
No, she won't. That would be *dishonorable.*
Do you really have to mess with her like that all the time?
Aw, but it's so fun, Pix! And she makes it so easy!!
She's just so...*serious* all the time.
Watch it, Cho!
Hey!
BUMP
Oh, look, it's the *Night Witches.* Because girl gangs are *totally* a thing that real people do in real life and not just something you saw in a movie one time.
With matching jackets too! Just in case anyone thought you *weren't trying hard enough.*
You're awfully sassy for someone who's gonna be dead meat in the Final Exam tomorrow.
Well, I have to fit it in while I still can, right?
You got a problem?
Easy there, bodyguard. We're going.
JUBILEE!!

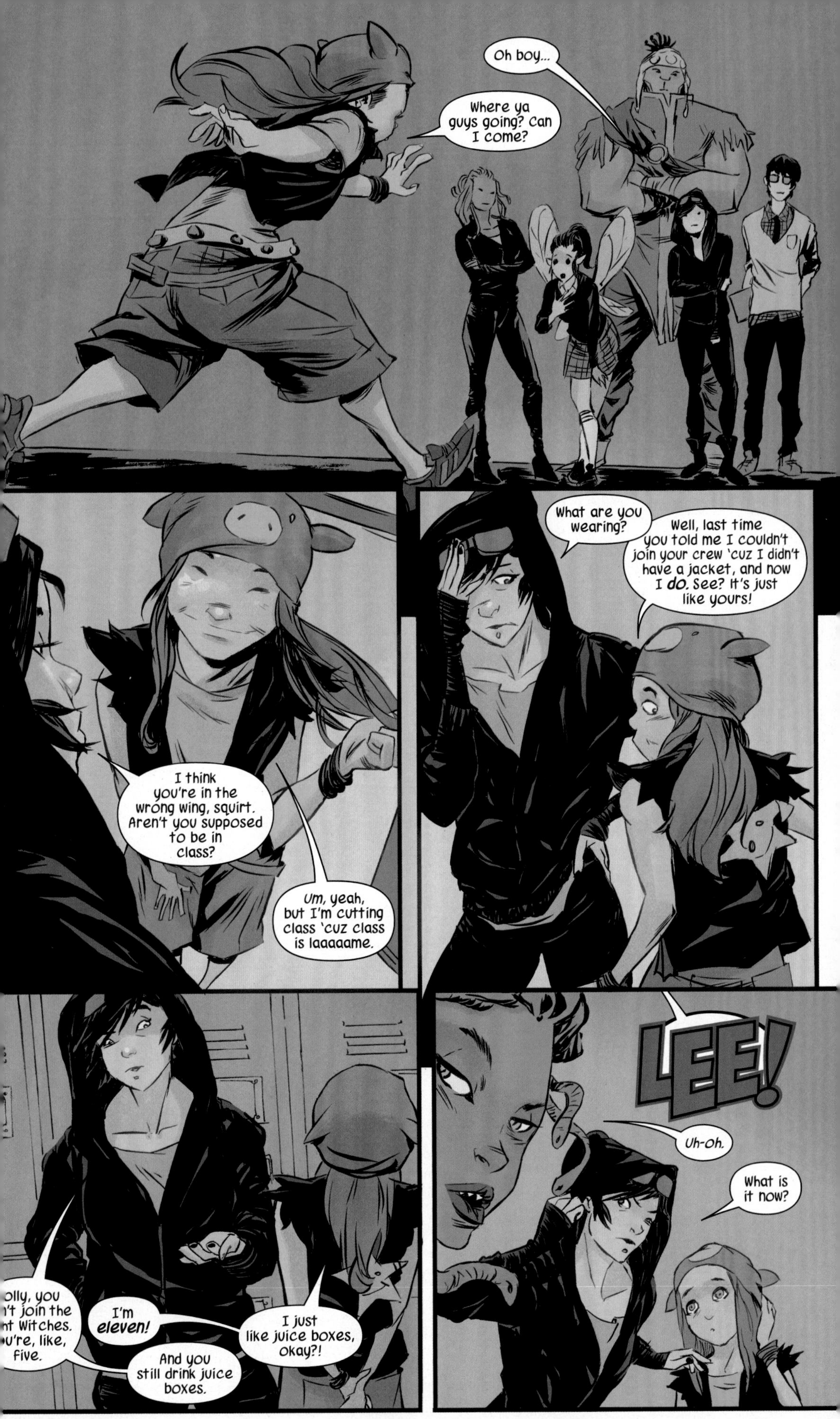
Oh boy...
Where ya guys going? Can I come?
What are you wearing?
Well, last time you told me I couldn't join your crew 'cuz I didn't have a jacket, and now I *do.* See? It's just like yours!
I think you're in the wrong wing, squirt. Aren't you supposed to be in class?
Um, yeah, but I'm cutting class 'cuz class is laaaaame.
I'm *eleven!*
And you still drink juice boxes.
I just like juice boxes, okay?!
LEE!
Uh-oh.
What is it now?

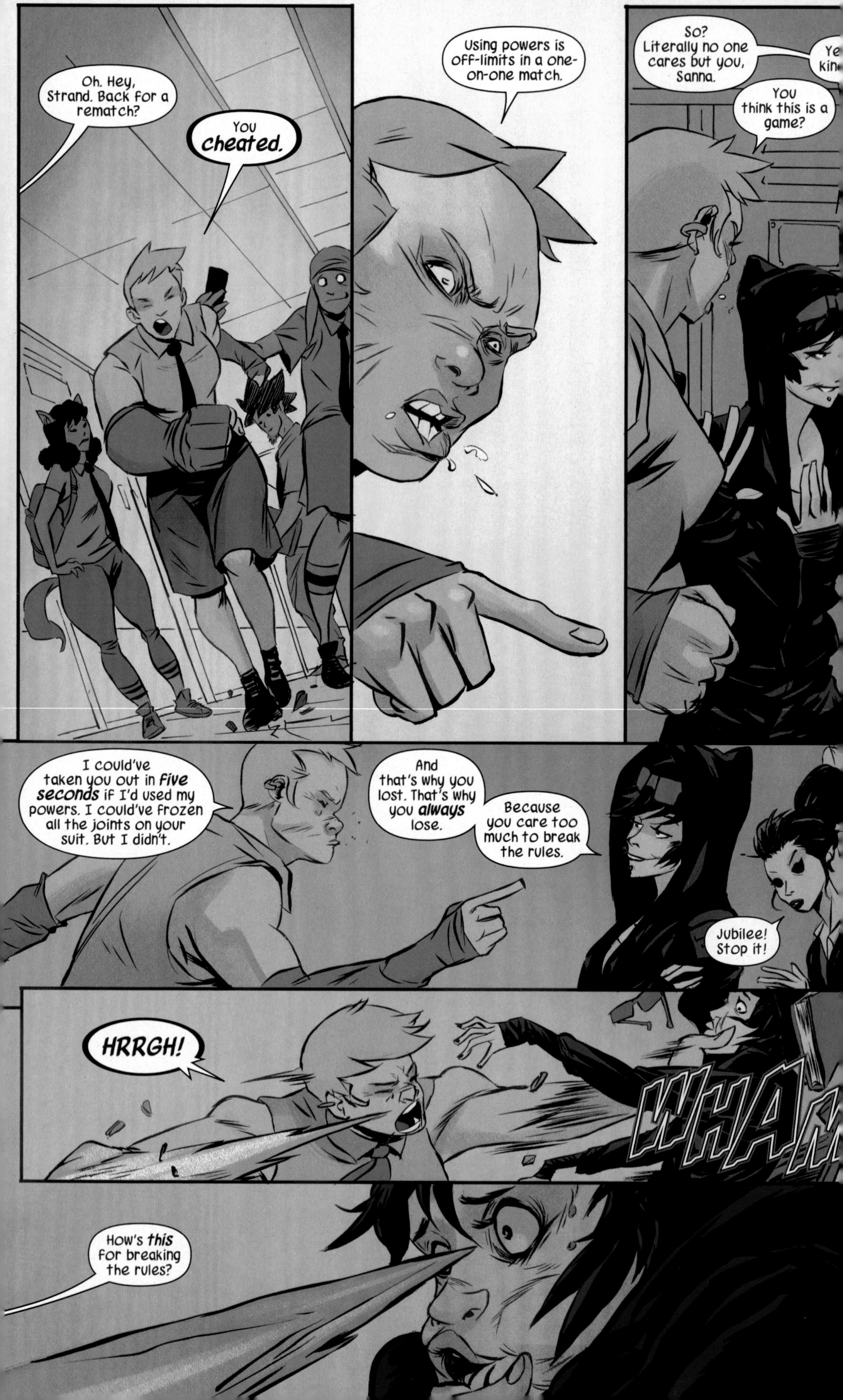
Oh. Hey, Strand. Back for a rematch?
You cheated.
Using powers is off-limits in a one-on-one match.
So? Literally no one cares but you, Sanna.
You think this is a game?
I could've taken you out in five seconds if I'd used my powers. I could've frozen all the joints on your suit. But I didn't.
And that's why you lost. That's why you always lose.
Because you care too much to break the rules.
Jubilee! Stop it!
HRRGH!
How's this for breaking the rules?

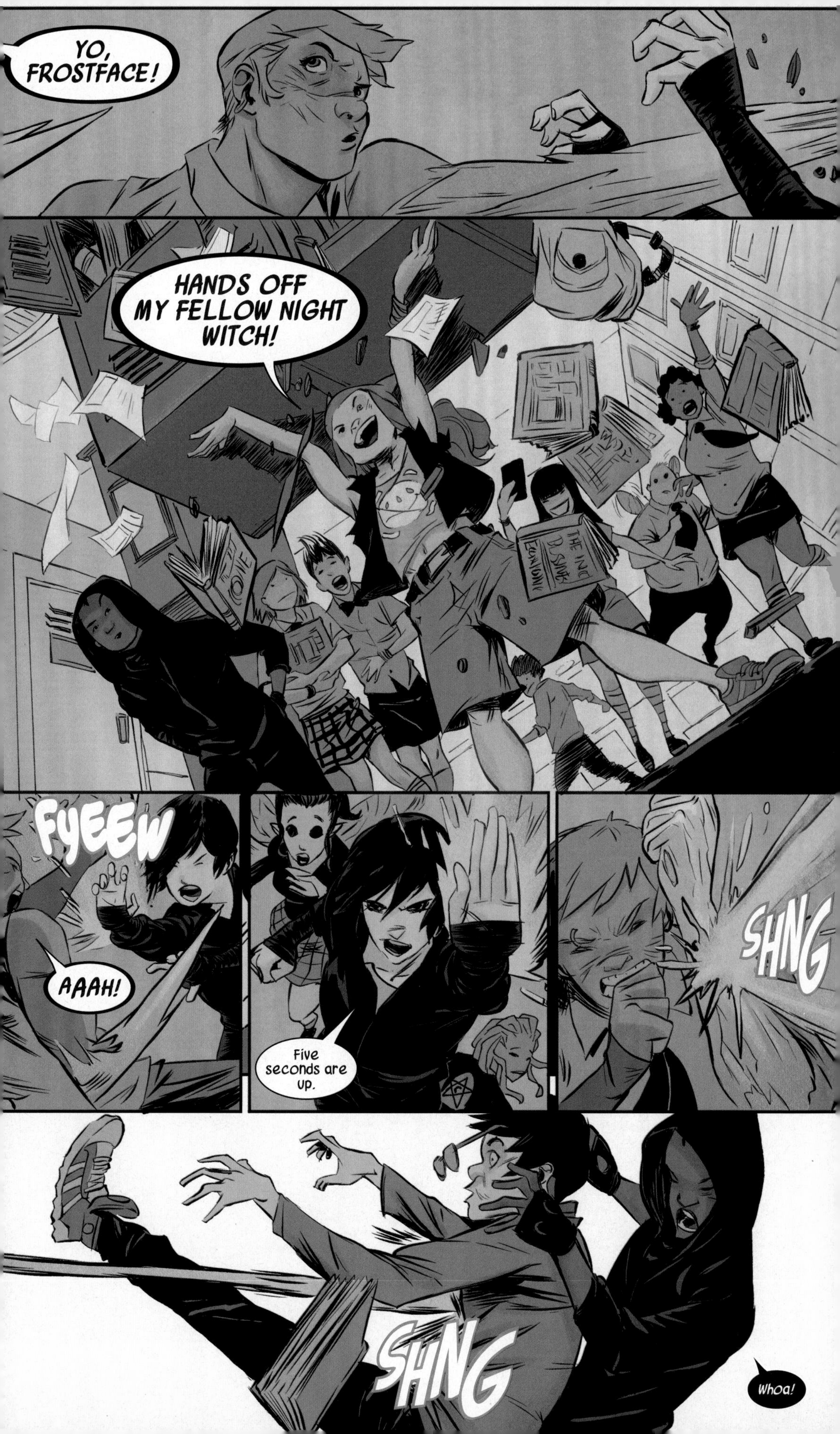
YO, FROSTFACE!
HANDS OFF MY FELLOW NIGHT WITCH!
FYEEW
AAAH!
Five seconds are up.
SHNG
SHNG
Whoa!

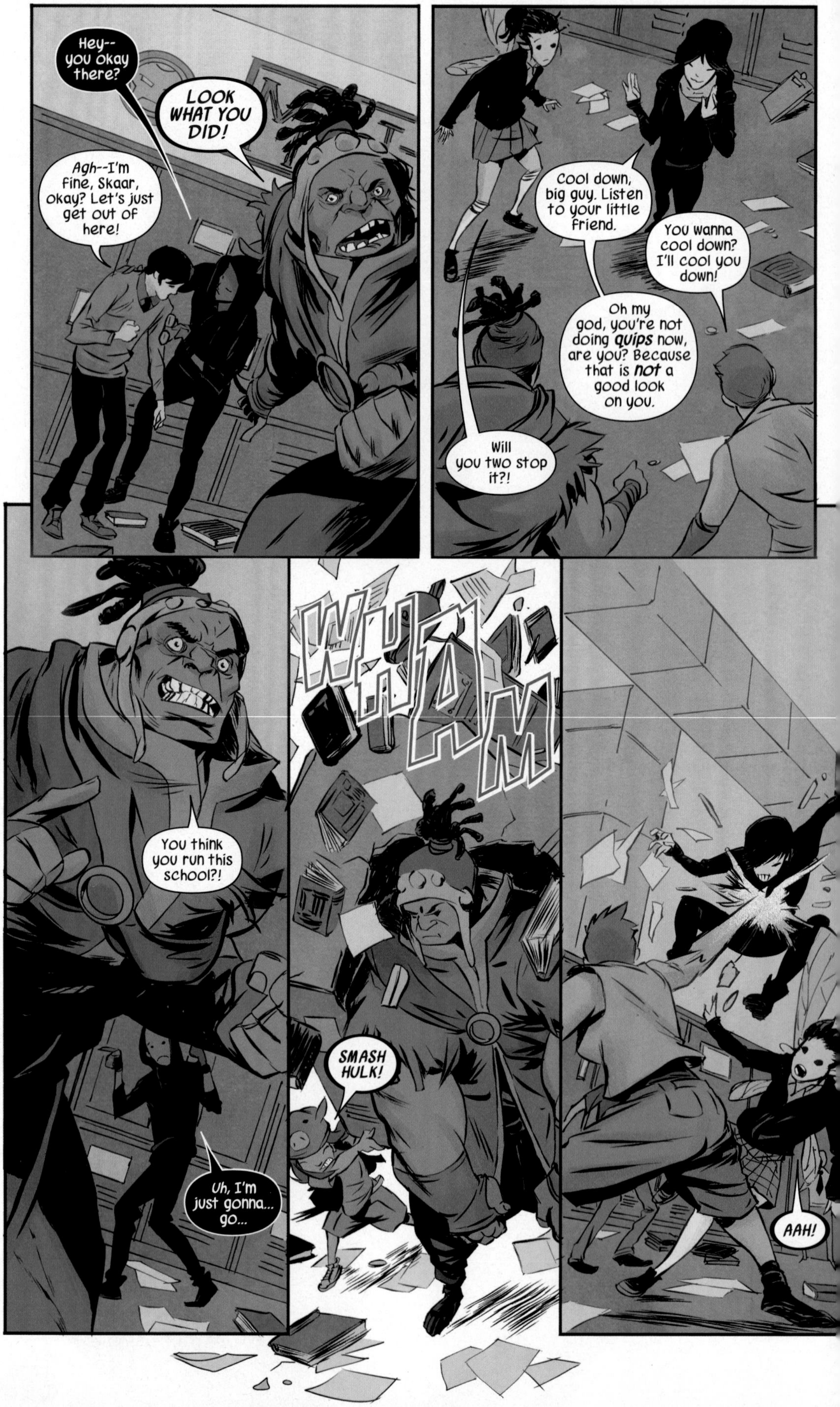
Hey-- you okay there?
LOOK WHAT YOU DID!
Agh--I'm fine, Skaar, okay? Let's just get out of here!
Cool down, big guy. Listen to your little friend.
You wanna cool down? I'll cool you down!
Oh my god, you're not doing quips now, are you? Because that is not a good look on you.
Will you two stop it?!
You think you run this school?!
Uh, I'm just gonna... go...
WHAM
SMASH HULK!
AAH!

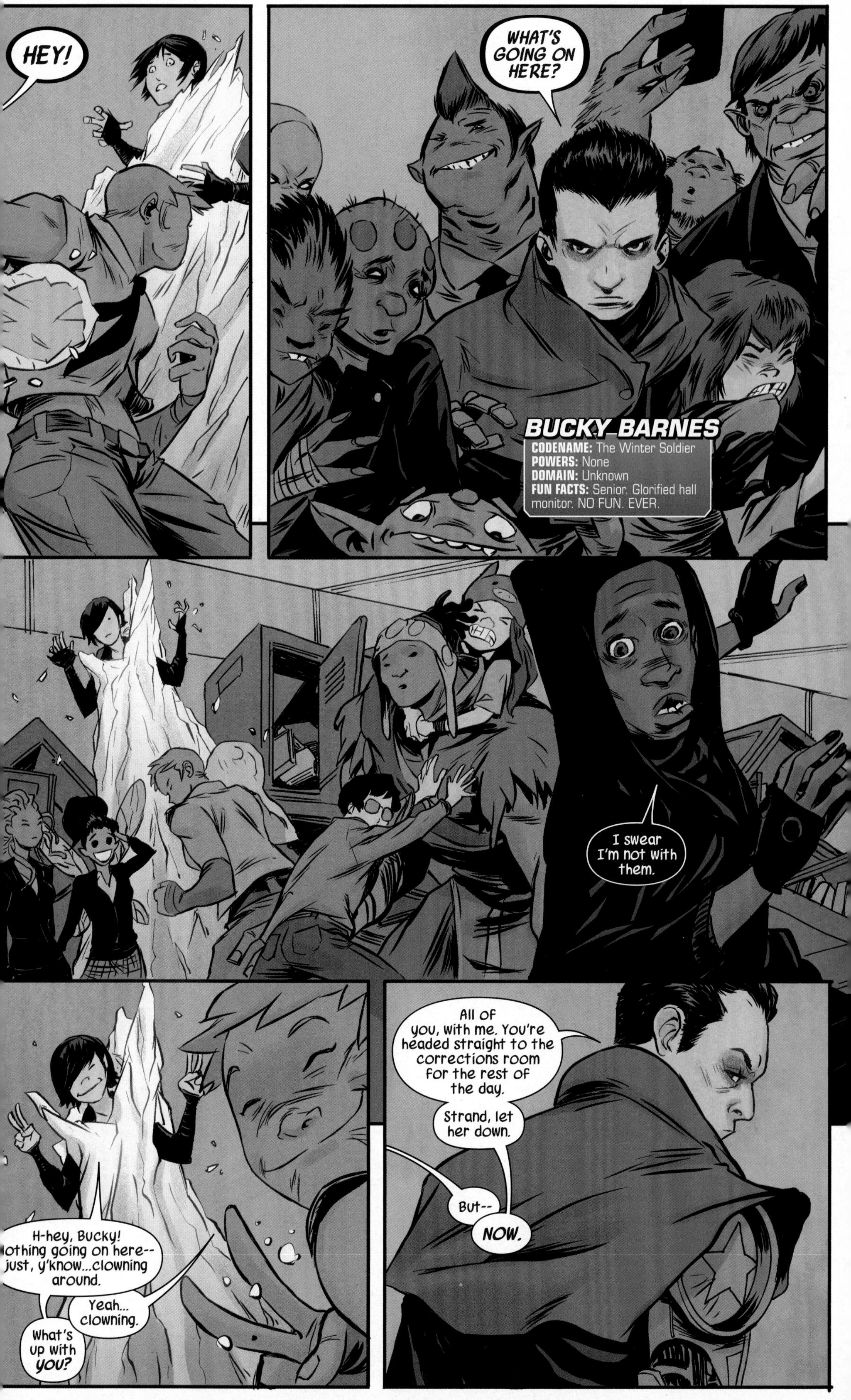
HEY!
WHAT'S GOING ON HERE?
BUCKY BARNES
CODENAME: The Winter Soldier
POWERS: None
DOMAIN: Unknown
FUN FACTS: Senior. Glorified hall monitor. NO FUN. EVER.
I swear I'm not with them.
H-hey, Bucky! othing going on here--just, y'know...clowning around.
Yeah... clowning.
What's up with you?
All of you, with me. You're headed straight to the corrections room for the rest of the day.
Strand, let her down.
But--
NOW.

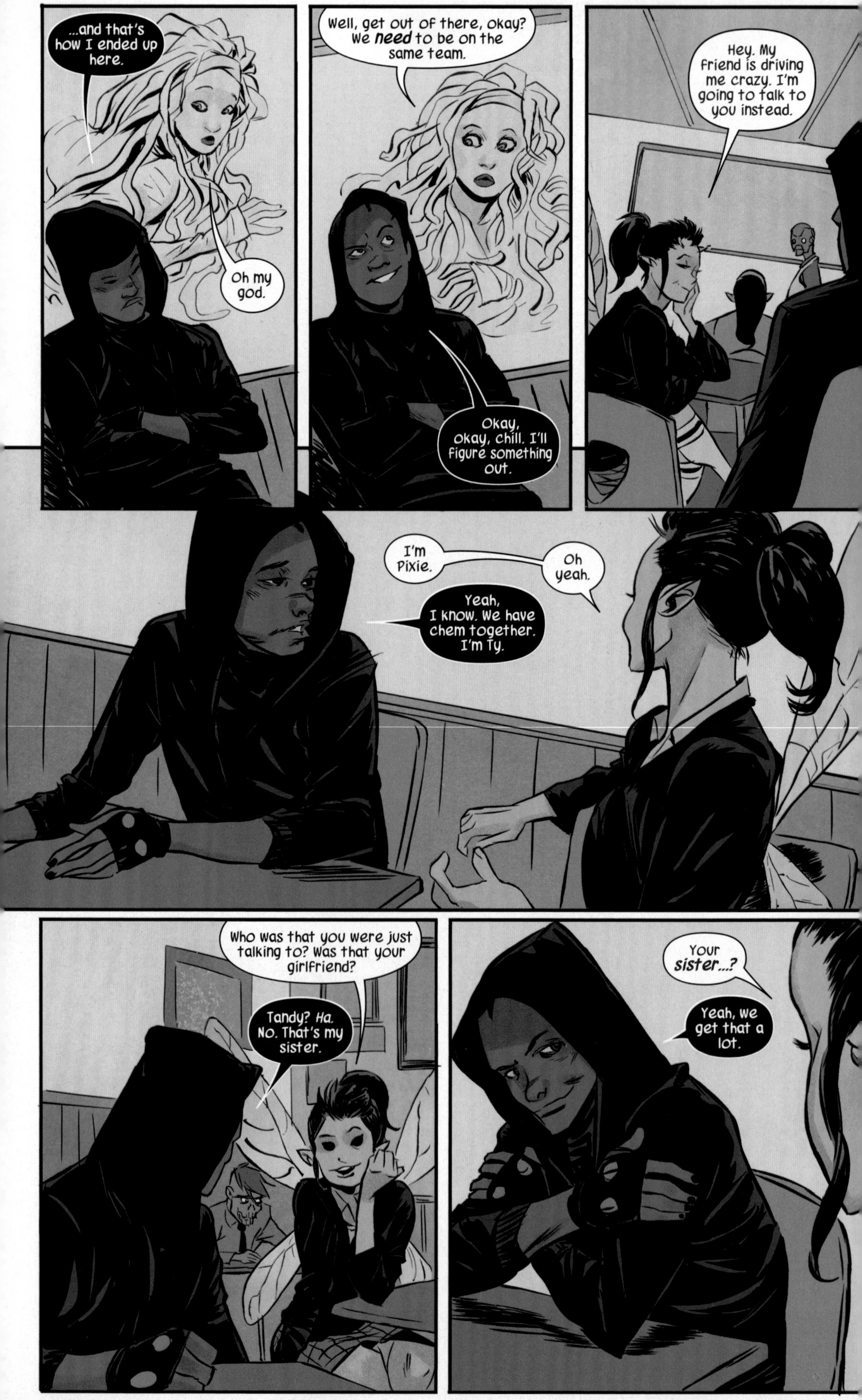
...and that's how I ended up here.
Oh my god.
Well, get out of there, okay? We *need* to be on the same team.
Okay, okay, chill. I'll figure something out.
Hey. My friend is driving me crazy. I'm going to talk to you instead.
I'm Pixie.
Oh yeah.
Yeah, I know. We have chem together. I'm Ty.
Who was that you were just talking to? Was that your girlfriend?
Tandy? *Ha.* No. That's my sister.
Your *sister...?*
Yeah, we get that a lot.

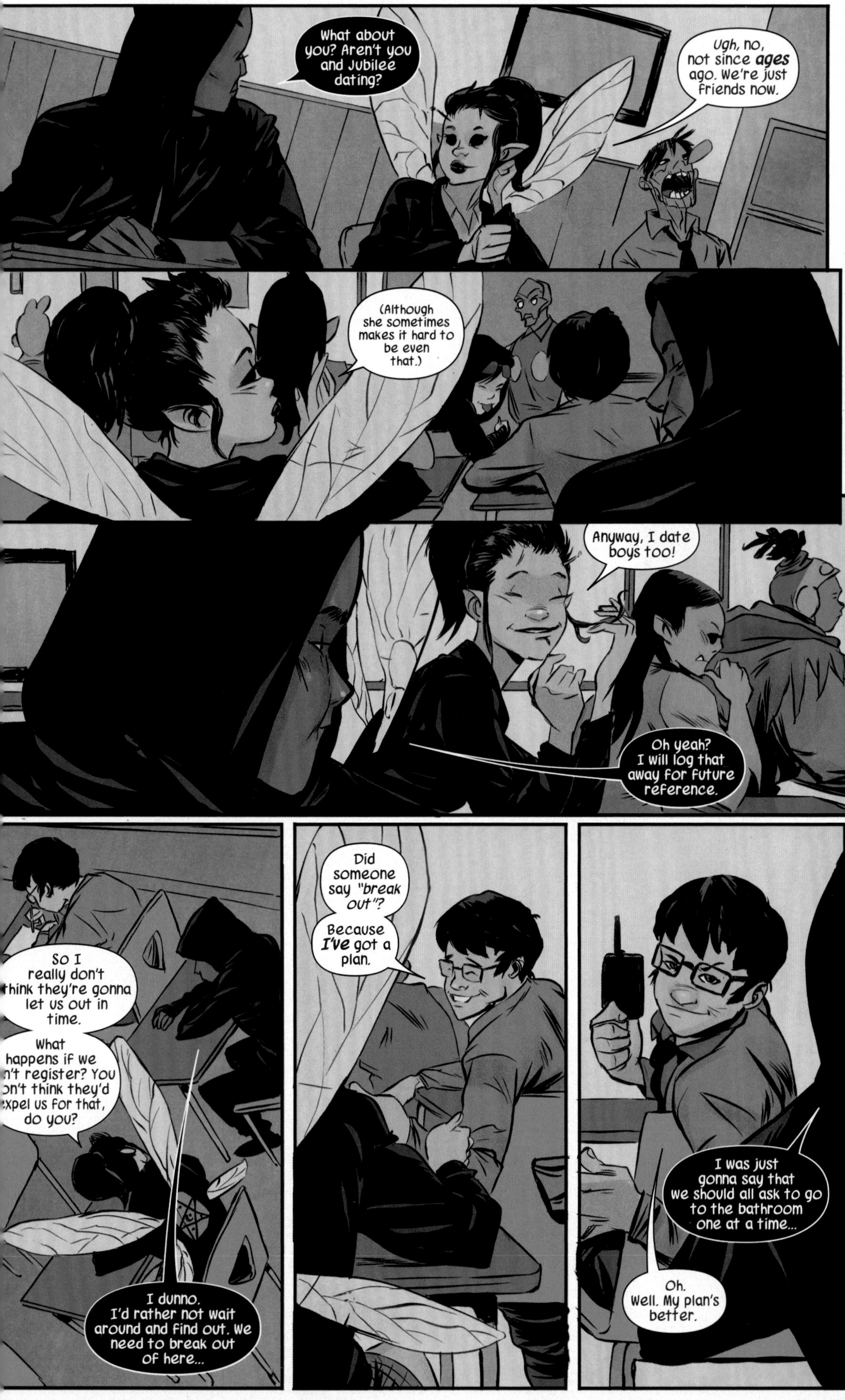
What about you? Aren't you and Jubilee dating?
Ugh, no, not since **ages** ago. We're just friends now.
(Although she sometimes makes it hard to be even that.)
Anyway, I date boys too!
Oh yeah? I will log that away for future reference.
So I really don't think they're gonna let us out in time.
What happens if we n't register? You on't think they'd xpel us for that, do you?
I dunno. I'd rather not wait around and find out. We need to break out of here...
Did someone say "*break out*"?
Because ***I've*** got a plan.
I was just gonna say that we should all ask to go to the bathroom one at a time...
Oh. Well. My plan's better.

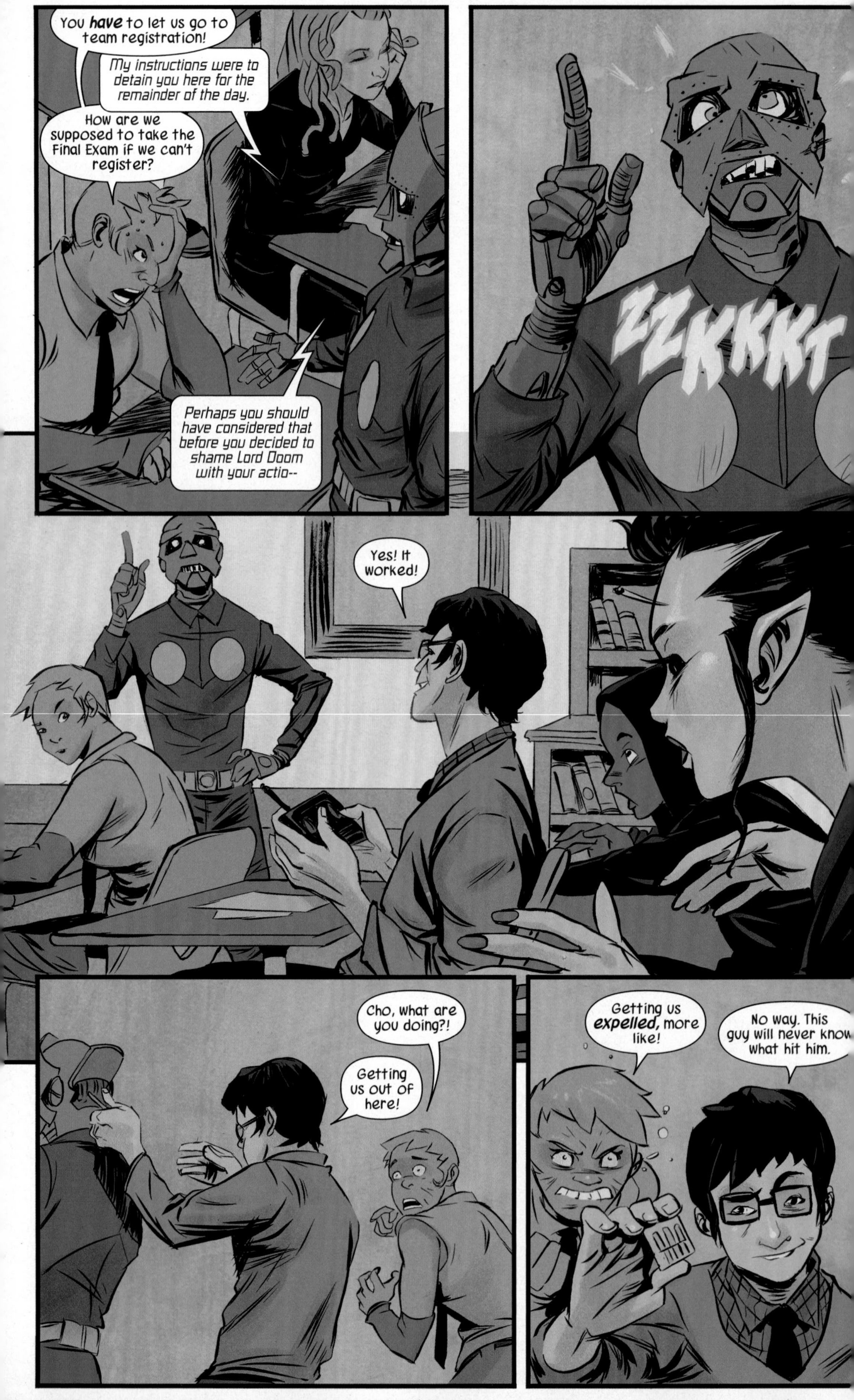
You **have** to let us go to team registration!
My instructions were to detain you here for the remainder of the day.
How are we supposed to take the Final Exam if we can't register?
Perhaps you should have considered that before you decided to shame Lord Doom with your actio--
ZZKKKT
Yes! It worked!
Cho, what are you doing?!
Getting us out of here!
Getting us **expelled,** more like!
No way. This guy will never know what hit him.

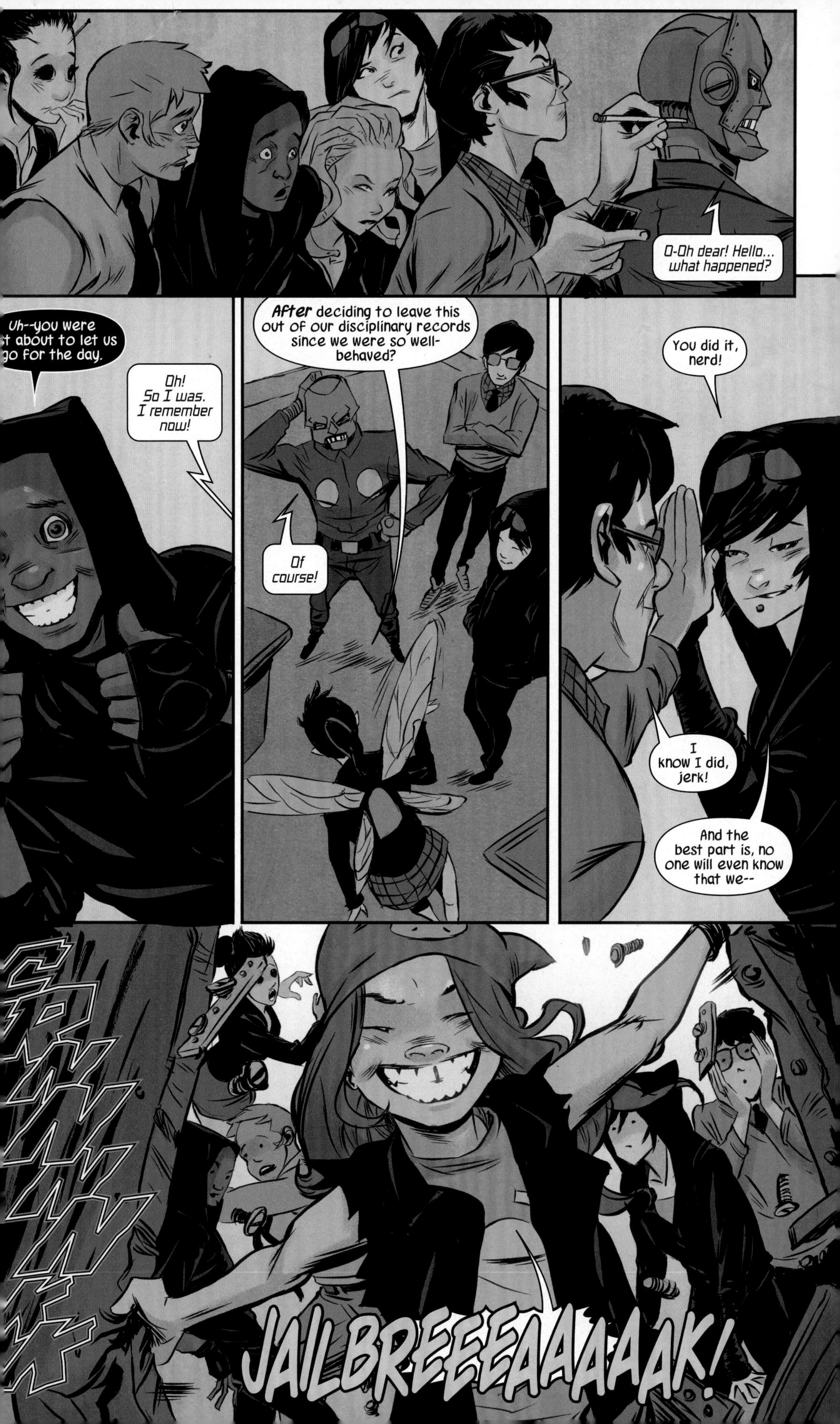

O-Oh dear! Hello... ...what happened?
Uh--you were t about to let us go for the day.
Oh! So I was. I remember now!
After deciding to leave this out of our disciplinary records since we were so well-behaved?
Of course!
You did it, nerd!
I know I did, jerk!
And the best part is, no one will even know that we--
JAILBREEEAAAAAK!

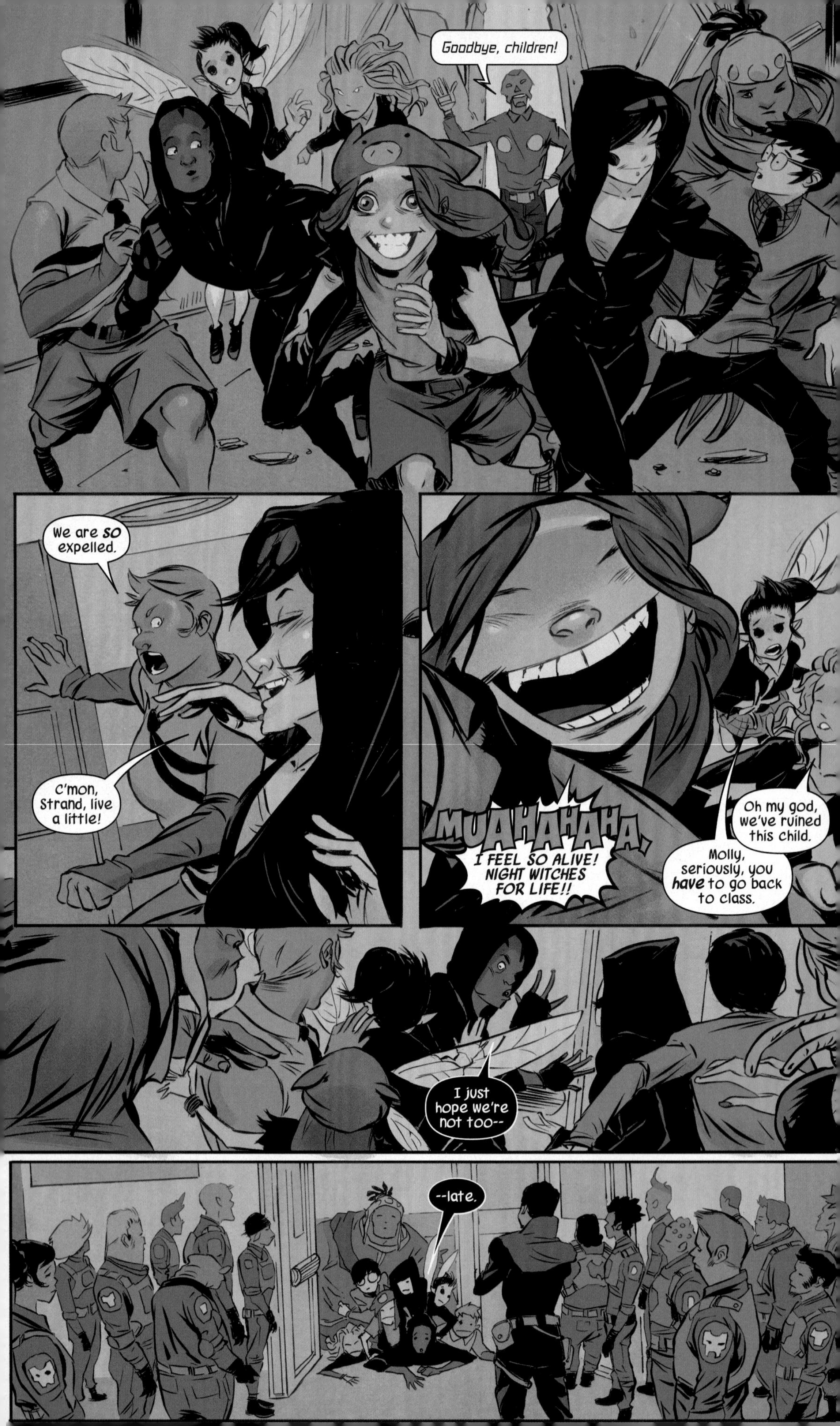
Goodbye, children!
We are SO expelled.
C'mon, Strand, live a little!
MUAHAHAHA, I FEEL SO ALIVE! NIGHT WITCHES FOR LIFE!!
Oh my god, we've ruined this child.
Molly, seriously, you have to go back to class.
I just hope we're not too--
--late.

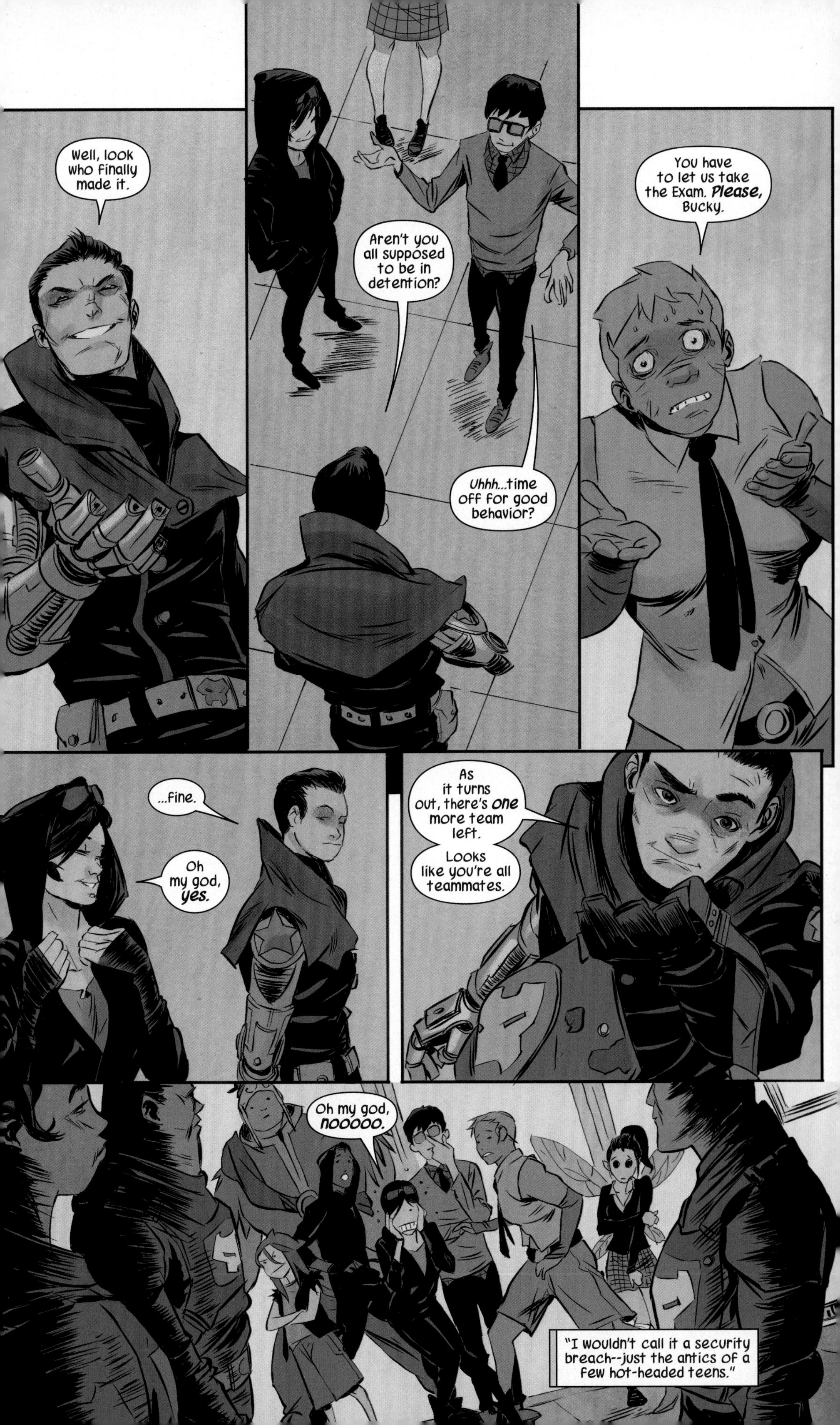
Well, look who finally made it.
Aren't you all supposed to be in detention?
Uhhh...time off for good behavior?
You have to let us take the Exam. *Please,* Bucky.
...fine.
Oh my god, *yes.*
As it turns out, there's *one* more team left.
Looks like you're all teammates.
Oh my god, *nooooo.*
"I wouldn't call it a security breach--just the antics of a few hot-headed teens."

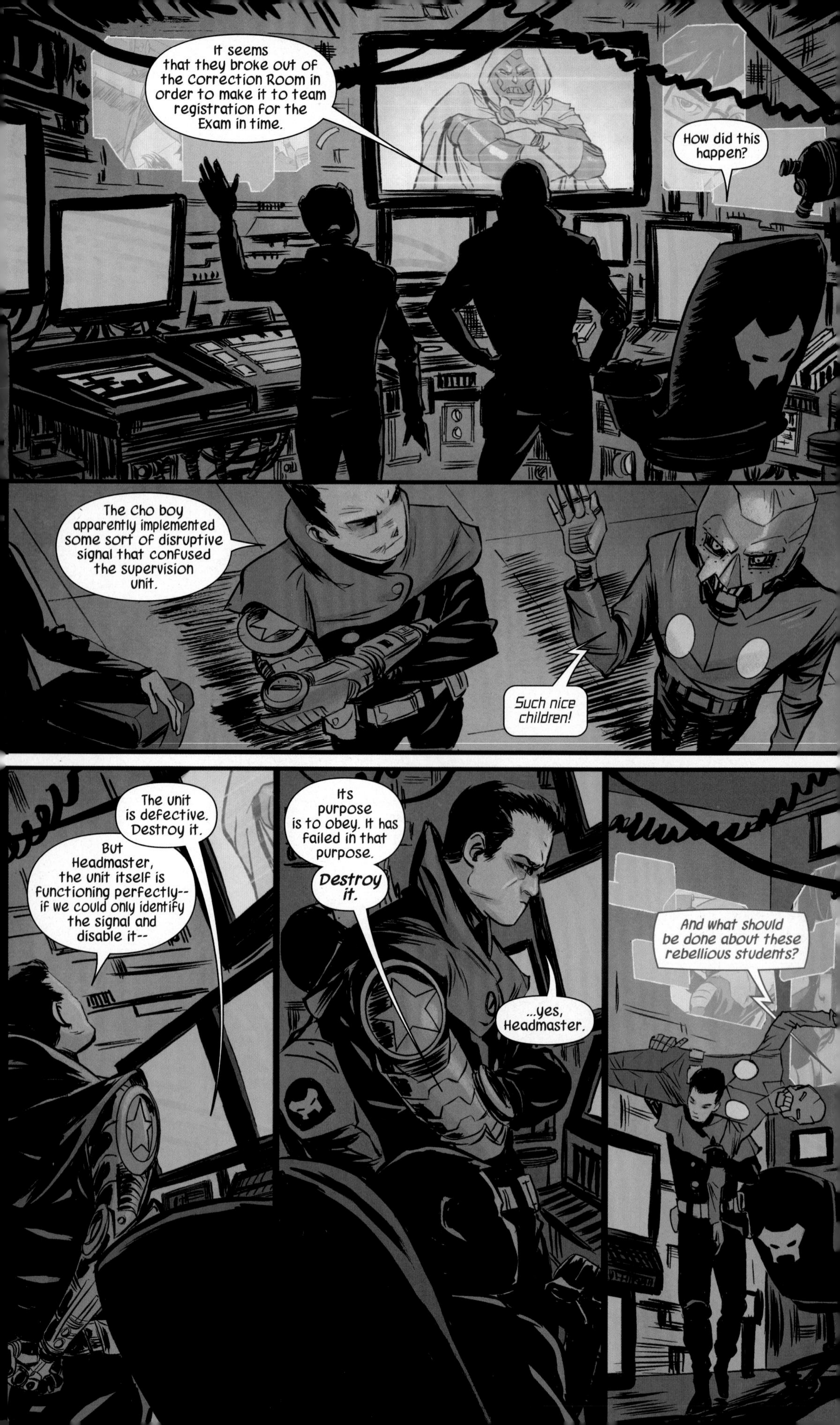
It seems that they broke out of the Correction Room in order to make it to team registration for the Exam in time.
How did this happen?
The Cho boy apparently implemented some sort of disruptive signal that confused the supervision unit.
Such nice children!
The unit is defective. Destroy it.
But Headmaster, the unit itself is functioning perfectly-- if we could only identify the signal and disable it--
Its purpose is to obey. It has failed in that purpose.
Destroy it.
...yes, Headmaster.
And what should be done about these rebellious students?

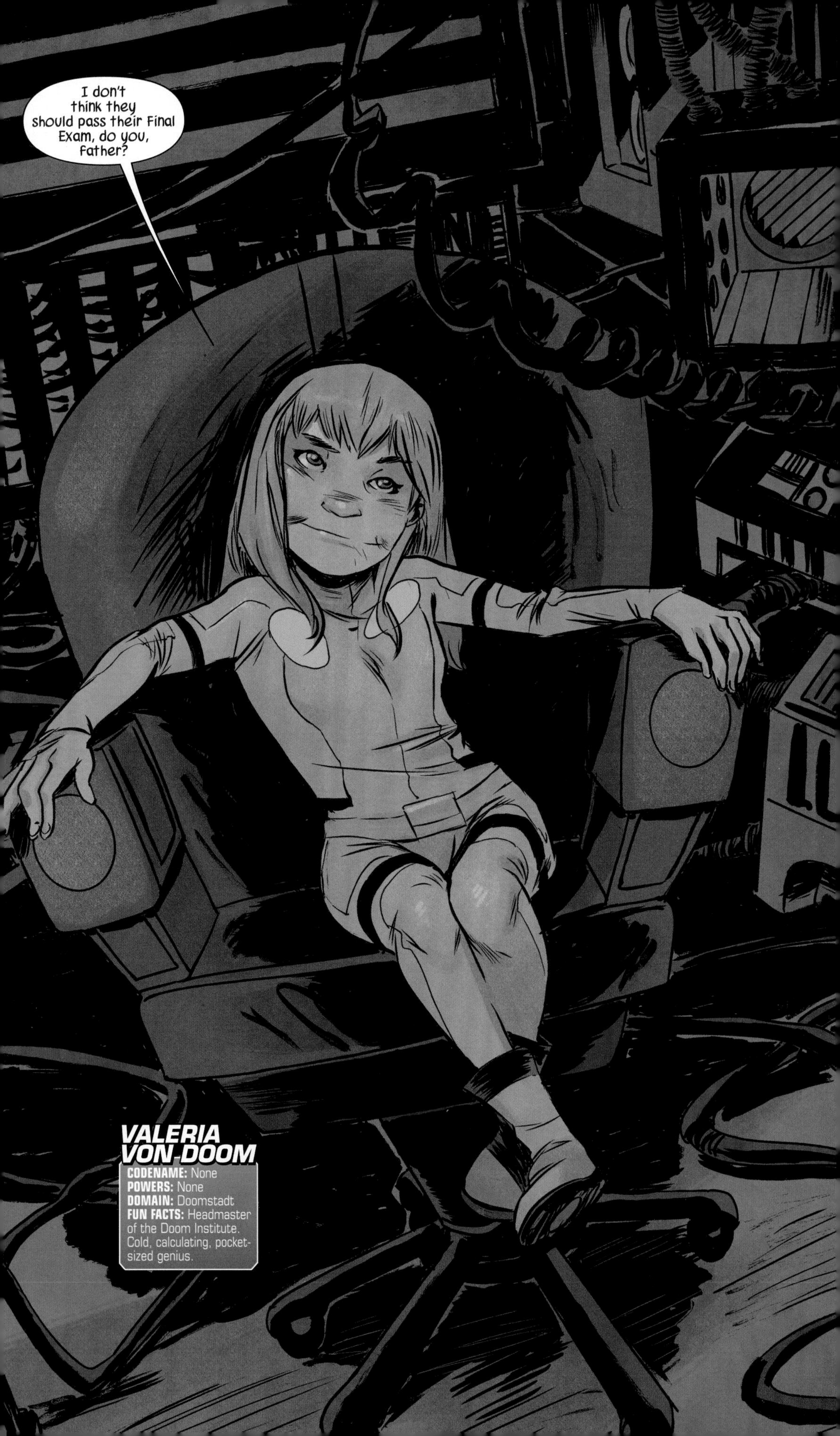

I don't think they should pass their Final Exam, do you, Father?
VALERIA VON-DOOM
CODENAME: None
POWERS: None
DOMAIN: Doomstadt
FUN FACTS: Headmaster of the Doom Institute. Cold, calculating, pocket-sized genius.

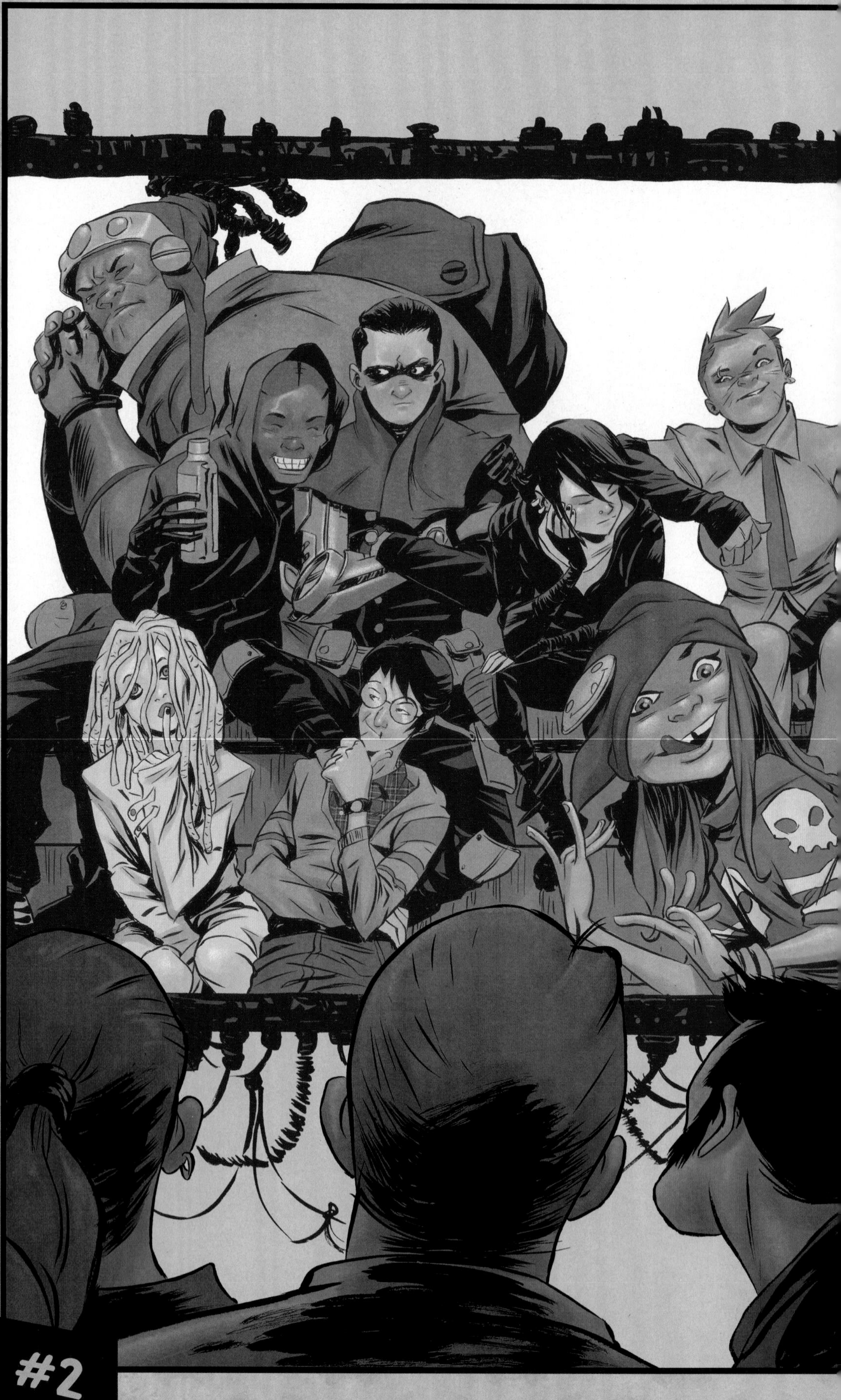

#2

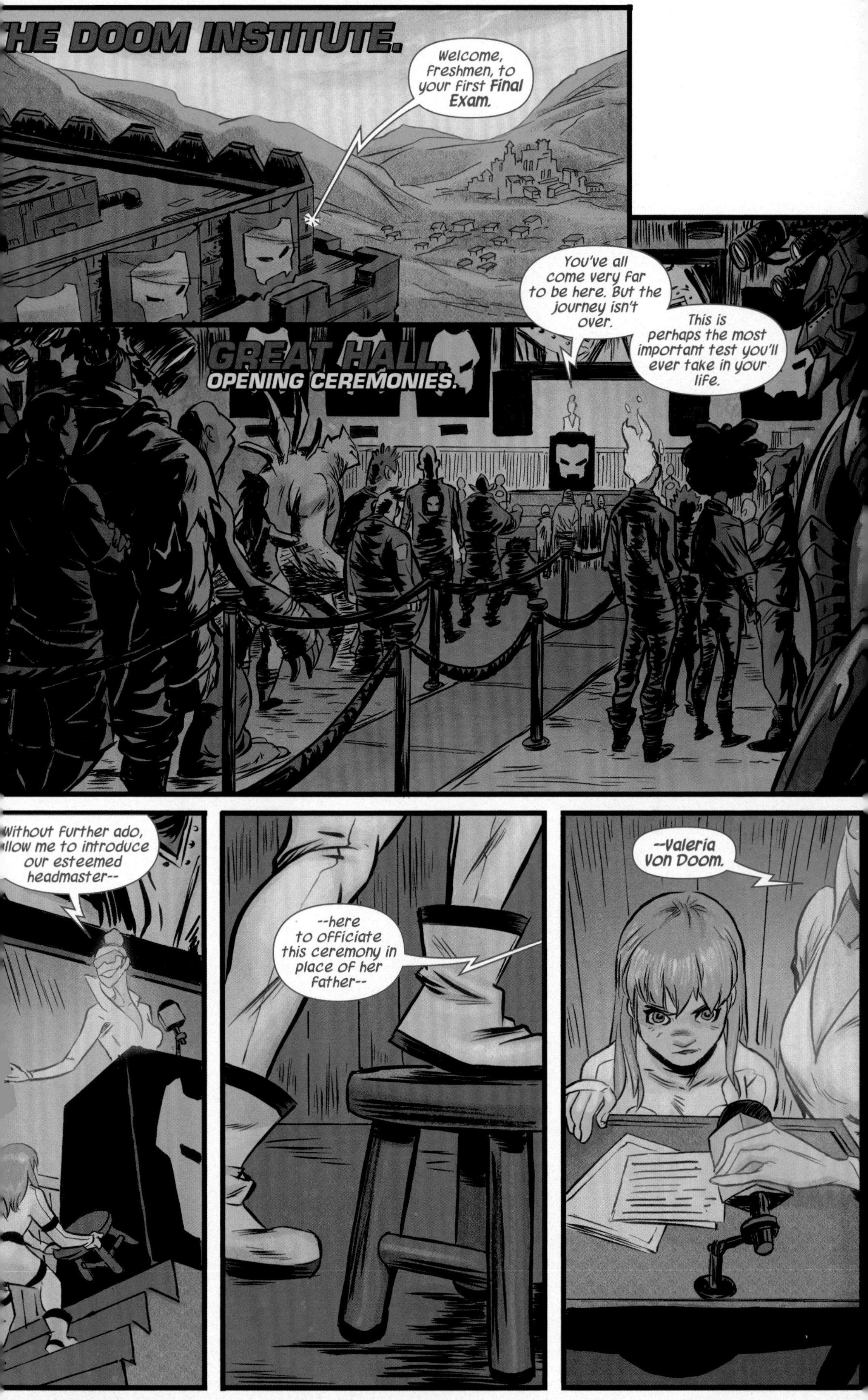

THE DOOM INSTITUTE.
Welcome, freshmen, to your first Final Exam.
You've all come very far to be here. But the journey isn't over.
This is perhaps the most important test you'll ever take in your life.
GREAT HALL. OPENING CEREMONIES.
Without further ado, allow me to introduce our esteemed headmaster--
--here to officiate this ceremony in place of her father--
--Valeria Von Doom.

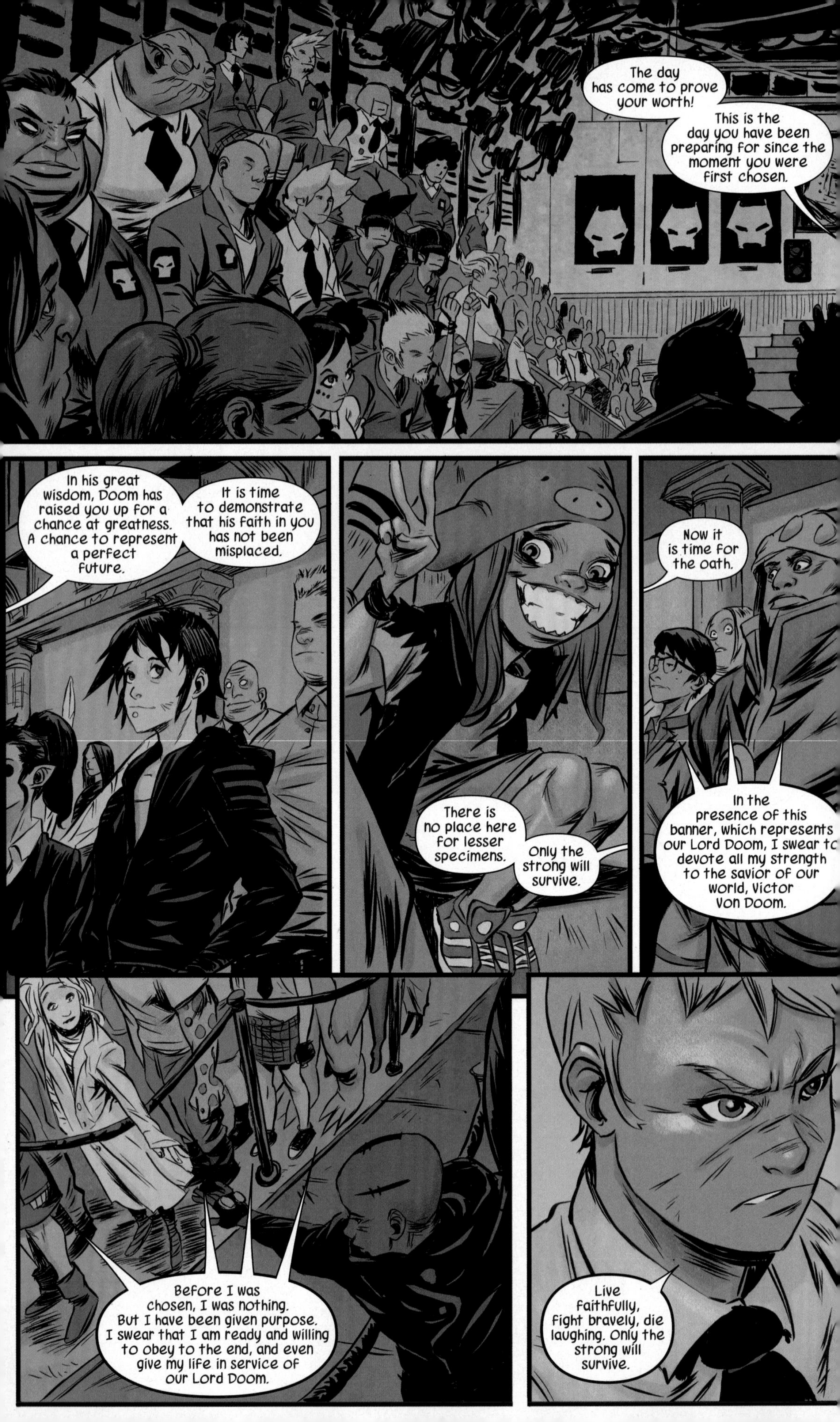
The day has come to prove your worth!
This is the day you have been preparing for since the moment you were first chosen.
In his great wisdom, Doom has raised you up for a chance at greatness. A chance to represent a perfect future.
It is time to demonstrate that his faith in you has not been misplaced.
There is no place here for lesser specimens.
Only the strong will survive.
Now it is time for the oath.
In the presence of this banner, which represents our Lord Doom, I swear to devote all my strength to the savior of our world, Victor Von Doom.
Before I was chosen, I was nothing. But I have been given purpose. I swear that I am ready and willing to obey to the end, and even give my life in service of our Lord Doom.
Live faithfully, fight bravely, die laughing. Only the strong will survive.

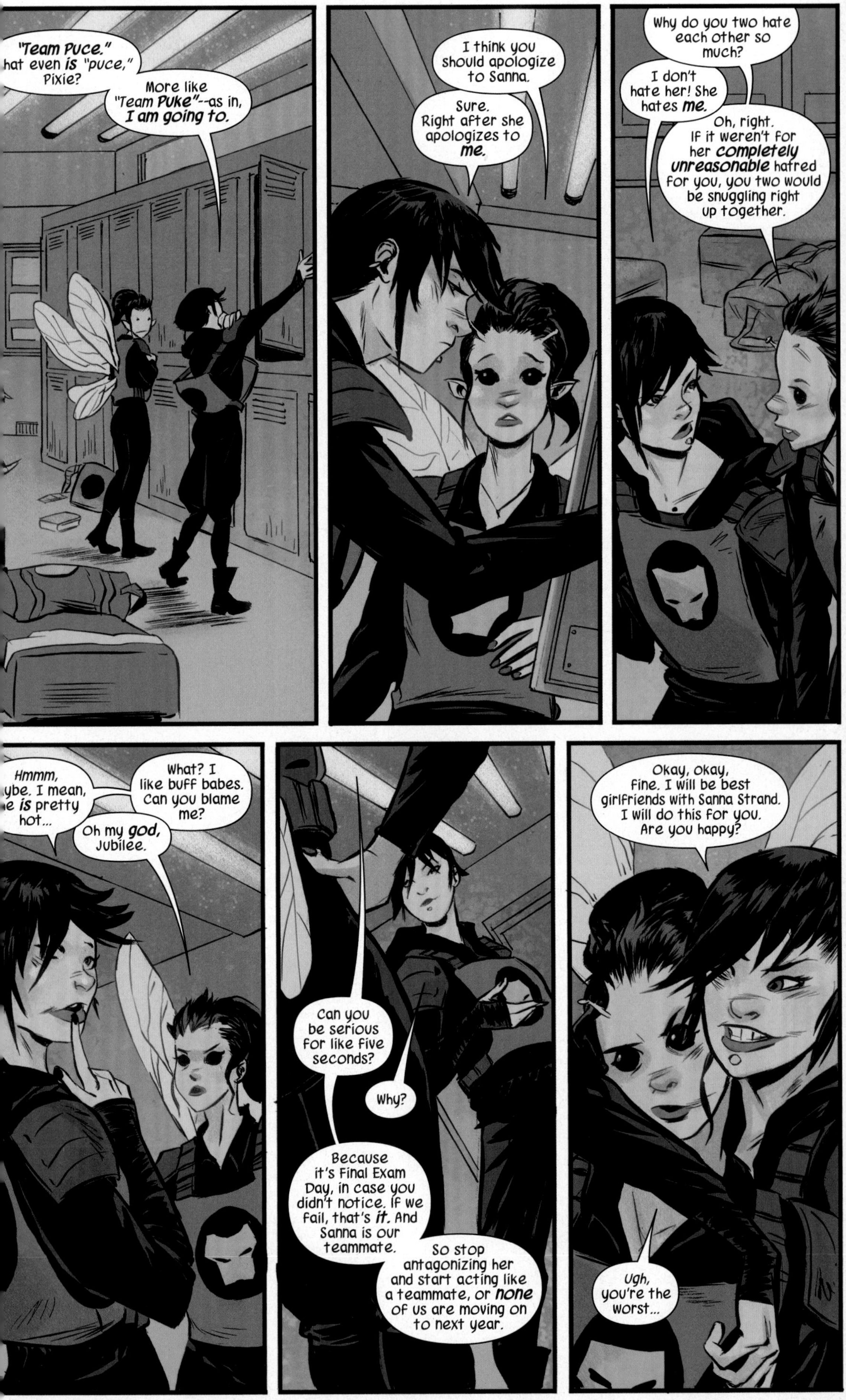
"Team Puce."
hat even is "puce," Pixie?
More like "Team Puke"--as in, I am going to.
I think you should apologize to Sanna.
Sure. Right after she apologizes to me.
Why do you two hate each other so much?
I don't hate her! She hates me.
Oh, right. If it weren't for her completely unreasonable hatred for you, you two would be snuggling right up together.
Hmmm, ybe. I mean, e is pretty hot...
What? I like buff babes. Can you blame me?
Oh my god, Jubilee.
Can you be serious for like five seconds?
Why?
Because it's Final Exam Day, in case you didn't notice. If we fail, that's it. And Sanna is our teammate.
So stop antagonizing her and start acting like a teammate, or none of us are moving on to next year.
Okay, okay, fine. I will be best girlfriends with Sanna Strand. I will do this for you. Are you happy?
Ugh, you're the worst...

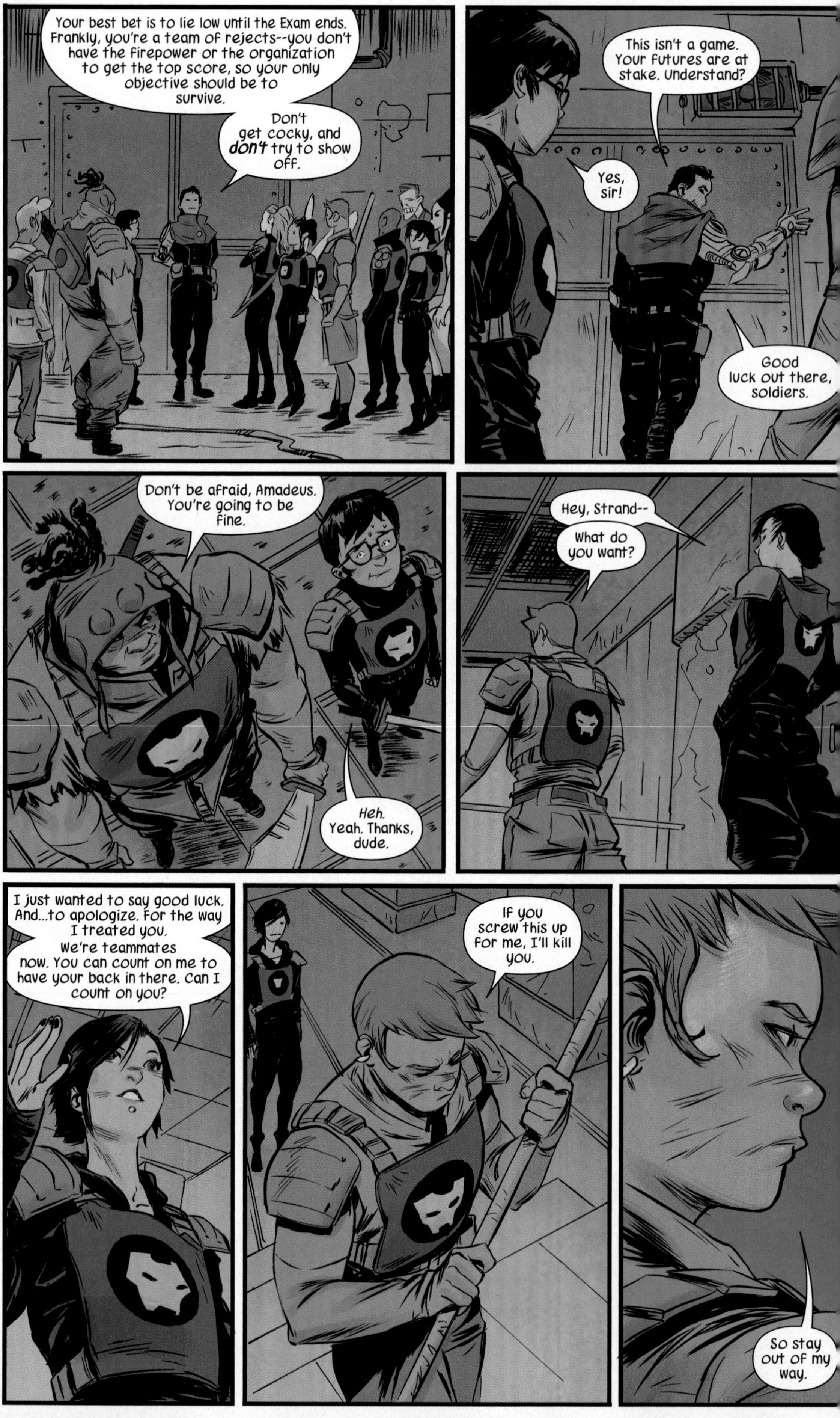
Your best bet is to lie low until the Exam ends. Frankly, you're a team of rejects--you don't have the firepower or the organization to get the top score, so your only objective should be to survive.
Don't get cocky, and **don't** try to show off.
This isn't a game. Your futures are at stake. Understand?
Yes, sir!
Good luck out there, soldiers.
Don't be afraid, Amadeus. You're going to be fine.
Heh. Yeah. Thanks, dude.
Hey, Strand--
What do you want?
I just wanted to say good luck. And...to apologize. For the way I treated you.
We're teammates now. You can count on me to have your back in there. Can I count on you?
If you screw this up for me, I'll kill you.
So stay out of my way.

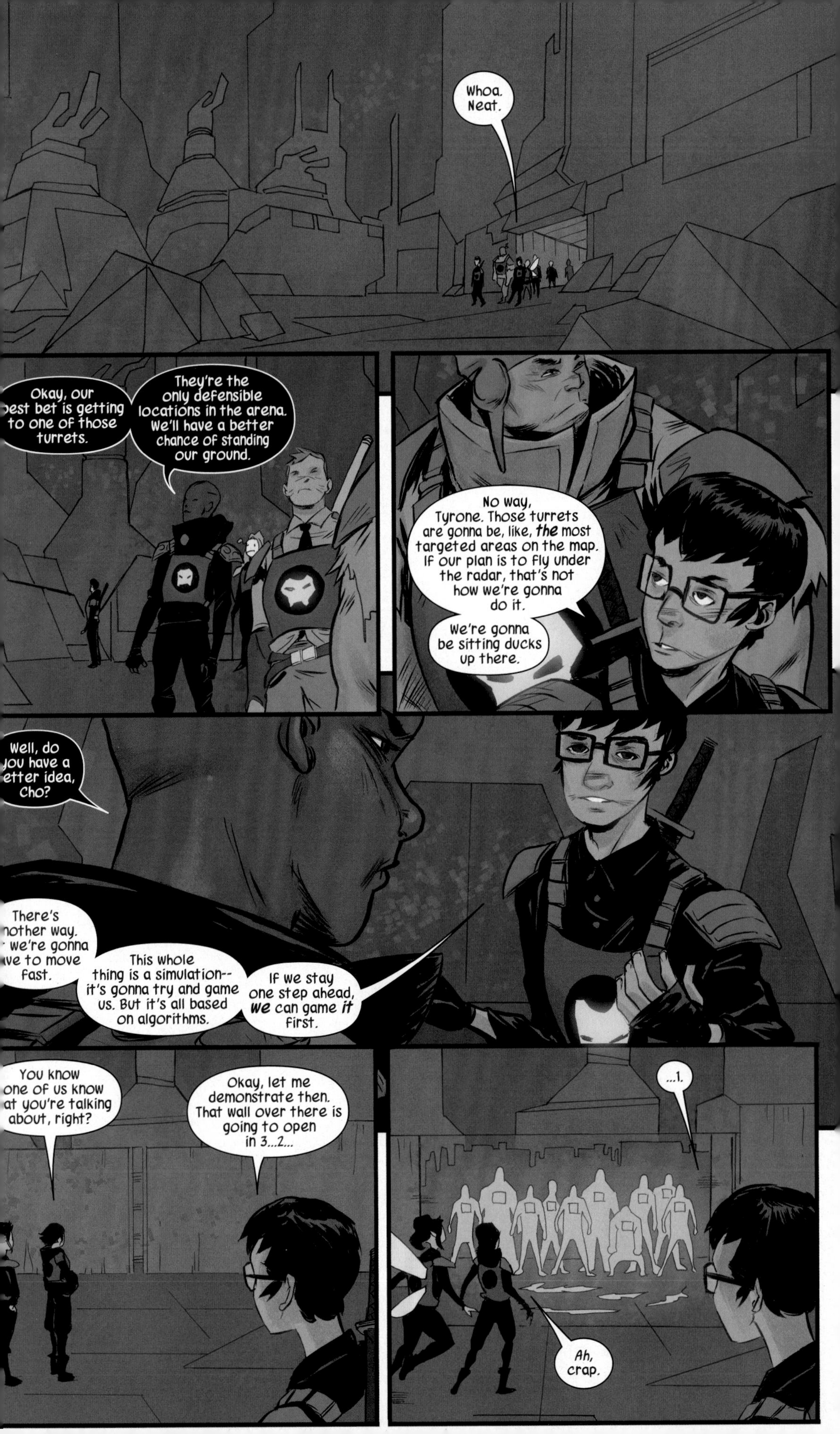

Whoa. Neat.
Okay, our
best bet is getting to one of those turrets.
They're the only defensible locations in the arena. We'll have a better chance of standing our ground.
No way, Tyrone. Those turrets are gonna be, like, *the* most targeted areas on the map. If our plan is to fly under the radar, that's not how we're gonna do it.
We're gonna be sitting ducks up there.
Well, do you have a etter idea, Cho?
There's nother way. we're gonna ve to move fast.
This whole thing is a simulation-- it's gonna try and game us. But it's all based on algorithms.
If we stay one step ahead, *we* can game *it* first.
You know one of us know at you're talking about, right?
Okay, let me demonstrate then. That wall over there is going to open in 3...2...
...1.
Ah, crap.

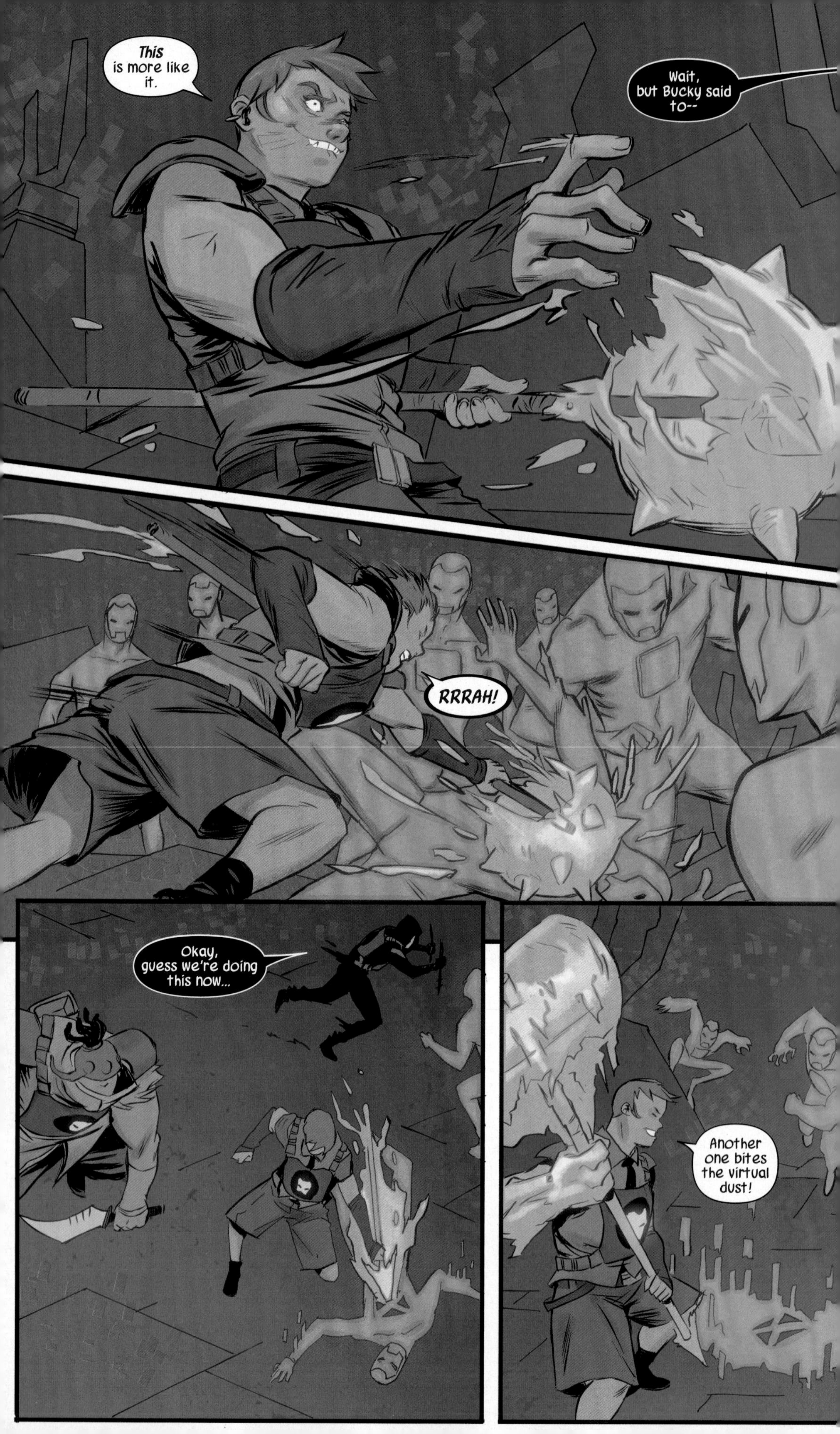

This is more like it.
Wait, but Bucky said to--
RRRAH!
Okay, guess we're doing this now...
Another one bites the virtual dust!

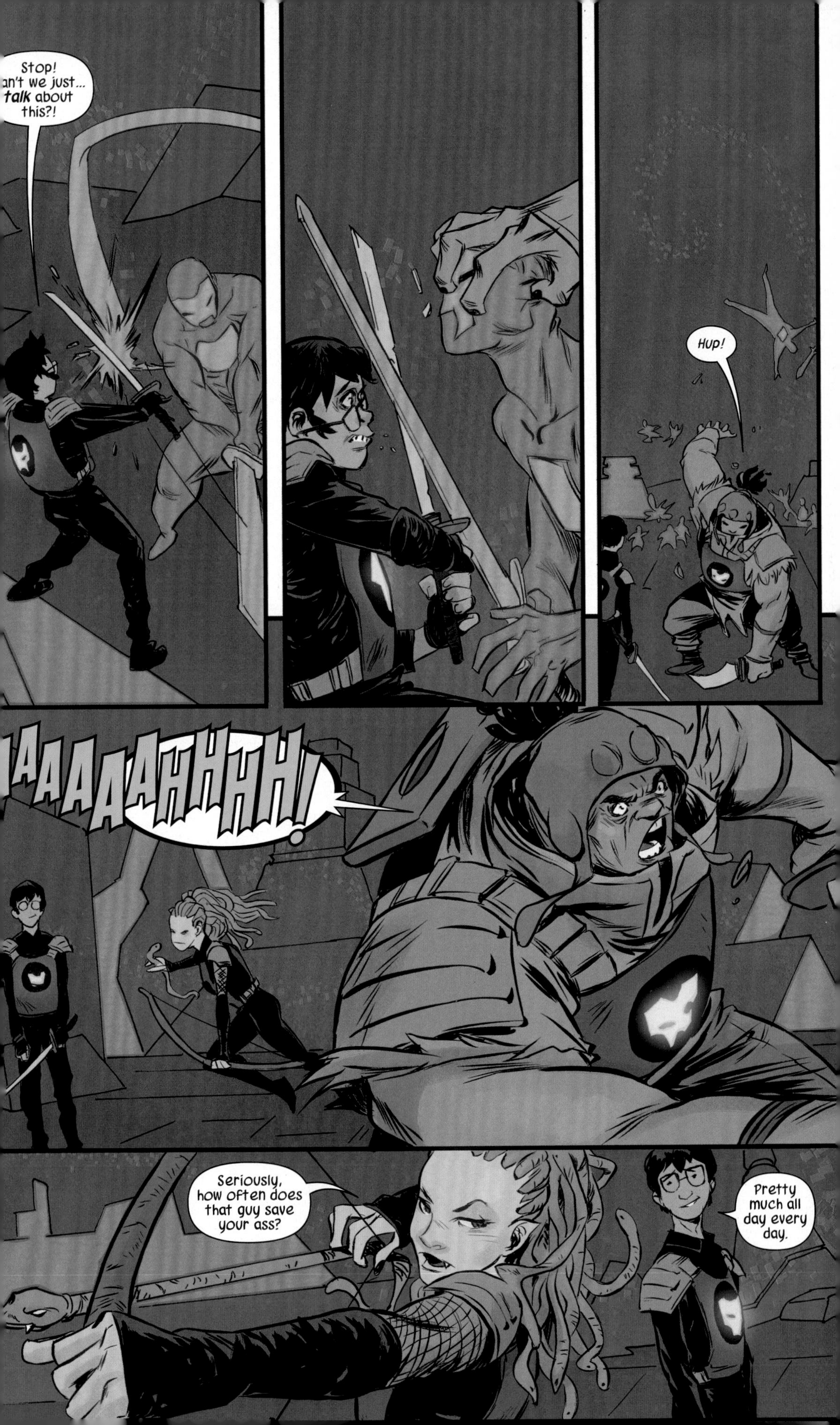
Stop!
an't we just... **talk** about this?!
Hup!
AAAAAAHHHH!
Seriously, how often does that guy save your ass?
Pretty much all day every day.

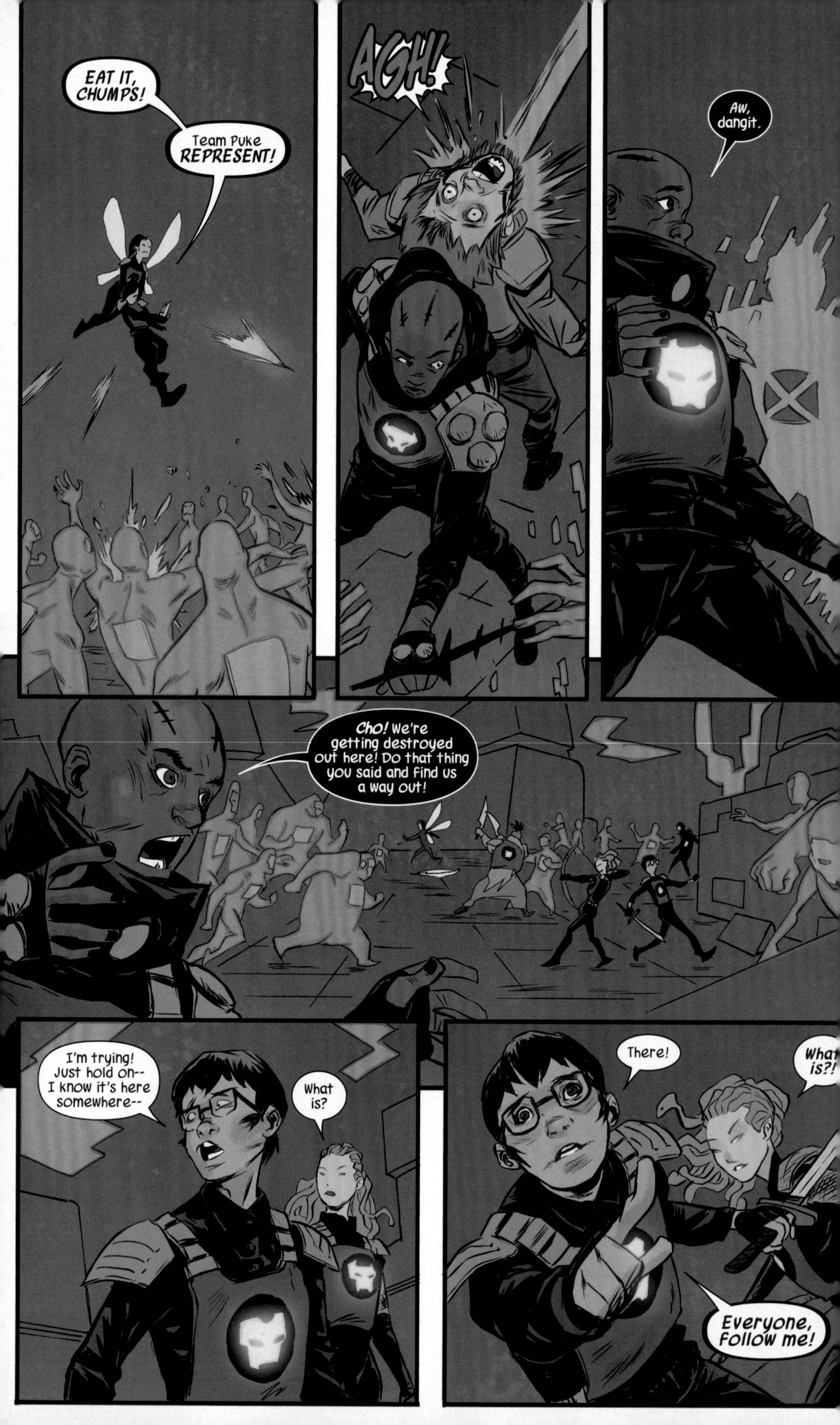
EAT IT, CHUMPS!
Team Puke REPRESENT!
AGH!
Aw, dangit.
Cho! We're getting destroyed out here! Do that thing you said and find us a way out!
I'm trying! Just hold on-- I know it's here somewhere--
What is?
There!
What is?!
Everyone, follow me!

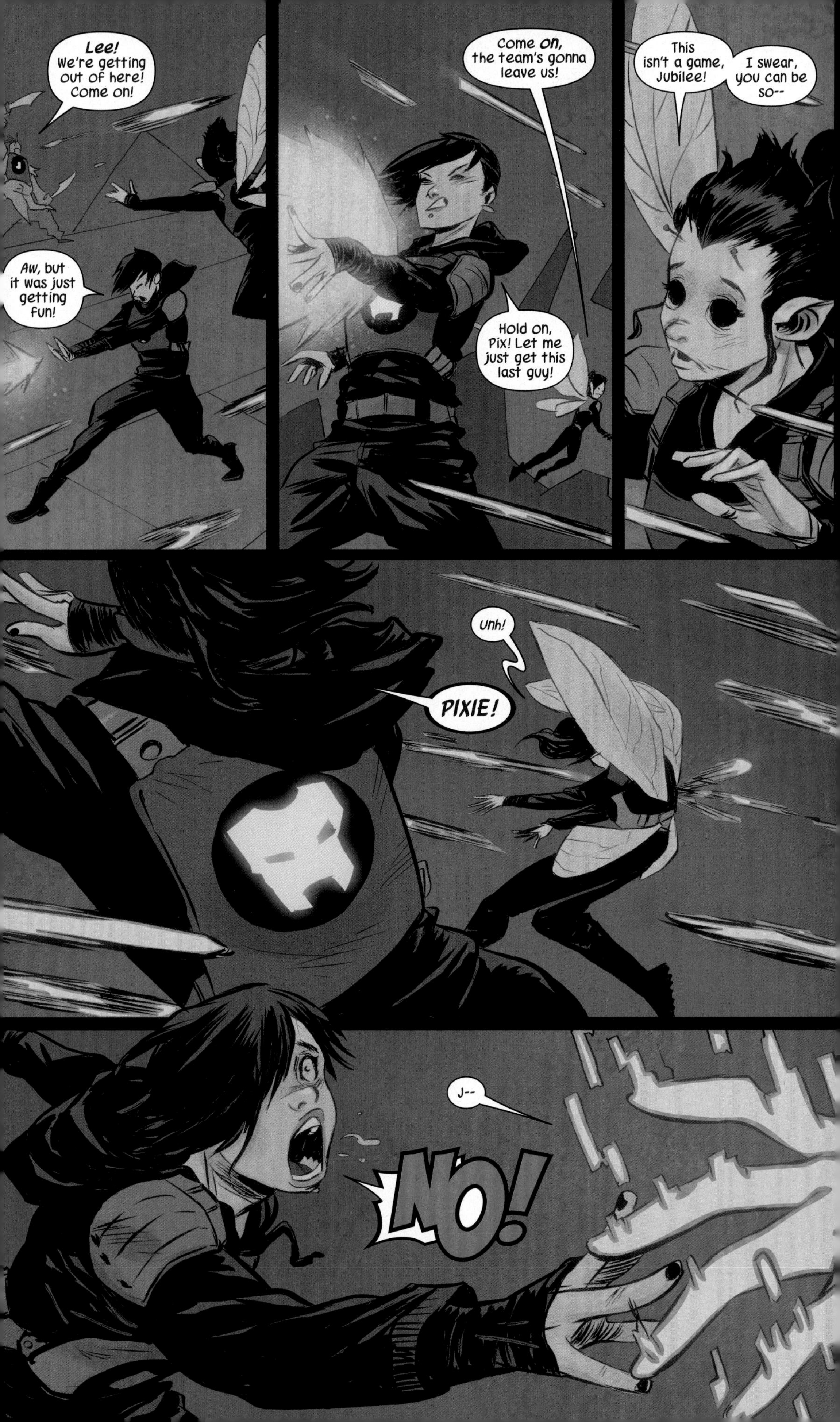
Lee! We're getting out of here! Come on!
Aw, but it was just getting fun!
Come on, the team's gonna leave us!
Hold on, Pix! Let me just get this last guy!
This isn't a game, Jubilee!
I swear, you can be so--
Unh!
PIXIE!
J--
NO!

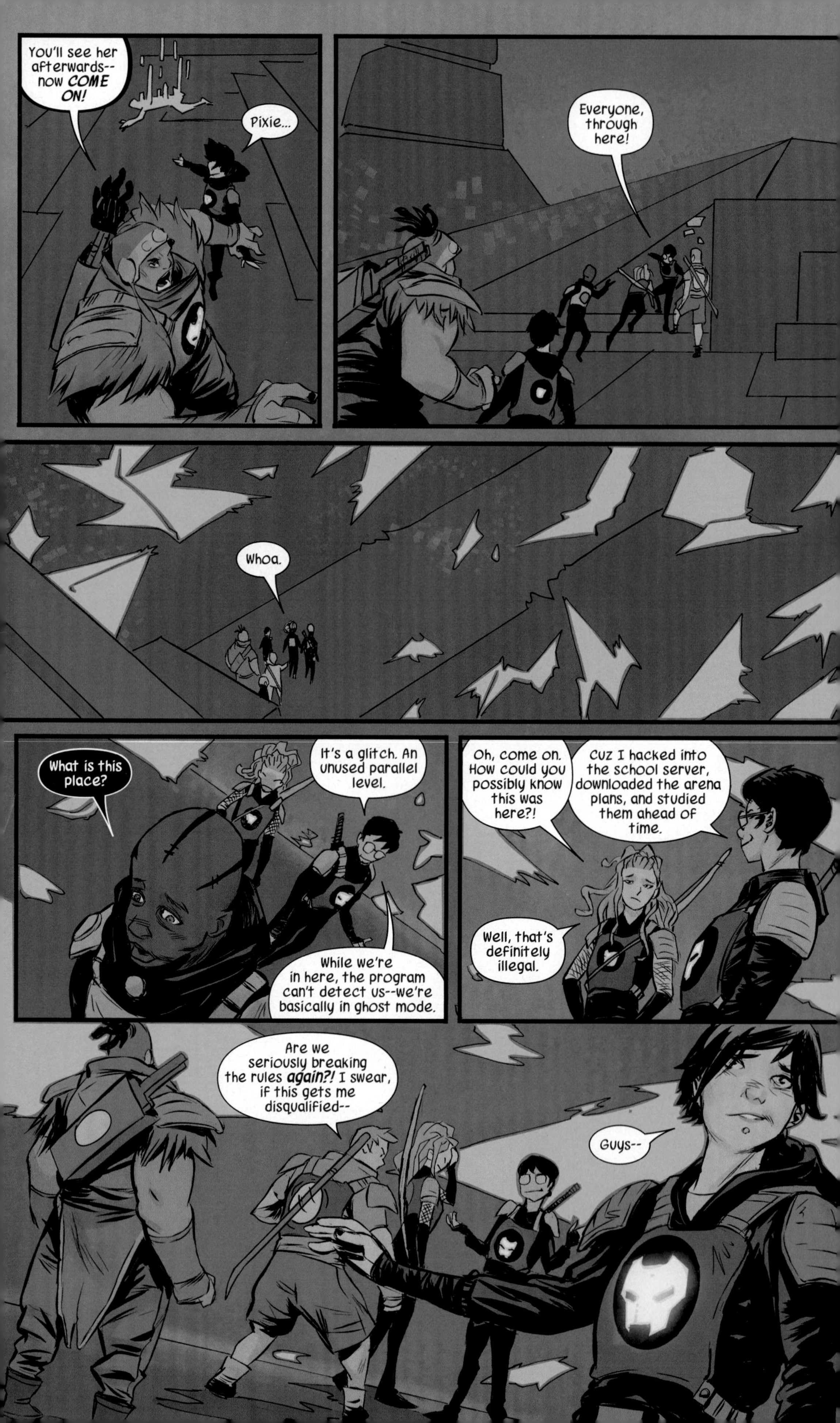

You'll see her afterwards--now COME ON!
Pixie...
Everyone, through here!
Whoa.
What is this place?
It's a glitch. An unused parallel level.
While we're in here, the program can't detect us--we're basically in ghost mode.
Oh, come on. How could you possibly know this was here?!
Cuz I hacked into the school server, downloaded the arena plans, and studied them ahead of time.
Well, that's definitely illegal.
Are we seriously breaking the rules again?! I swear, if this gets me disqualified--
Guys--

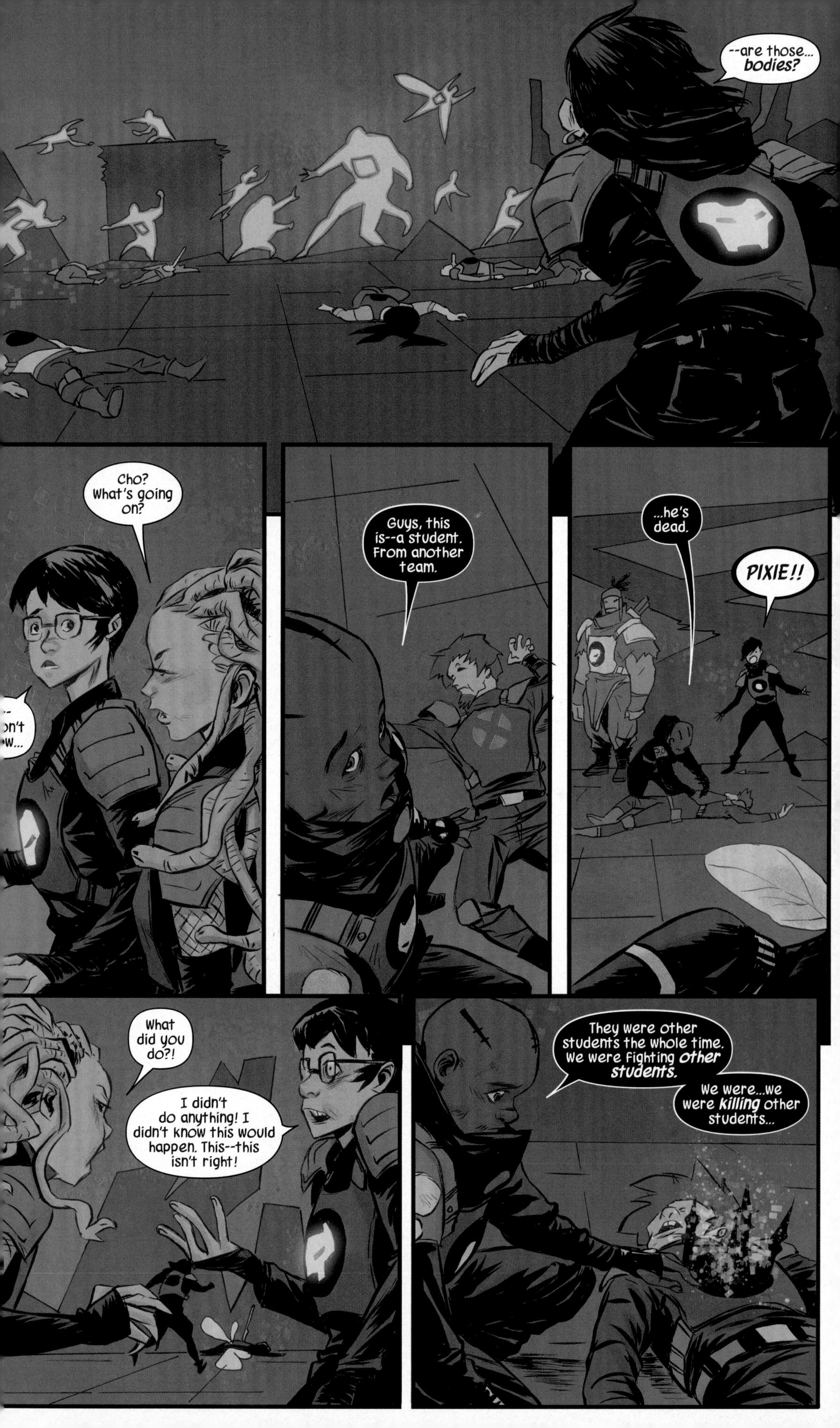
--are those... bodies?
Cho? What's going on?
Guys, this is--a student. From another team.
...he's dead.
PIXIE!!
What did you do?!
I didn't do anything! I didn't know this would happen. This--this isn't right!
They were other students the whole time. We were fighting other students.
We were...we were killing other students...

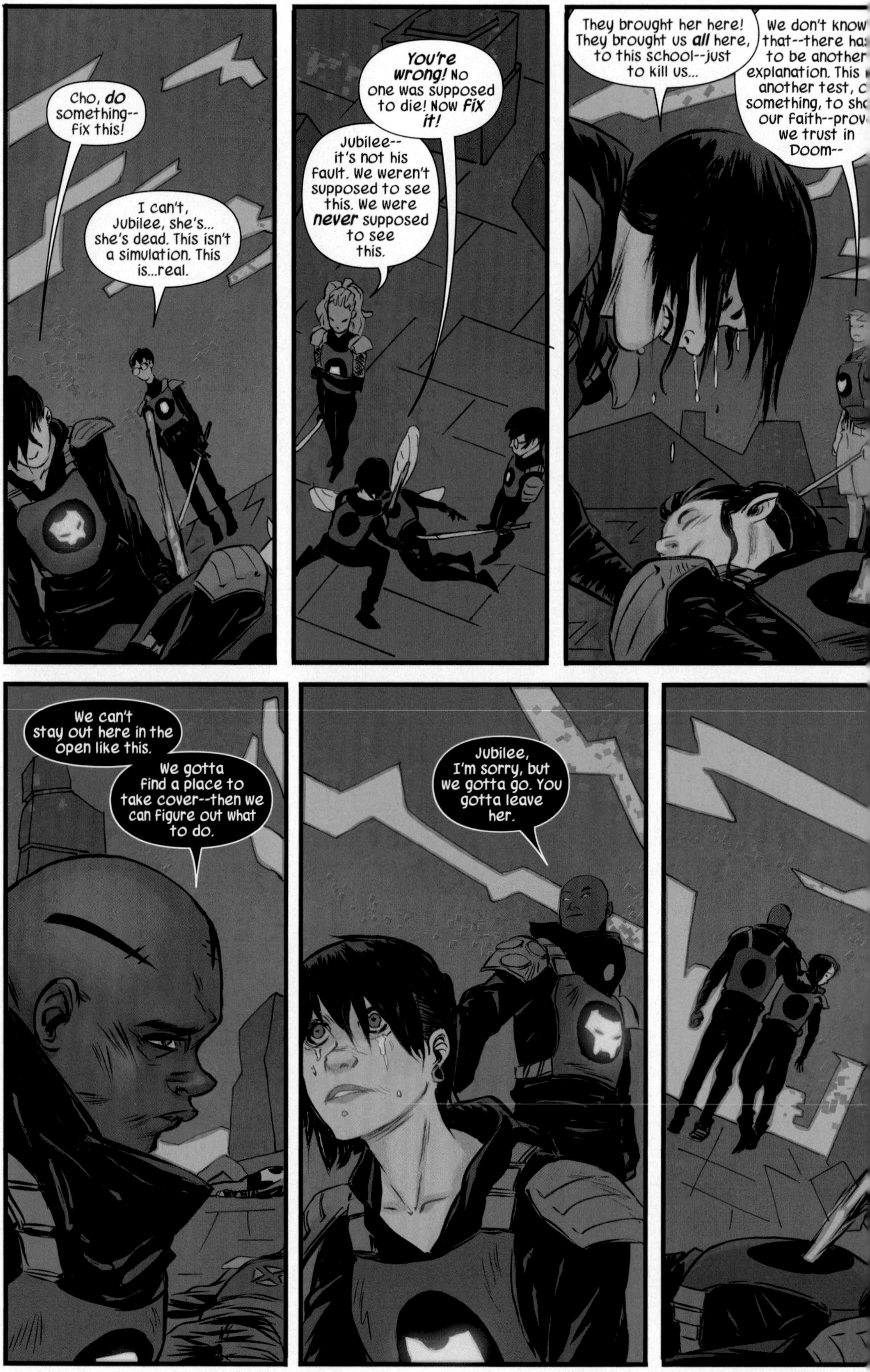
Cho, **do** something--fix this!
I can't, Jubilee, she's... she's dead. This isn't a simulation. This is...real.
You're wrong! No one was supposed to die! Now **fix it!**
Jubilee--it's not his fault. We weren't supposed to see this. We were **never** supposed to see this.
They brought her here! They brought us **all** here, to this school--just to kill us...
We don't know that--there ha to be another explanation. This another test, c something, to sh our faith--prov we trust in Doom--
We can't stay out here in the open like this.
We gotta find a place to take cover--then we can figure out what to do.
Jubilee, I'm sorry, but we gotta go. You gotta leave her.

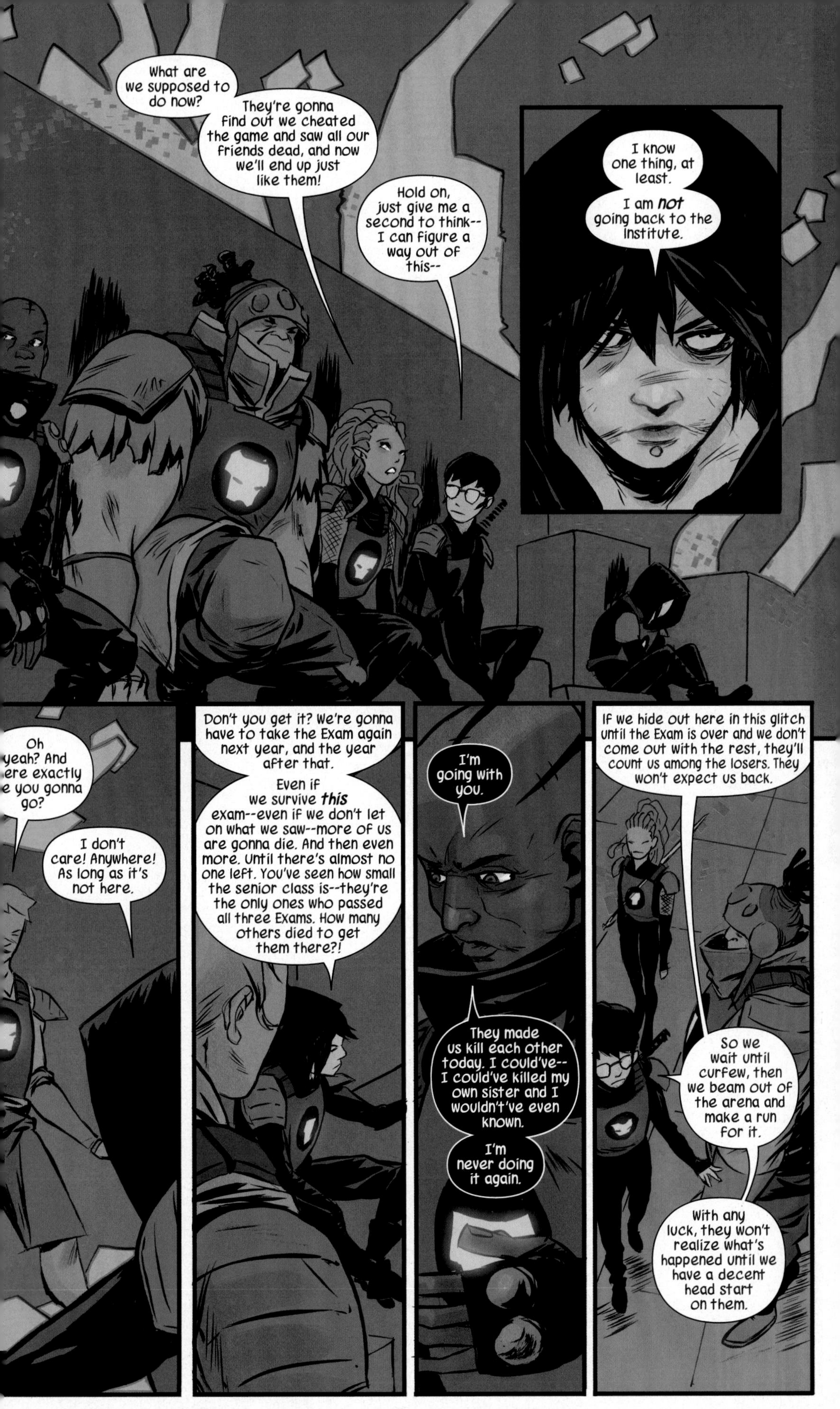
What are we supposed to do now?
They're gonna find out we cheated the game and saw all our friends dead, and now we'll end up just like them!
Hold on, just give me a second to think-- I can figure a way out of this--
I know one thing, at least.
I am *not* going back to the institute.
Oh yeah? And ere exactly e you gonna go?
I don't care! Anywhere! As long as it's not here.
Don't you get it? We're gonna have to take the Exam again next year, and the year after that.
Even if we survive *this* exam--even if we don't let on what we saw--more of us are gonna die. And then even more. Until there's almost no one left. You've seen how small the senior class is--they're the only ones who passed all three Exams. How many others died to get them there?!
I'm going with you.
They made us kill each other today. I could've-- I could've killed my own sister and I wouldn't've even known.
I'm never doing it again.
If we hide out here in this glitch until the Exam is over and we don't come out with the rest, they'll count us among the losers. They won't expect us back.
So we wait until curfew, then we beam out of the arena and make a run for it.
With any luck, they won't realize what's happened until we have a decent head start on them.

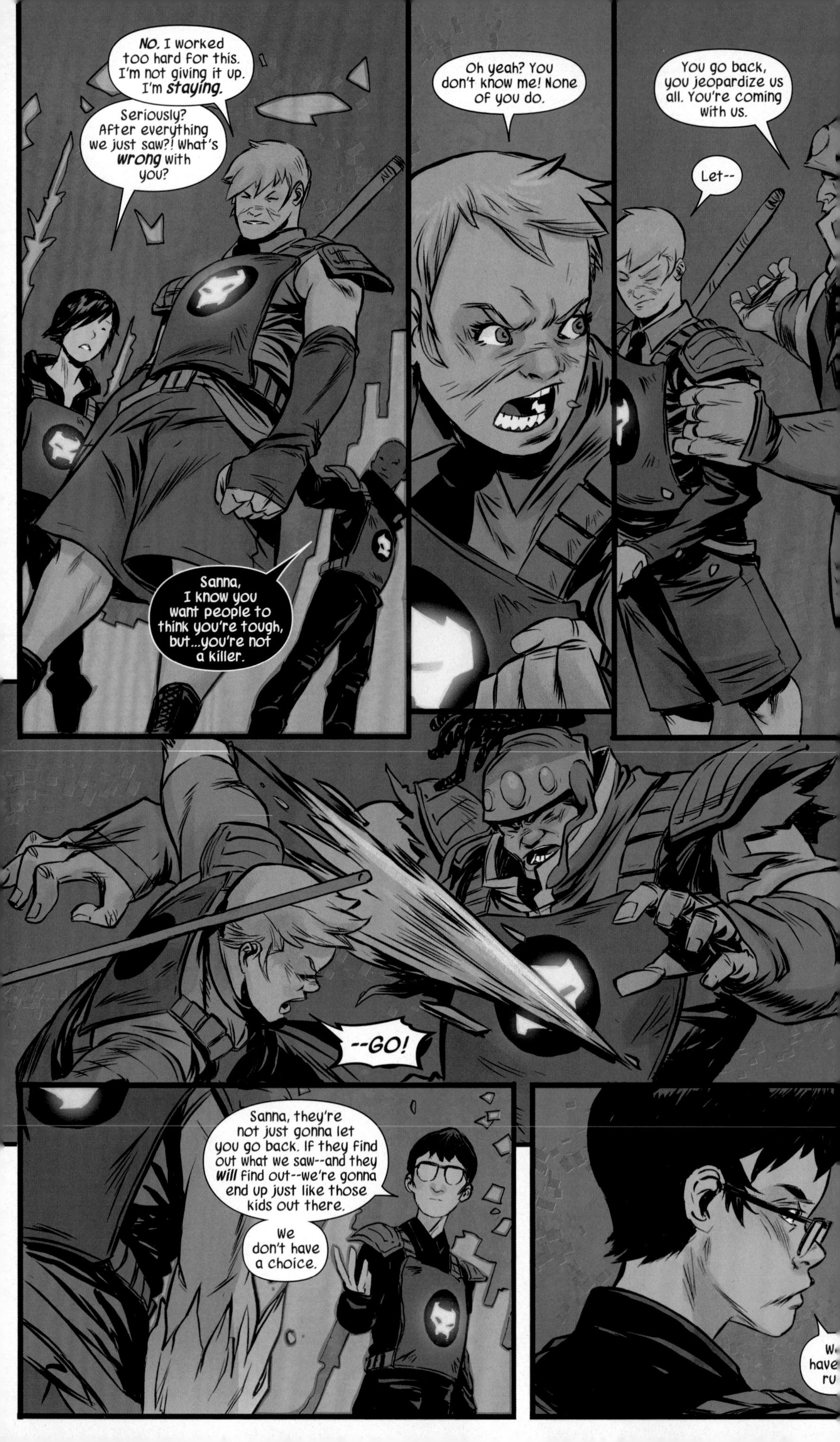
NO. I worked too hard for this. I'm not giving it up. I'm staying.
Seriously? After everything we just saw?! What's wrong with you?
Sanna, I know you want people to think you're tough, but...you're not a killer.
Oh yeah? You don't know me! None of you do.
You go back, you jeopardize us all. You're coming with us.
Let--
--GO!
Sanna, they're not just gonna let you go back. If they find out what we saw--and they will find out--we're gonna end up just like those kids out there.
We don't have a choice.

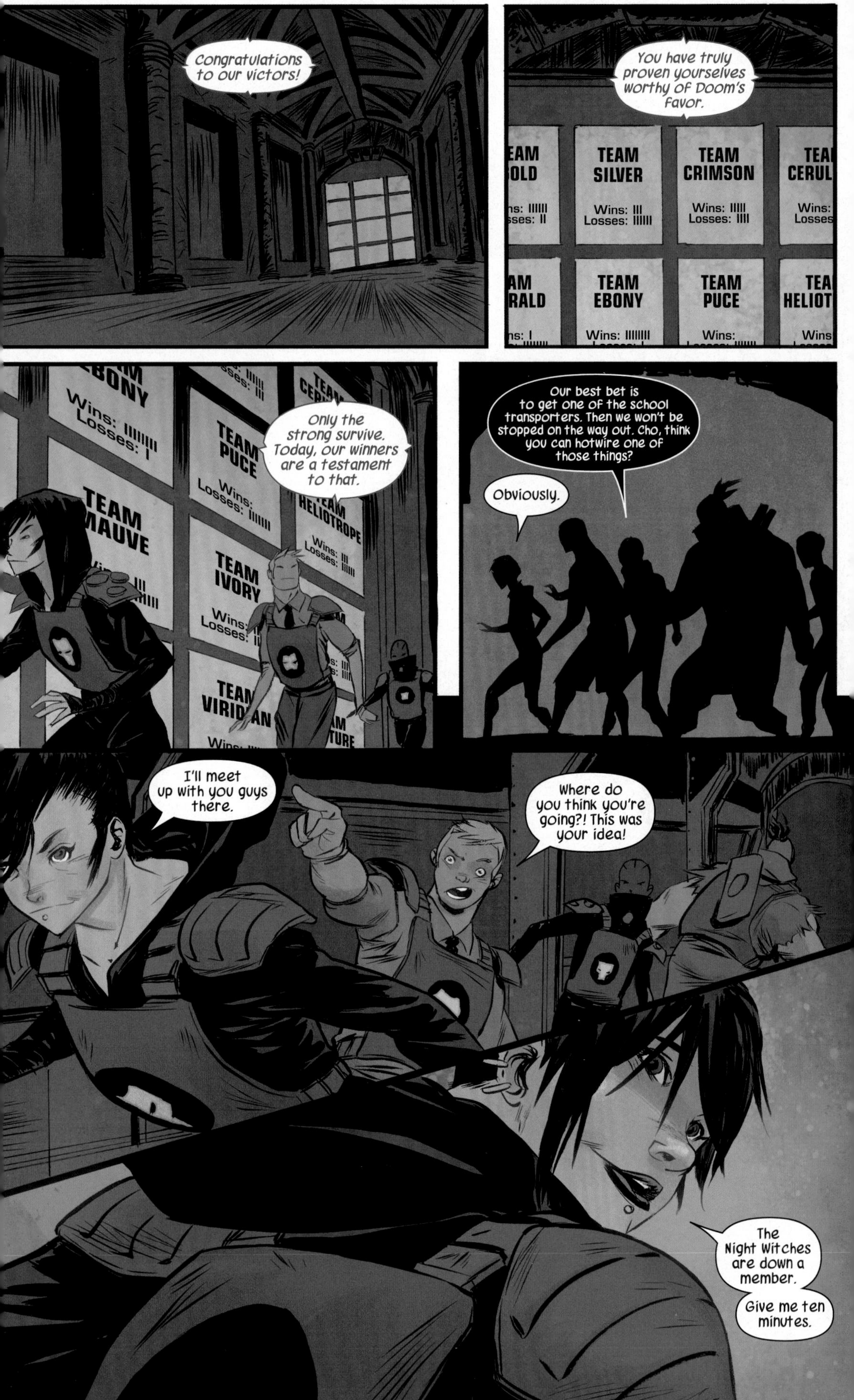
Congratulations to our victors!
You have truly proven yourselves worthy of Doom's favor.
TEAM SILVER
Wins: III
Losses: IIIIII
TEAM CRIMSON
Wins: IIIII
Losses: IIII
TEAM EBONY
Wins: IIIIIII
TEAM PUCE
Only the strong survive. Today, our winners are a testament to that.
TEAM MAUVE
TEAM IVORY
TEAM VIRIDIAN
TEAM HELIOTROPE
Our best bet is to get one of the school transporters. Then we won't be stopped on the way out. Cho, think you can hotwire one of those things?
Obviously.
I'll meet up with you guys there.
Where do you think you're going?! This was your idea!
The Night Witches are down a member.
Give me ten minutes.

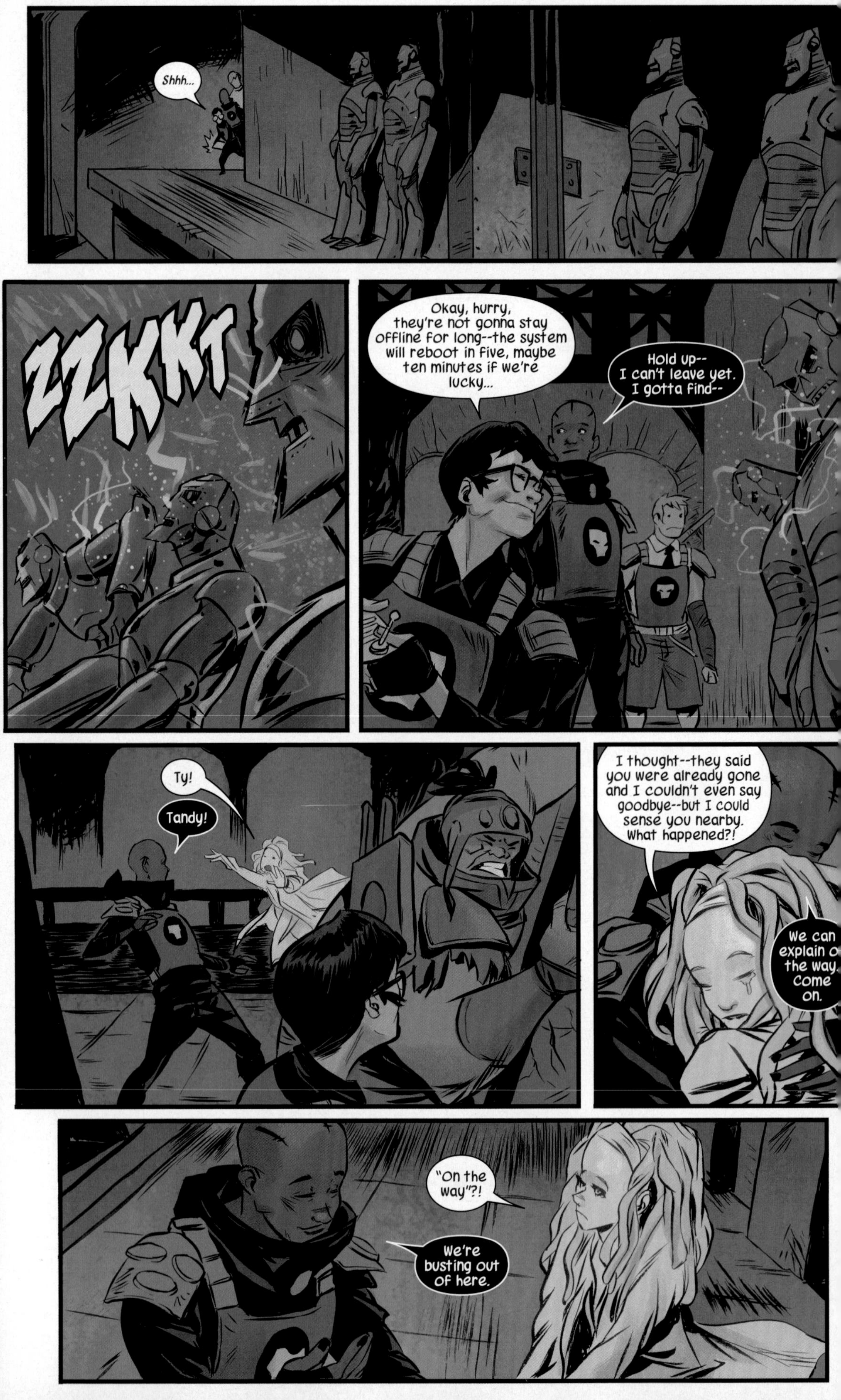
Shhh...
ZZKKT
Okay, hurry, they're not gonna stay offline for long--the system will reboot in five, maybe ten minutes if we're lucky...
Hold up-- I can't leave yet. I gotta find--
Ty!
Tandy!
I thought--they said you were already gone and I couldn't even say goodbye--but I could sense you nearby. What happened?!
We can explain o the way. Come on.
"On the way"?!
We're busting out of here.

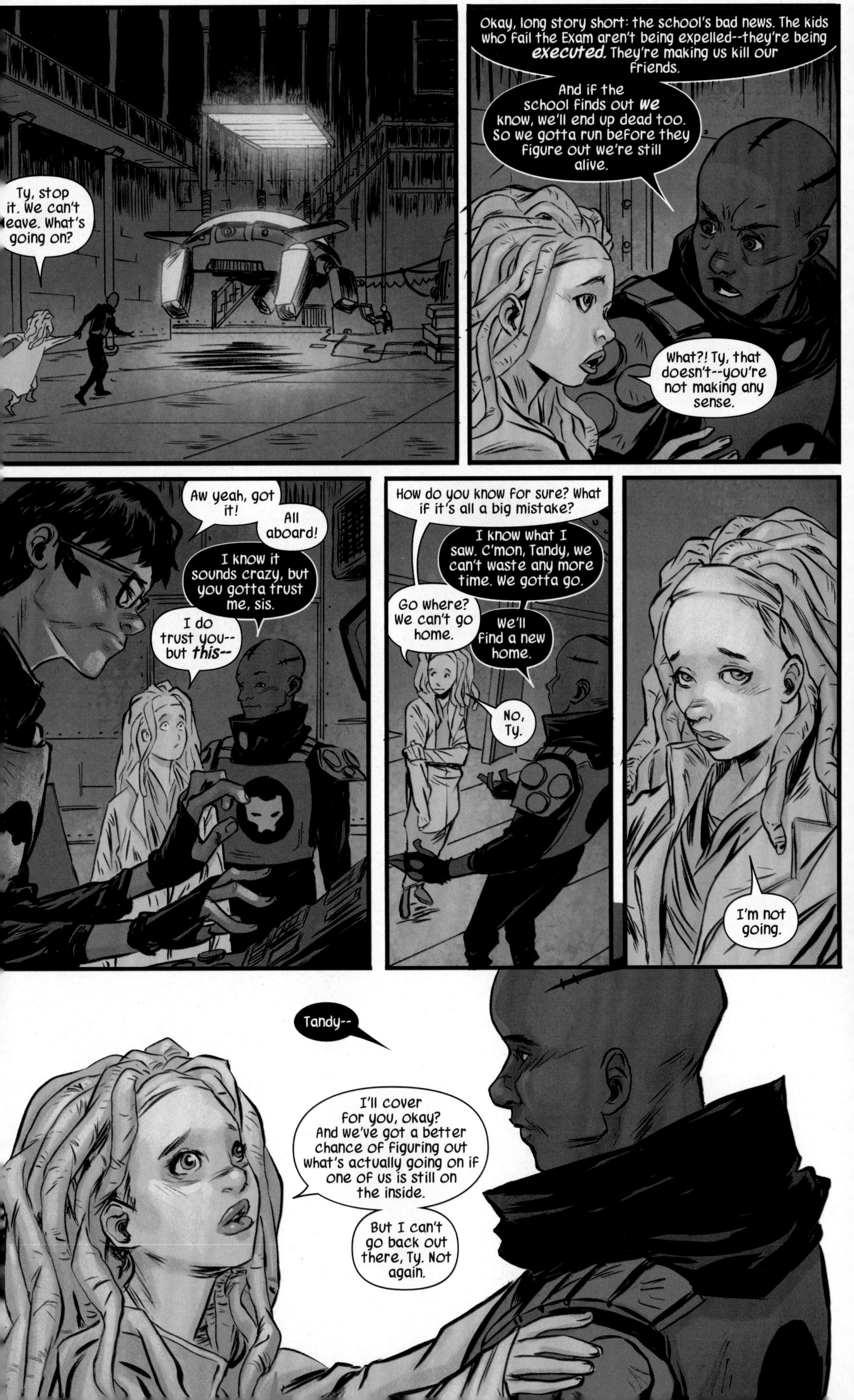
Ty, stop it. We can't leave. What's going on?
Okay, long story short: the school's bad news. The kids who fail the Exam aren't being expelled--they're being *executed*. They're making us kill our friends.
And if the school finds out *we* know, we'll end up dead too. So we gotta run before they figure out we're still alive.
What?! Ty, that doesn't--you're not making any sense.
Aw yeah, got it!
All aboard!
I know it sounds crazy, but you gotta trust me, sis.
I do trust you--but *this*--
How do you know for sure? What if it's all a big mistake?
I know what I saw. C'mon, Tandy, we can't waste any more time. We gotta go.
Go where? We can't go home.
We'll find a new home.
No, Ty.
I'm not going.
Tandy--
I'll cover for you, okay? And we've got a better chance of figuring out what's actually going on if one of us is still on the inside.
But I can't go back out there, Ty. Not again.

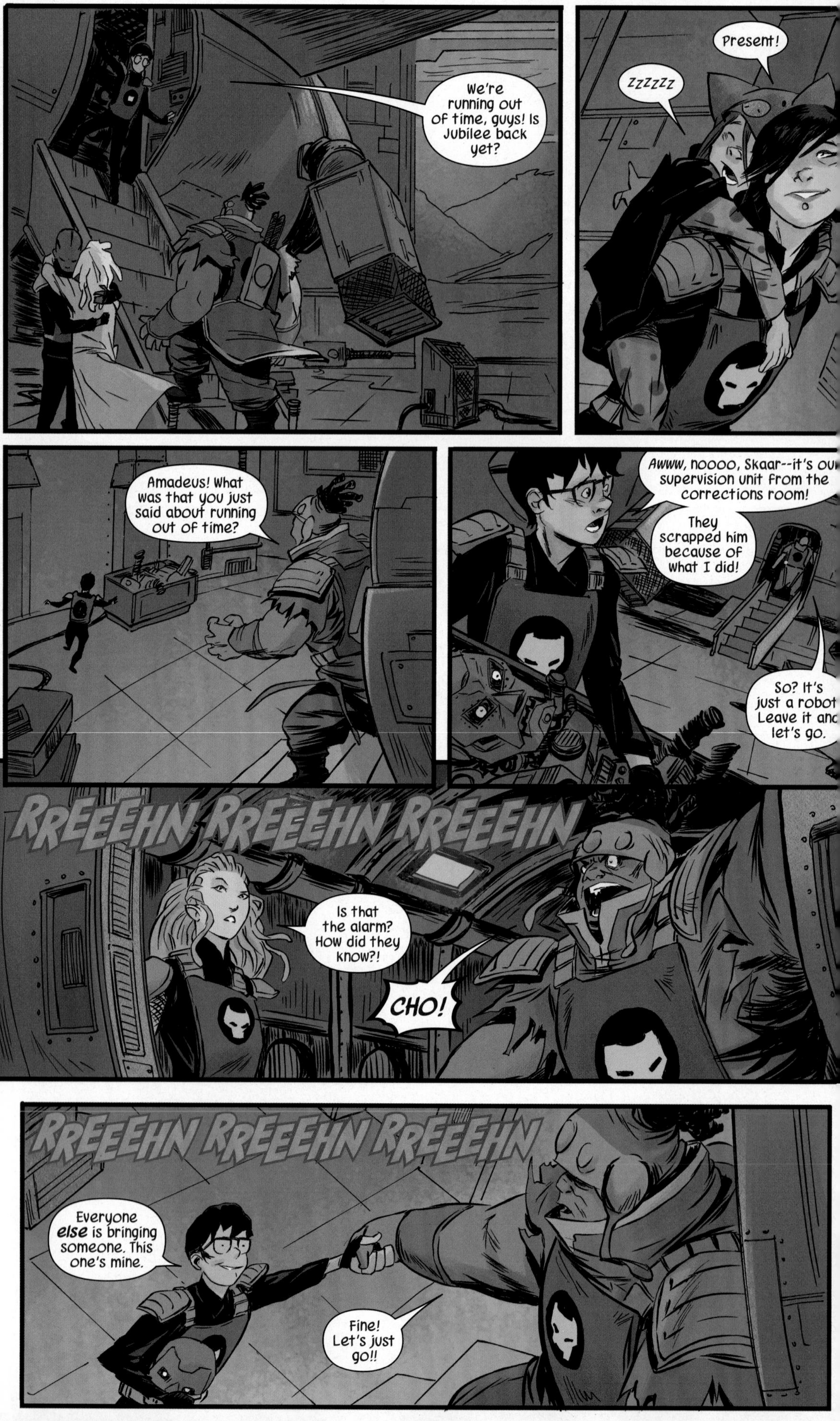
We're running out of time, guys! Is Jubilee back yet?
ZZZZZZ
Present!
Amadeus! What was that you just said about running out of time?
Awww, noooo, Skaar--it's our supervision unit from the corrections room!
They scrapped him because of what I did!
So? It's just a robot. Leave it and let's go.
RREEEHN RREEEHN RREEEHN
Is that the alarm? How did they know?!
CHO!
RREEEHN RREEEHN RREEEHN
Everyone *else* is bringing someone. This one's mine.
Fine! Let's just go!!

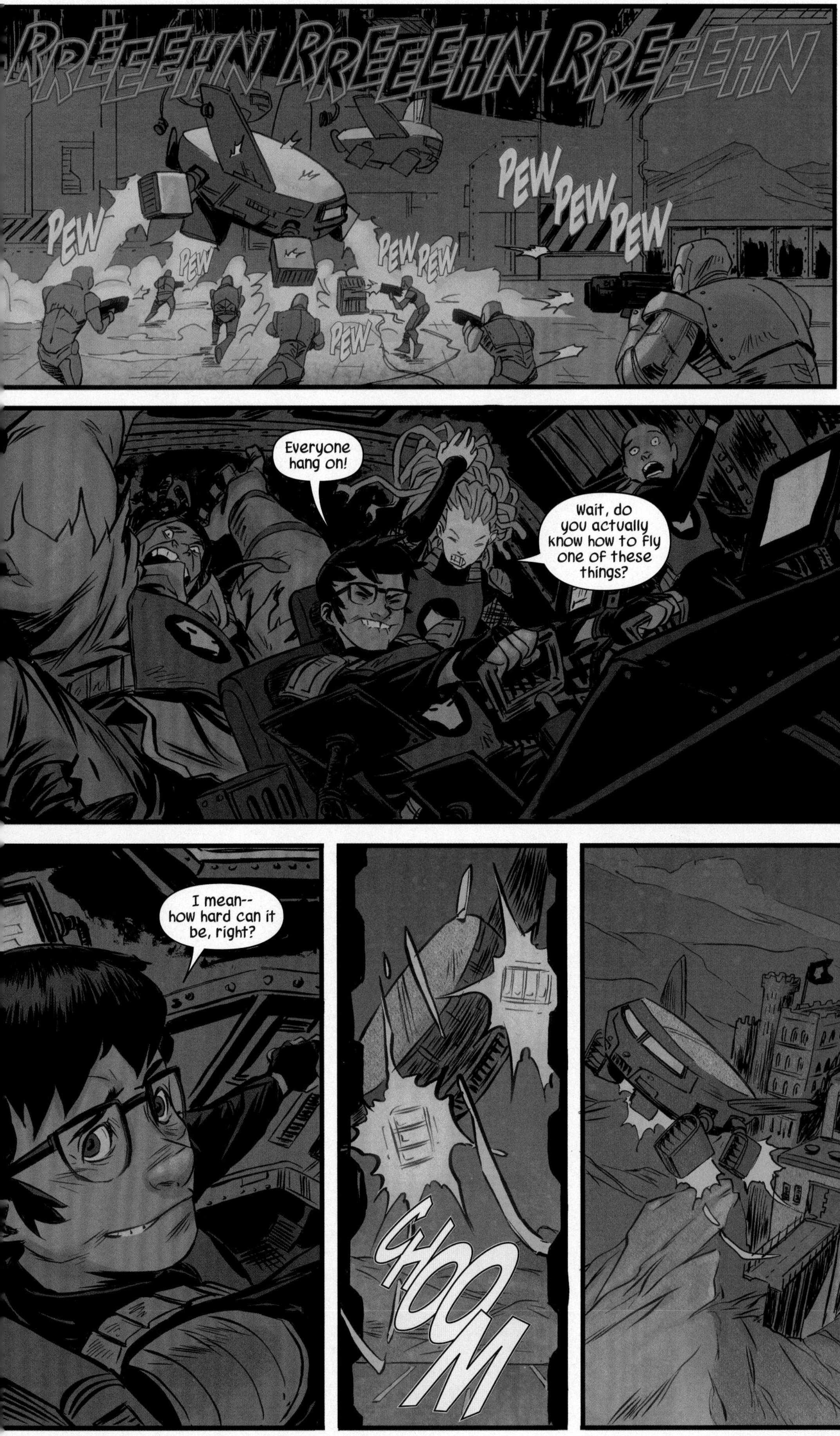
RREEEHN RREEEHN RREEEHN
PEW
PEW
PEW PEW
PEW
PEW PEW PEW
Everyone hang on!
Wait, do you actually know how to fly one of these things?
I mean-- how hard can it be, right?
CHOOM

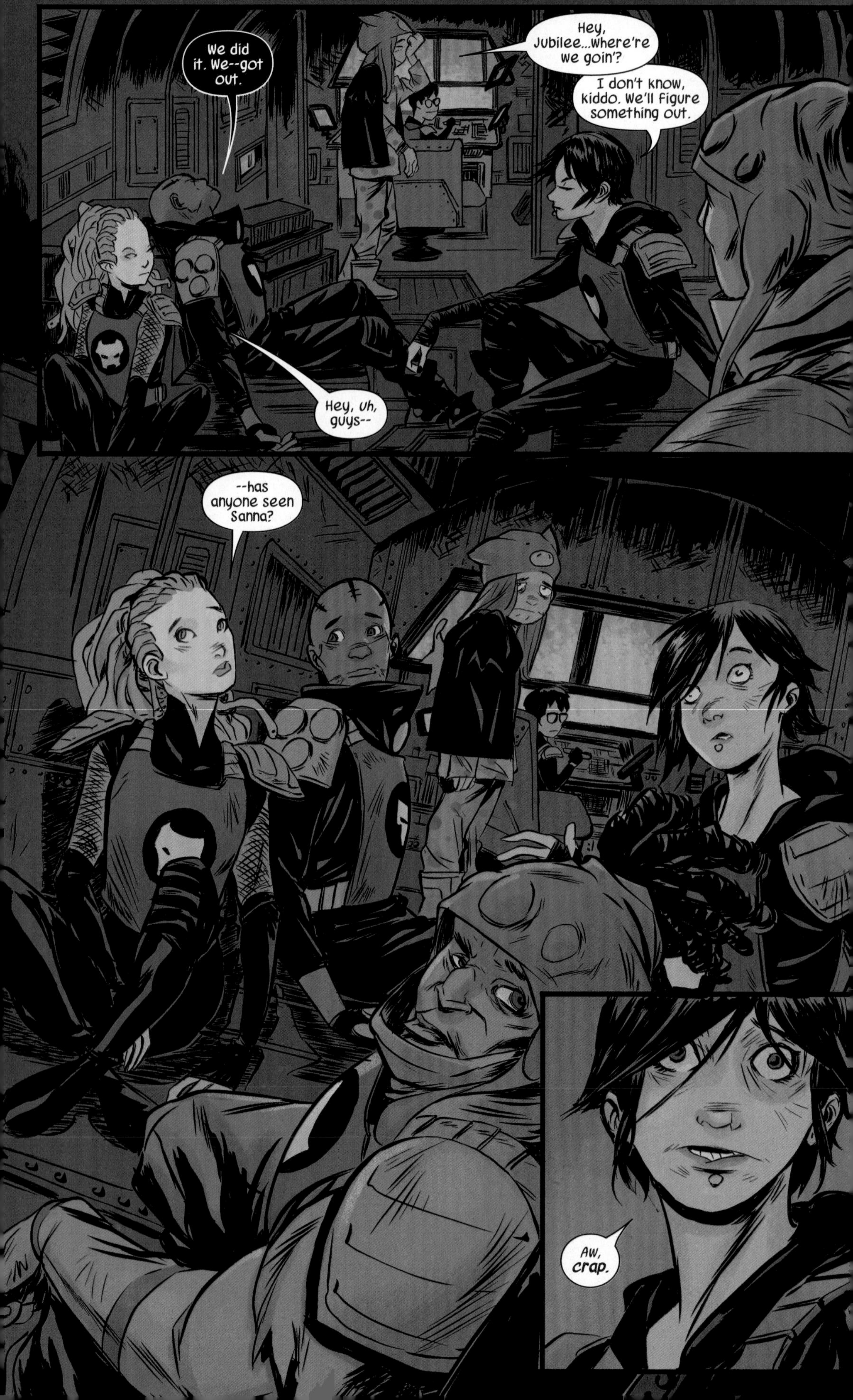
We did it. We--got out.
Hey, Jubilee...where're we goin'?
I don't know, kiddo. We'll figure something out.
Hey, uh, guys--
--has anyone seen Sanna?
Aw, crap.

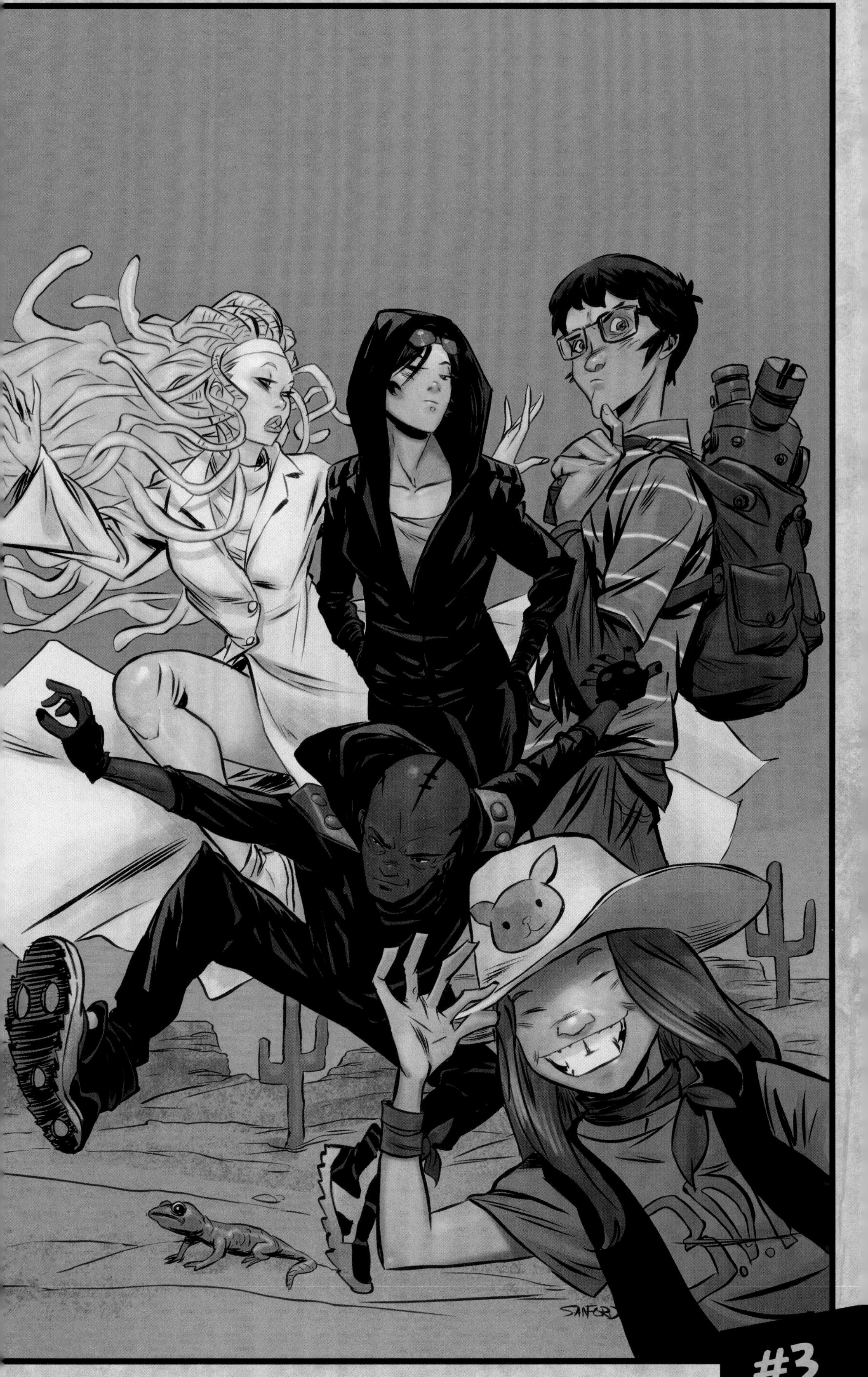
SANFORD
#3

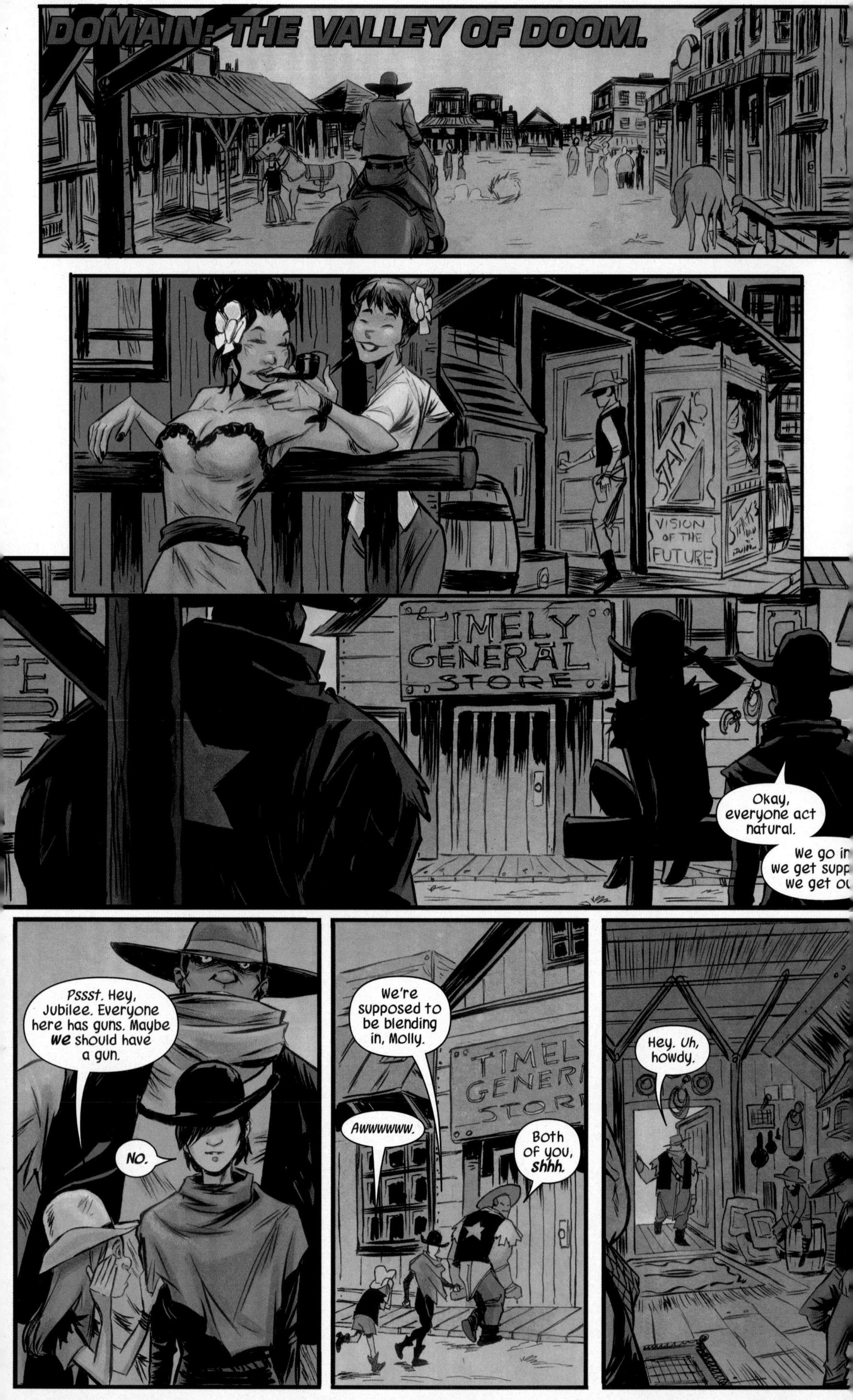
DOMAIN: THE VALLEY OF DOOM.
STARK'S
VISION OF THE FUTURE
TIMELY GENERAL STORE
Okay, everyone act natural.
We go in
we get supp
we get ou
Pssst. Hey, Jubilee. Everyone here has guns. Maybe we should have a gun.
NO.
We're supposed to be blending in, Molly.
Awwwwww.
Both of you, shhh.
Hey. Uh, howdy.

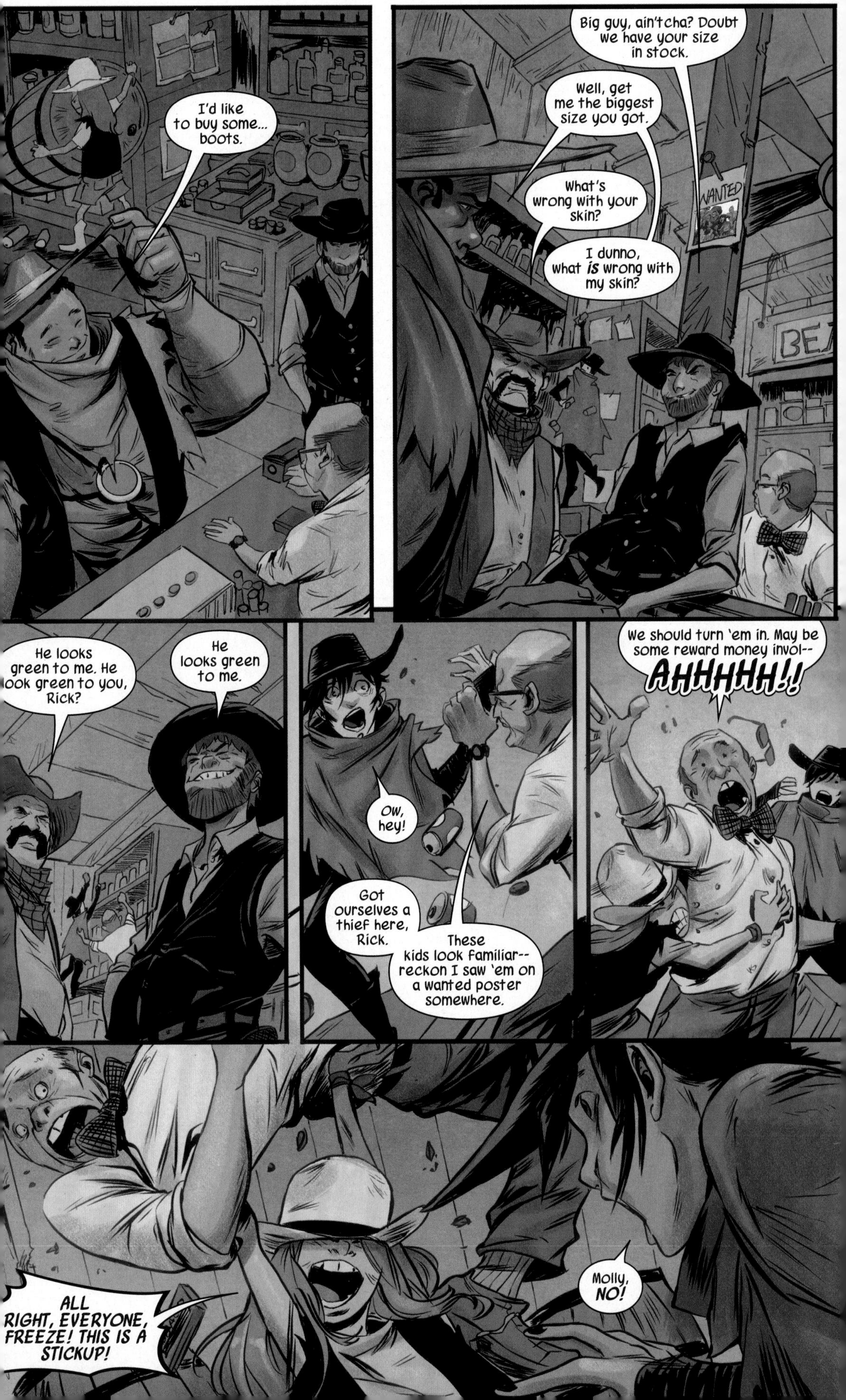
I'd like to buy some... boots.
Big guy, ain'tcha? Doubt we have your size in stock.
Well, get me the biggest size you got.
What's wrong with your skin?
I dunno, what *is* wrong with my skin?
WANTED
He looks green to me. He look green to you, Rick?
He looks green to me.
Ow, hey!
Got ourselves a thief here, Rick.
These kids look familiar-- reckon I saw 'em on a wanted poster somewhere.
We should turn 'em in. May be some reward money invol-- AHHHHH!!
ALL RIGHT, EVERYONE, FREEZE! THIS IS A STICKUP!
Molly, NO!

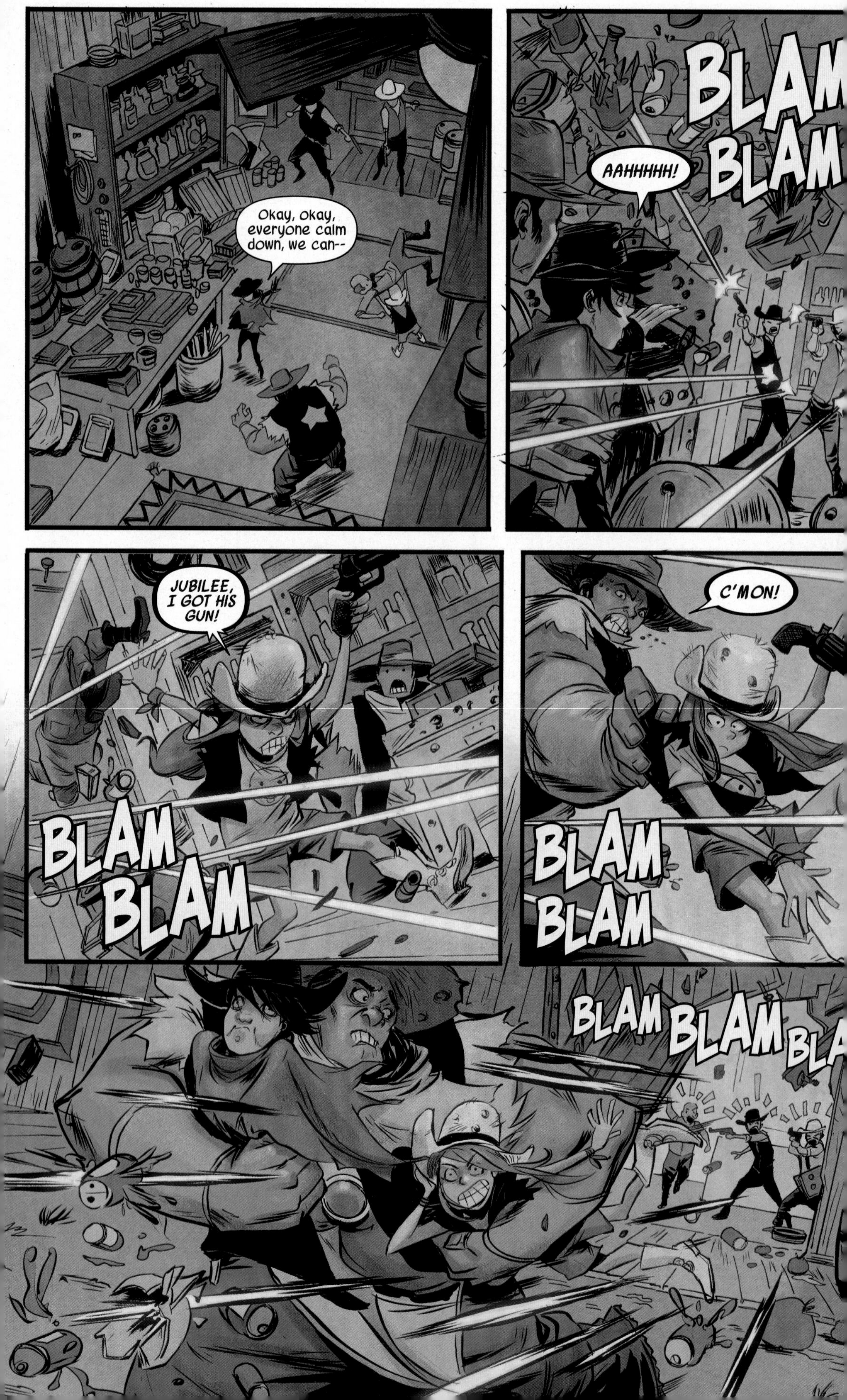
Okay, okay, everyone calm down, we can--
AAHHHHH!
BLAM
BLAM
JUBILEE, I GOT HIS GUN!
BLAM
BLAM
C'MON!
BLAM
BLAM
BLAM BLAM

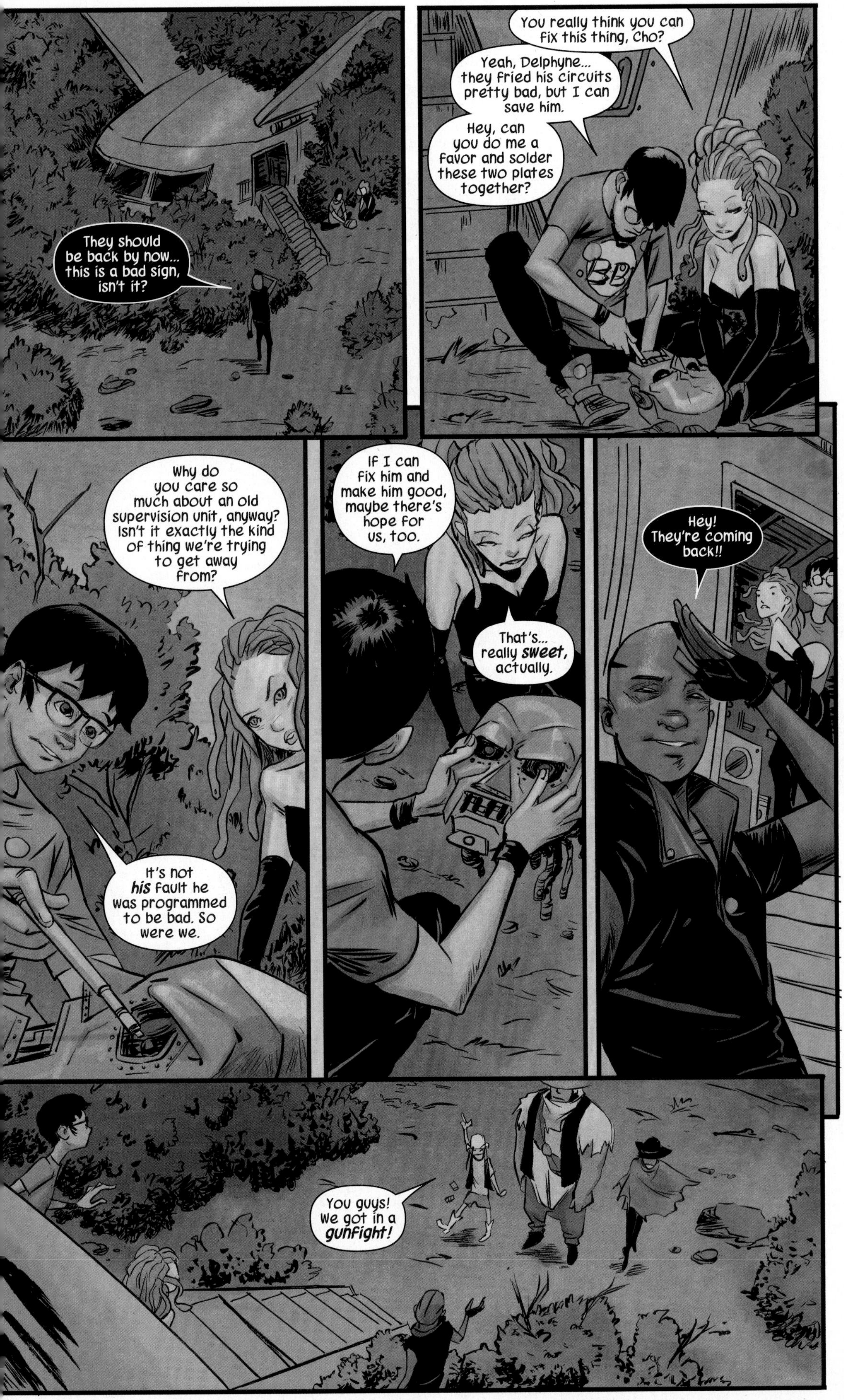
They should be back by now... this is a bad sign, isn't it?
You really think you can fix this thing, Cho?
Yeah, Delphyne... they fried his circuits pretty bad, but I can save him.
Hey, can you do me a favor and solder these two plates together?
Why do you care so much about an old supervision unit, anyway? Isn't it exactly the kind of thing we're trying to get away from?
It's not ***his*** fault he was programmed to be bad. So were we.
If I can fix him and make him good, maybe there's hope for us, too.
That's... really ***sweet,*** actually.
Hey! They're coming back!!
You guys! We got in a ***gunfight!***

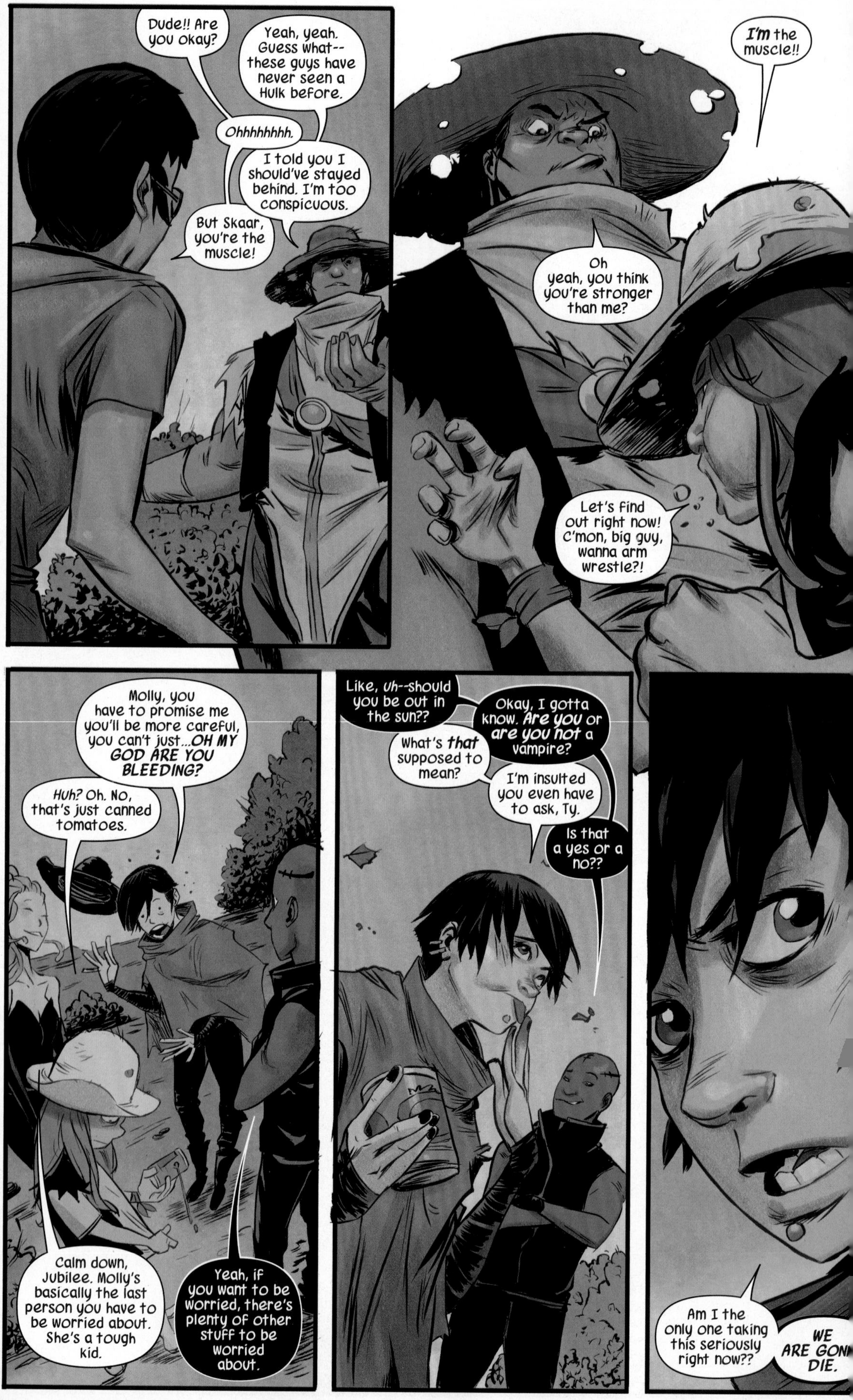

Dude!! Are you okay?
Yeah, yeah. Guess what-- these guys have never seen a Hulk before.
Ohhhhhhhh.
I told you I should've stayed behind. I'm too conspicuous.
But Skaar, you're the muscle!
I'm the muscle!!
Oh yeah, you think you're stronger than me?
Let's find out right now! C'mon, big guy, wanna arm wrestle?!
Molly, you have to promise me you'll be more careful, you can't just...OH MY GOD ARE YOU BLEEDING?
Huh? Oh. No, that's just canned tomatoes.
Calm down, Jubilee. Molly's basically the last person you have to be worried about. She's a tough kid.
Yeah, if you want to be worried, there's plenty of other stuff to be worried about.
Like, uh--should you be out in the sun??
Okay, I gotta know. Are you or are you not a vampire?
What's that supposed to mean?
I'm insulted you even have to ask, Ty.
Is that a yes or a no??
Am I the only one taking this seriously right now??
WE ARE GON DIE.

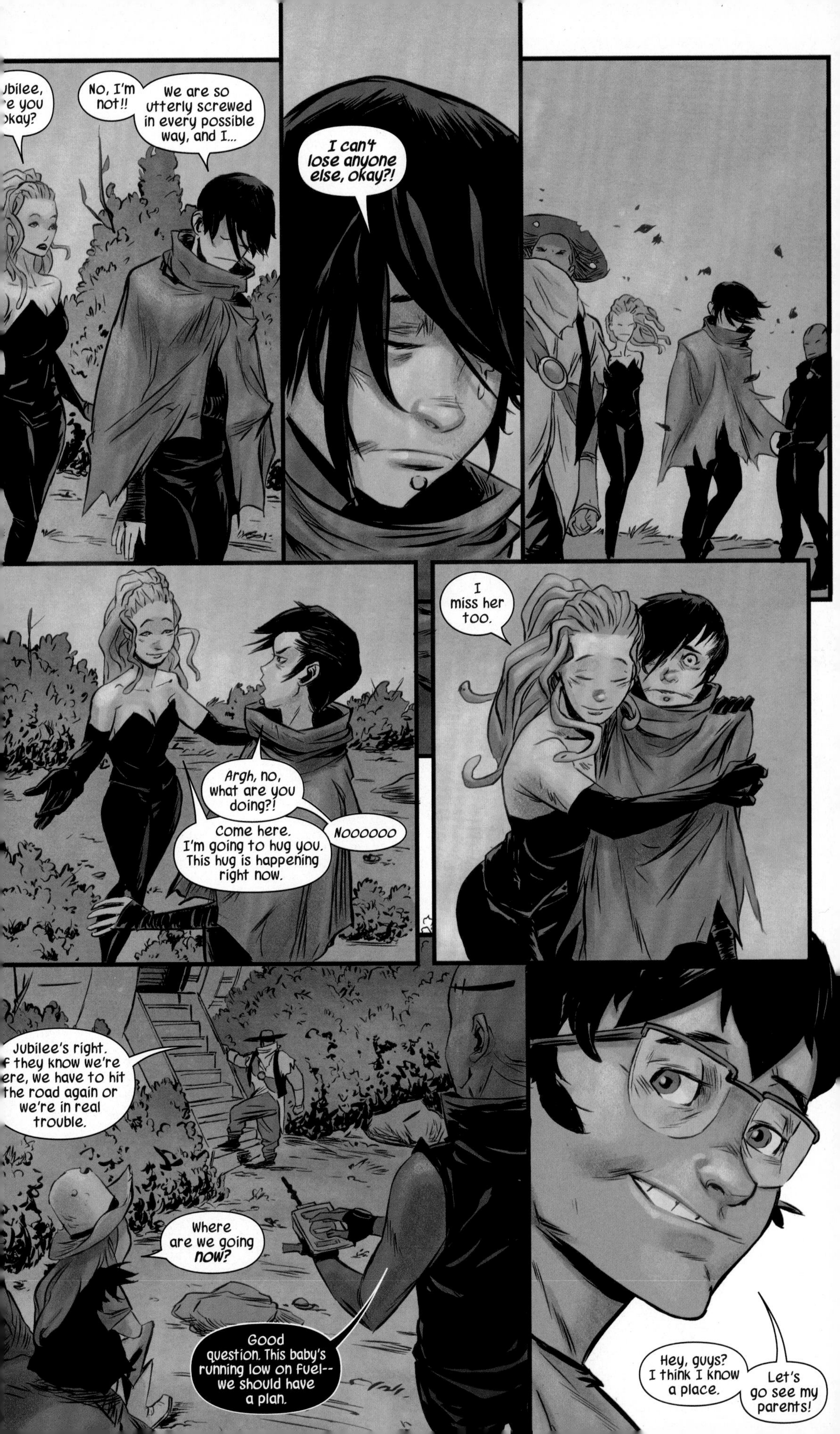

ubilee,
e you
okay?
No, I'm not!!
We are so utterly screwed in every possible way, and I...
I can't lose anyone else, okay?!
Argh, no, what are you doing?!
Come here. I'm going to hug you. This hug is happening right now.
NOOOOOO
I miss her too.
Jubilee's right.
f they know we're
ere, we have to hit
the road again or
we're in real
trouble.
Where are we going now?
Good question. This baby's running low on fuel-- we should have a plan.
Hey, guys? I think I know a place.
Let's go see my parents!

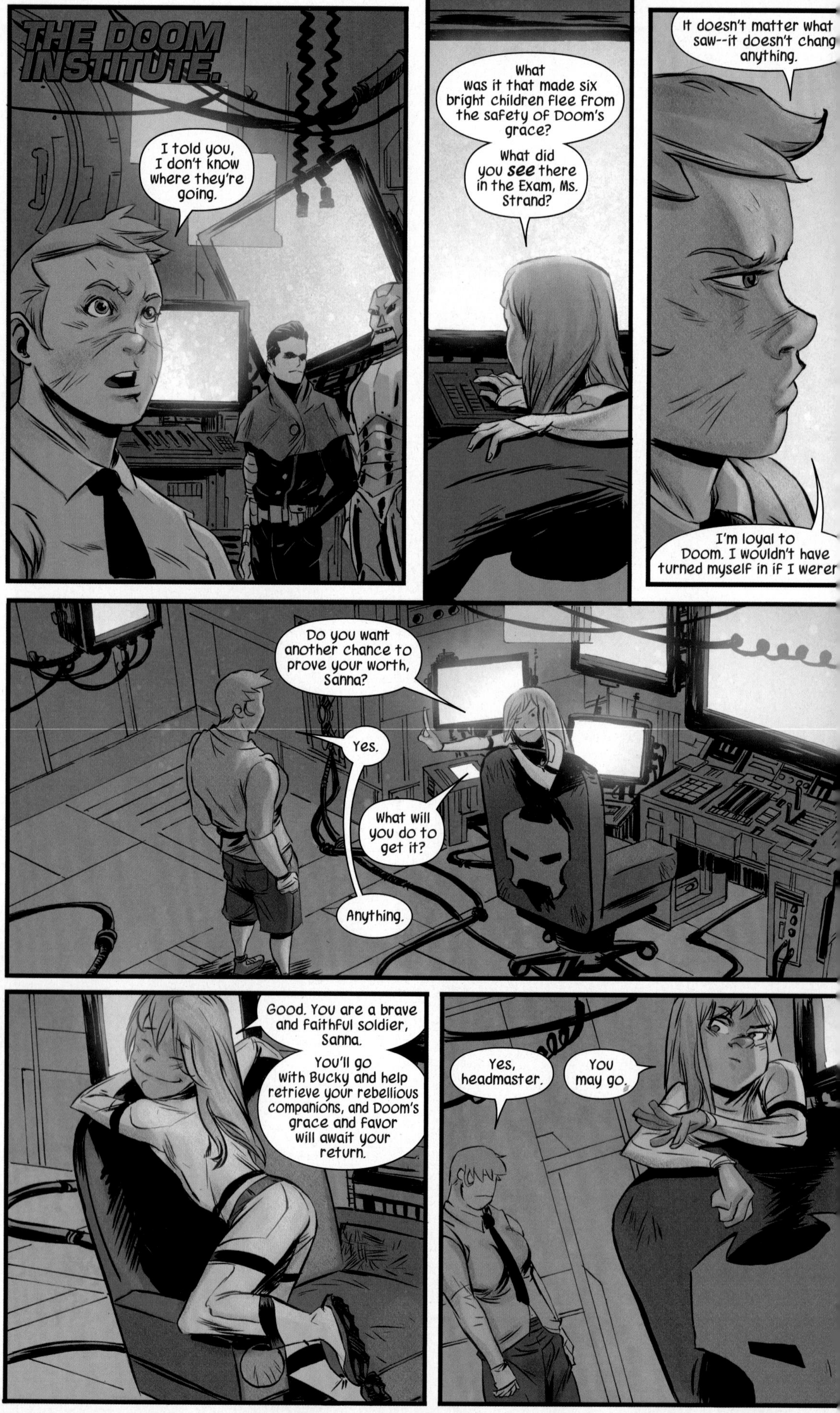
THE DOOM INSTITUTE.
I told you, I don't know where they're going.
What was it that made six bright children flee from the safety of Doom's grace?
What did you *see* there in the Exam, Ms. Strand?
It doesn't matter what saw--it doesn't chang anything.
I'm loyal to Doom. I wouldn't have turned myself in if I werer
Do you want another chance to prove your worth, Sanna?
Yes.
What will you do to get it?
Anything.
Good. You are a brave and faithful soldier, Sanna.
You'll go with Bucky and help retrieve your rebellious companions, and Doom's grace and favor will await your return.
Yes, headmaster.
You may go.

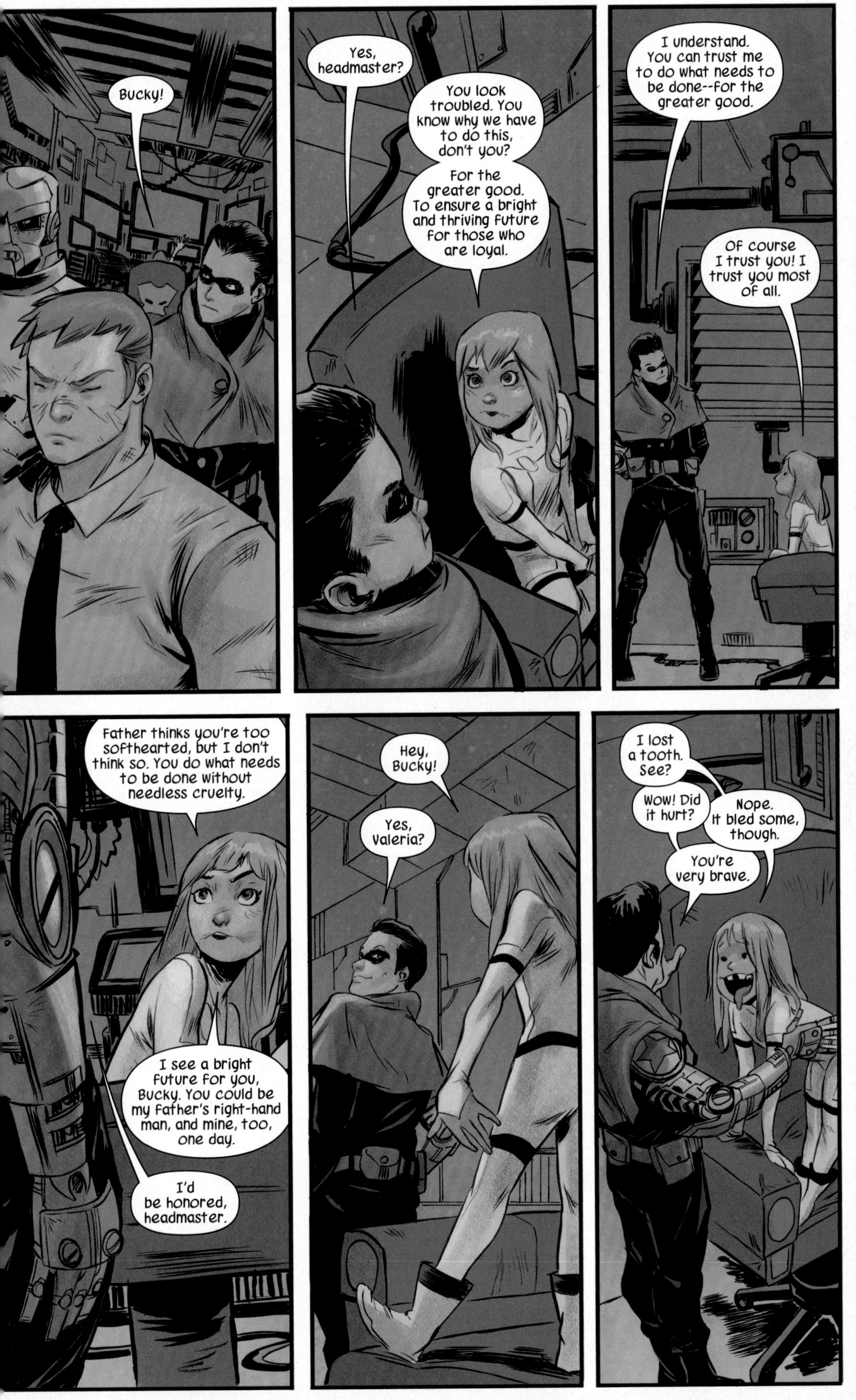
Bucky!
Yes, headmaster?
You look troubled. You know why we have to do this, don't you?
For the greater good. To ensure a bright and thriving future for those who are loyal.
I understand. You can trust me to do what needs to be done--for the greater good.
Of course I trust you! I trust you most of all.
Father thinks you're too softhearted, but I don't think so. You do what needs to be done without needless cruelty.
I see a bright future for you, Bucky. You could be my father's right-hand man, and mine, too, one day.
I'd be honored, headmaster.
Hey, Bucky!
Yes, Valeria?
I lost a tooth. See?
Wow! Did it hurt?
Nope. It bled some, though.
You're very brave.

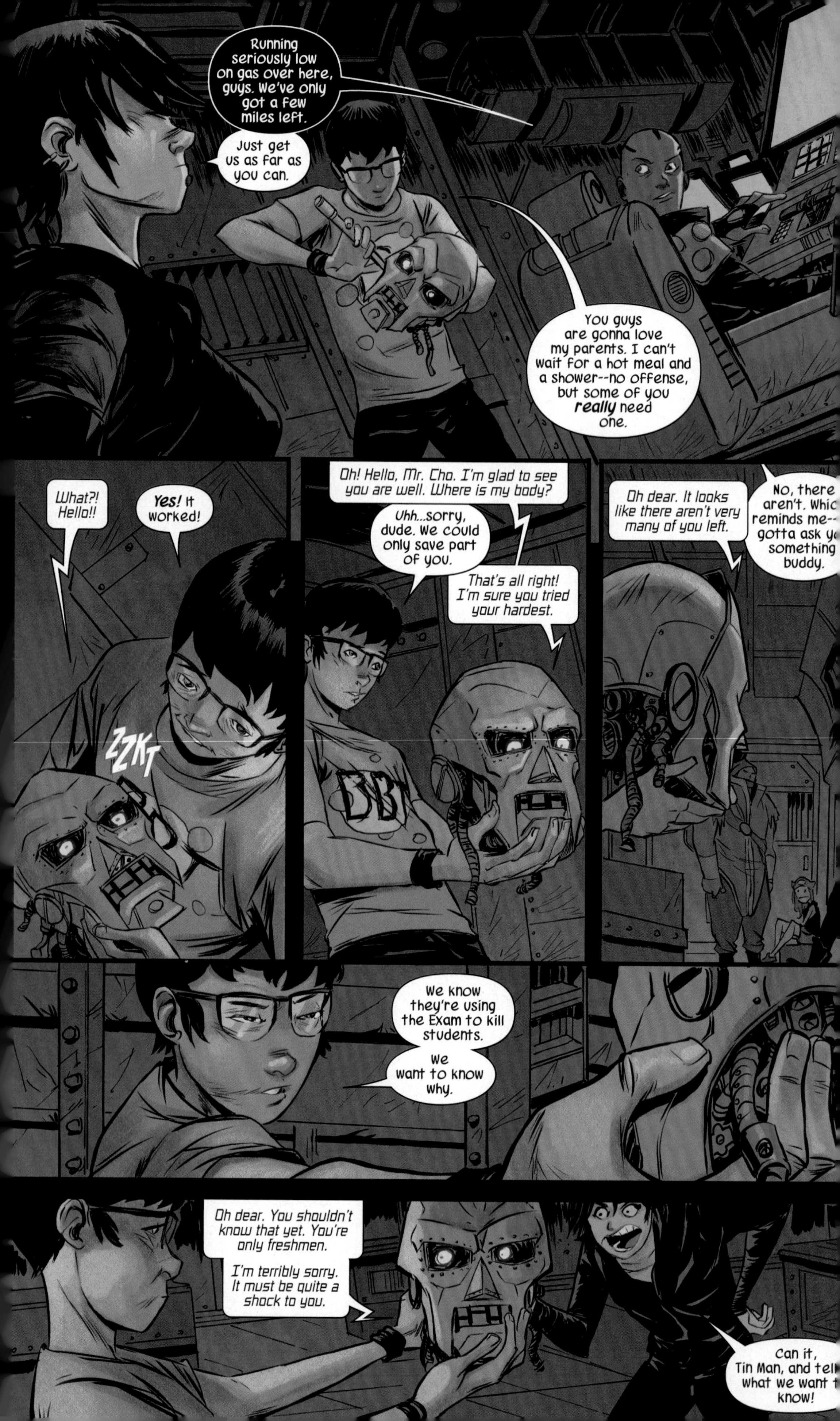
Running seriously low on gas over here, guys. We've only got a few miles left.
Just get us as far as you can.
You guys are gonna love my parents. I can't wait for a hot meal and a shower--no offense, but some of you *really* need one.
What?! Hello!!
Yes! It worked!
ZZKT
Oh! Hello, Mr. Cho. I'm glad to see you are well. Where is my body?
Uhh...sorry, dude. We could only save part of you.
That's all right! I'm sure you tried your hardest.
Oh dear. It looks like there aren't very many of you left.
We know they're using the Exam to kill students.
We want to know why.
Oh dear. You shouldn't know that yet. You're only freshmen.
I'm terribly sorry. It must be quite a shock to you.

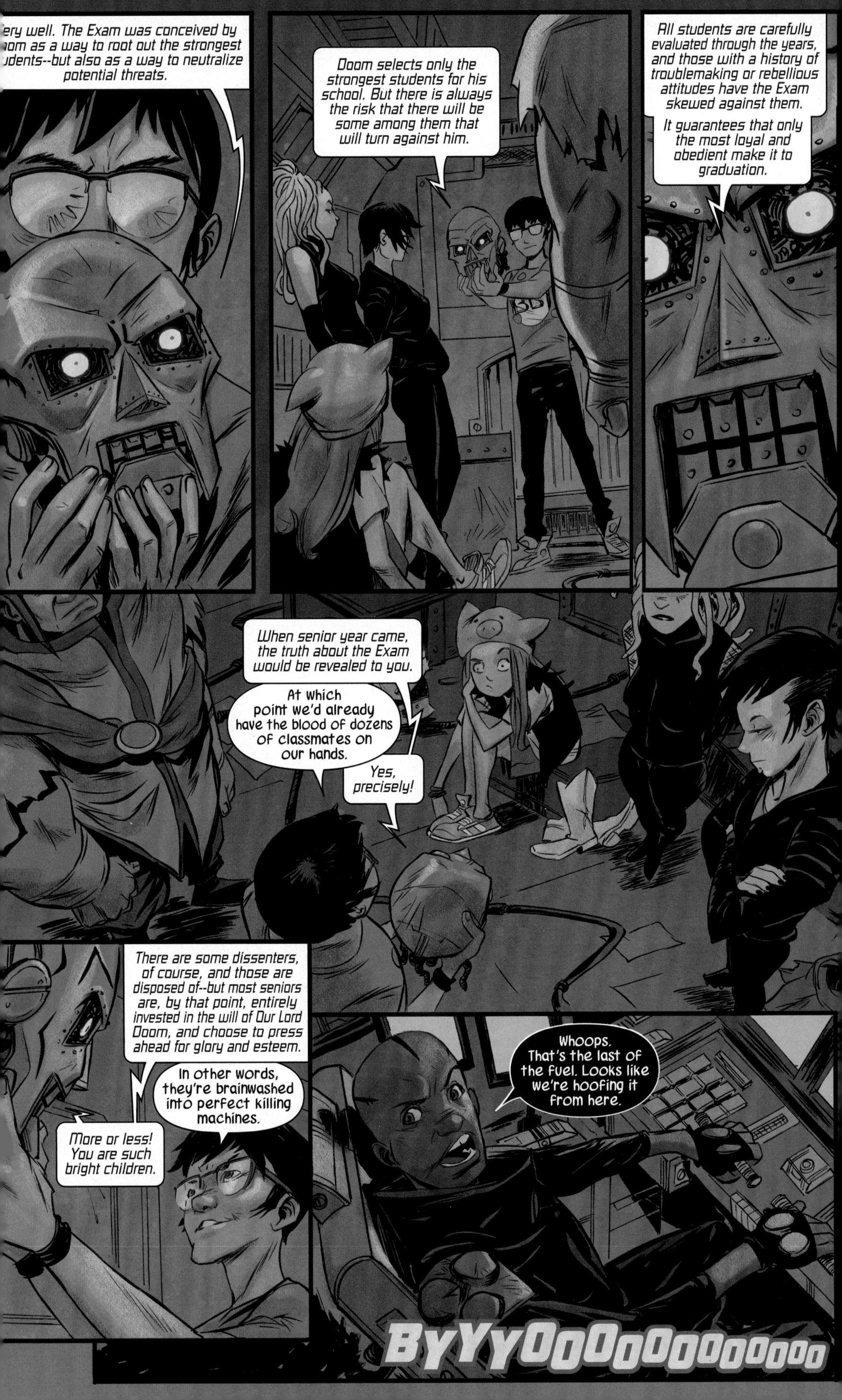

ery well. The Exam was conceived by oom as a way to root out the strongest udents--but also as a way to neutralize potential threats.
Doom selects only the strongest students for his school. But there is always the risk that there will be some among them that will turn against him.
All students are carefully evaluated through the years, and those with a history of troublemaking or rebellious attitudes have the Exam skewed against them.
It guarantees that only the most loyal and obedient make it to graduation.
When senior year came, the truth about the Exam would be revealed to you.
At which point we'd already have the blood of dozens of classmates on our hands.
Yes, precisely!
There are some dissenters, of course, and those are disposed of--but most seniors are, by that point, entirely invested in the will of Our Lord Doom, and choose to press ahead for glory and esteem.
In other words, they're brainwashed into perfect killing machines.
More or less! You are such bright children.
Whoops. That's the last of the fuel. Looks like we're hoofing it from here.
ByYyOoooooooooooo

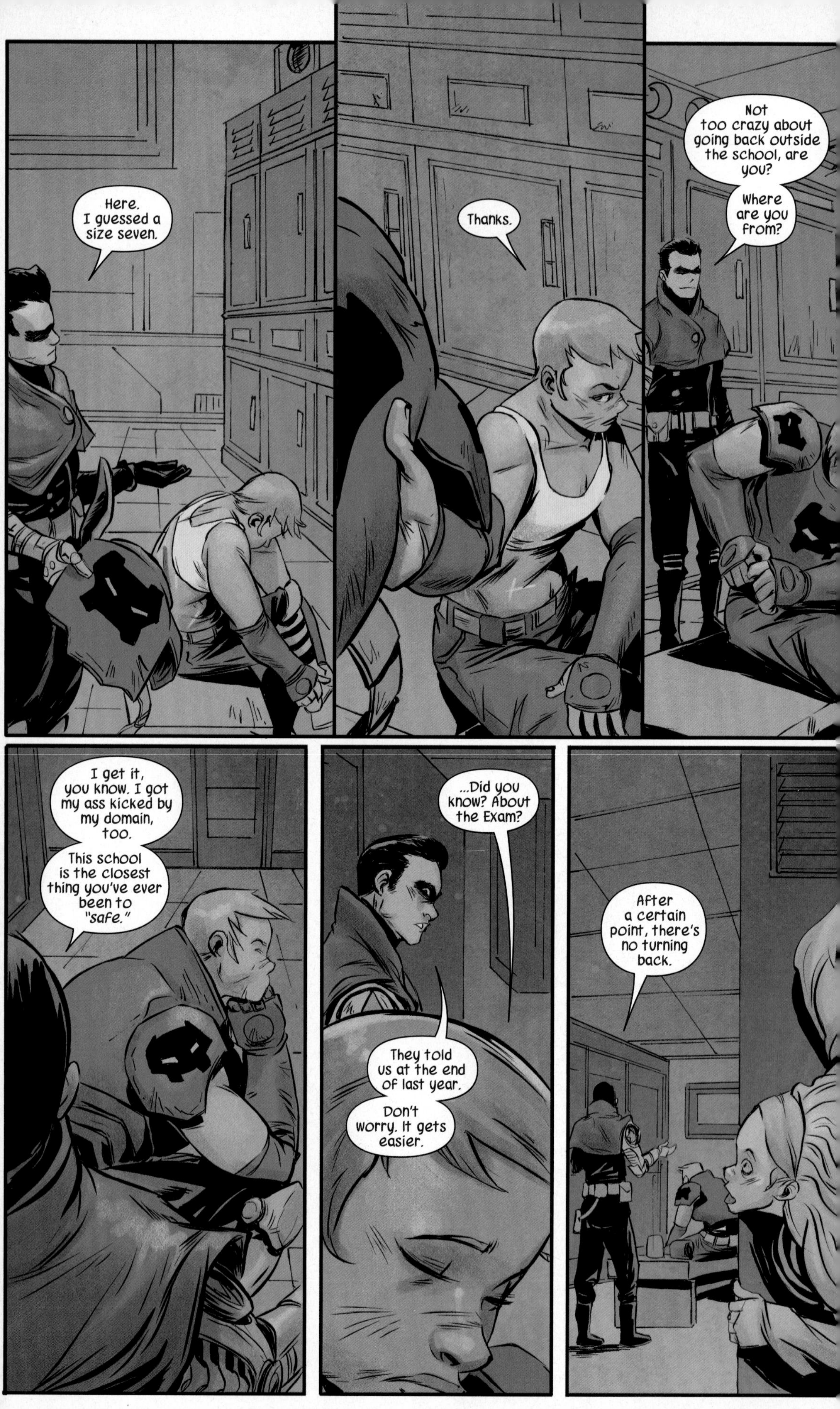
Here. I guessed a size seven.
Thanks.
Not too crazy about going back outside the school, are you?
Where are you from?
I get it, you know. I got my ass kicked by my domain, too.
This school is the closest thing you've ever been to "safe."
...Did you know? About the Exam?
They told us at the end of last year.
Don't worry. It gets easier.
After a certain point, there's no turning back.

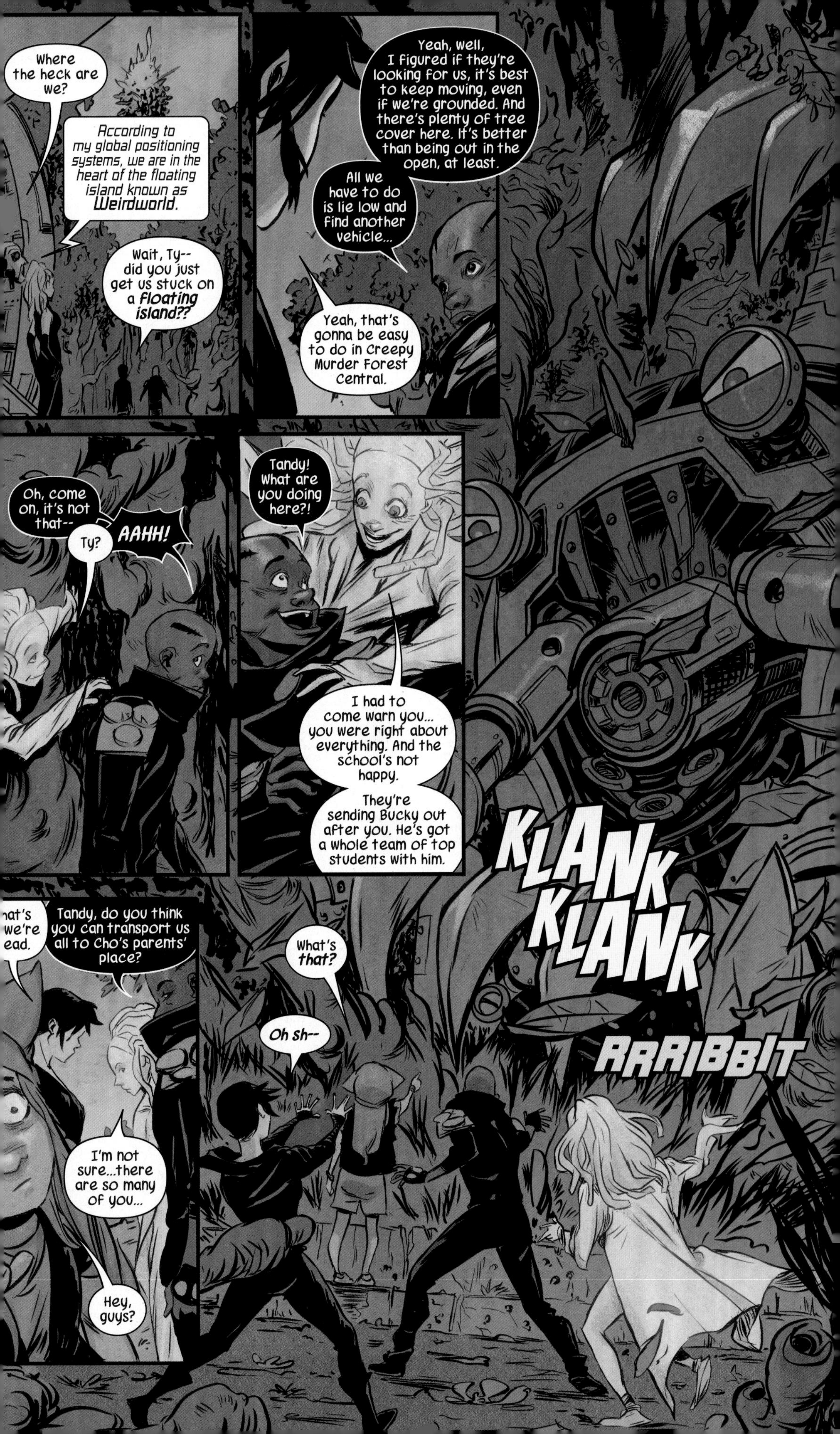

Where the heck are we?
According to my global positioning systems, we are in the heart of the floating island known as Weirdworld.
Wait, Ty-- did you just get us stuck on a floating island??
Yeah, well, I figured if they're looking for us, it's best to keep moving, even if we're grounded. And there's plenty of tree cover here. It's better than being out in the open, at least.
All we have to do is lie low and find another vehicle...
Yeah, that's gonna be easy to do in Creepy Murder Forest Central.
Oh, come on, it's not that--
Ty?
AAHH!
Tandy! What are you doing here?!
I had to come warn you... you were right about everything. And the school's not happy.
They're sending Bucky out after you. He's got a whole team of top students with him.
Tandy, do you think you can transport us all to Cho's parents' place?
I'm not sure...there are so many of you...
Hey, guys?
What's that?
Oh sh--
KLANK KLANK
RRRIBBIT

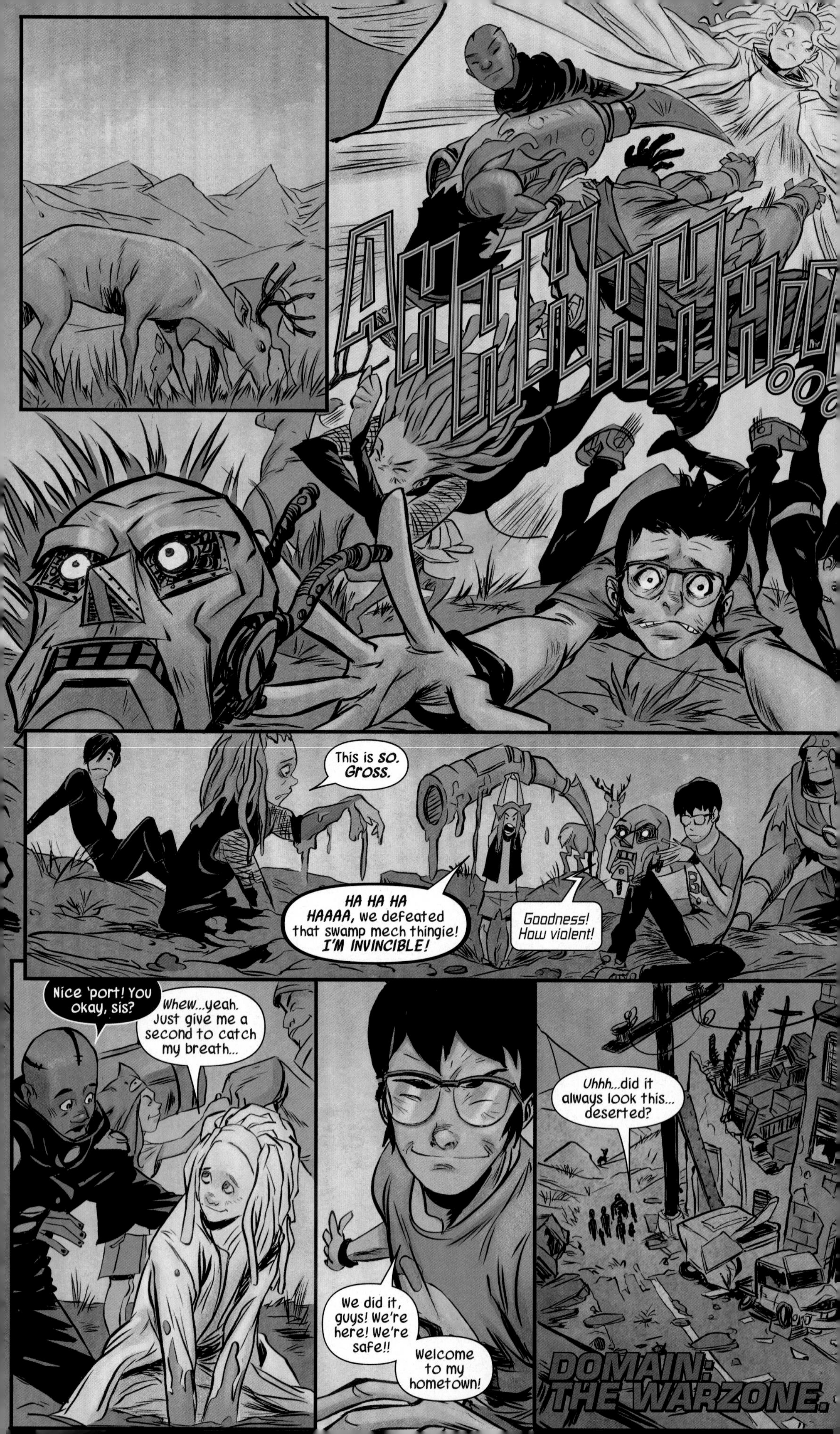
AHHHHHHHHHooo!
This is SO. GROSS.
HA HA HA HAAAA, we defeated that swamp mech thingie! I'M INVINCIBLE!
Goodness! How violent!
Nice 'port! You okay, sis?
Whew...yeah. Just give me a second to catch my breath...
We did it, guys! We're here! We're safe!!
Welcome to my hometown!
Uhhh...did it always look this... deserted?
DOMAIN: THE WARZONE.

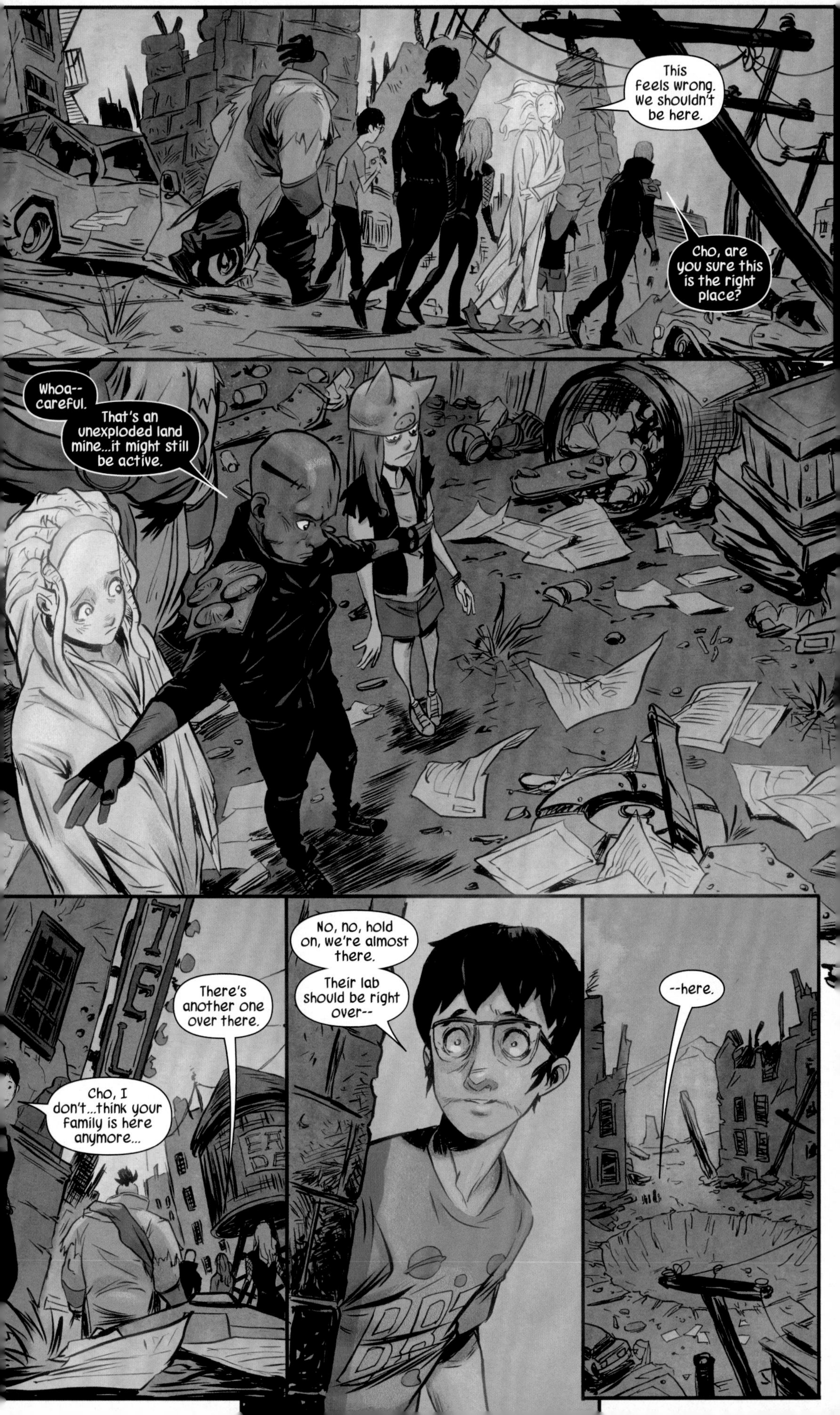
This feels wrong. We shouldn't be here.
Cho, are you sure this is the right place?
Whoa--careful.
That's an unexploded land mine...it might still be active.
There's another one over there.
Cho, I don't...think your family is here anymore...
No, no, hold on, we're almost there.
Their lab should be right over--
--here.

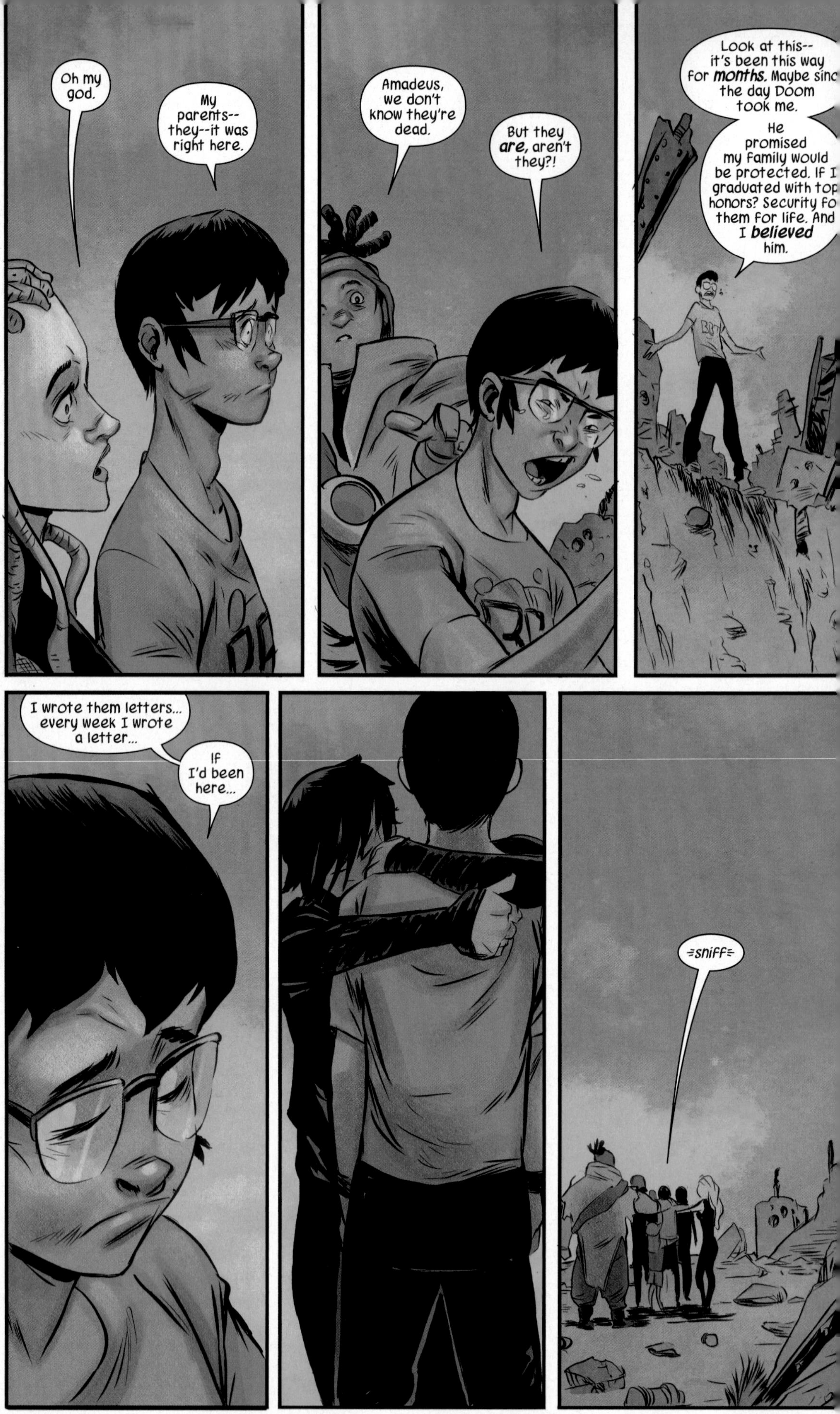
Oh my god.
My parents--they--it was right here.
Amadeus, we don't know they're dead.
But they are, aren't they?!
Look at this--it's been this way for months. Maybe sinc the day Doom took me.
He promised my family would be protected. If I graduated with top honors? Security fo them for life. And I believed him.
I wrote them letters... every week I wrote a letter...
If I'd been here...
=sniff=

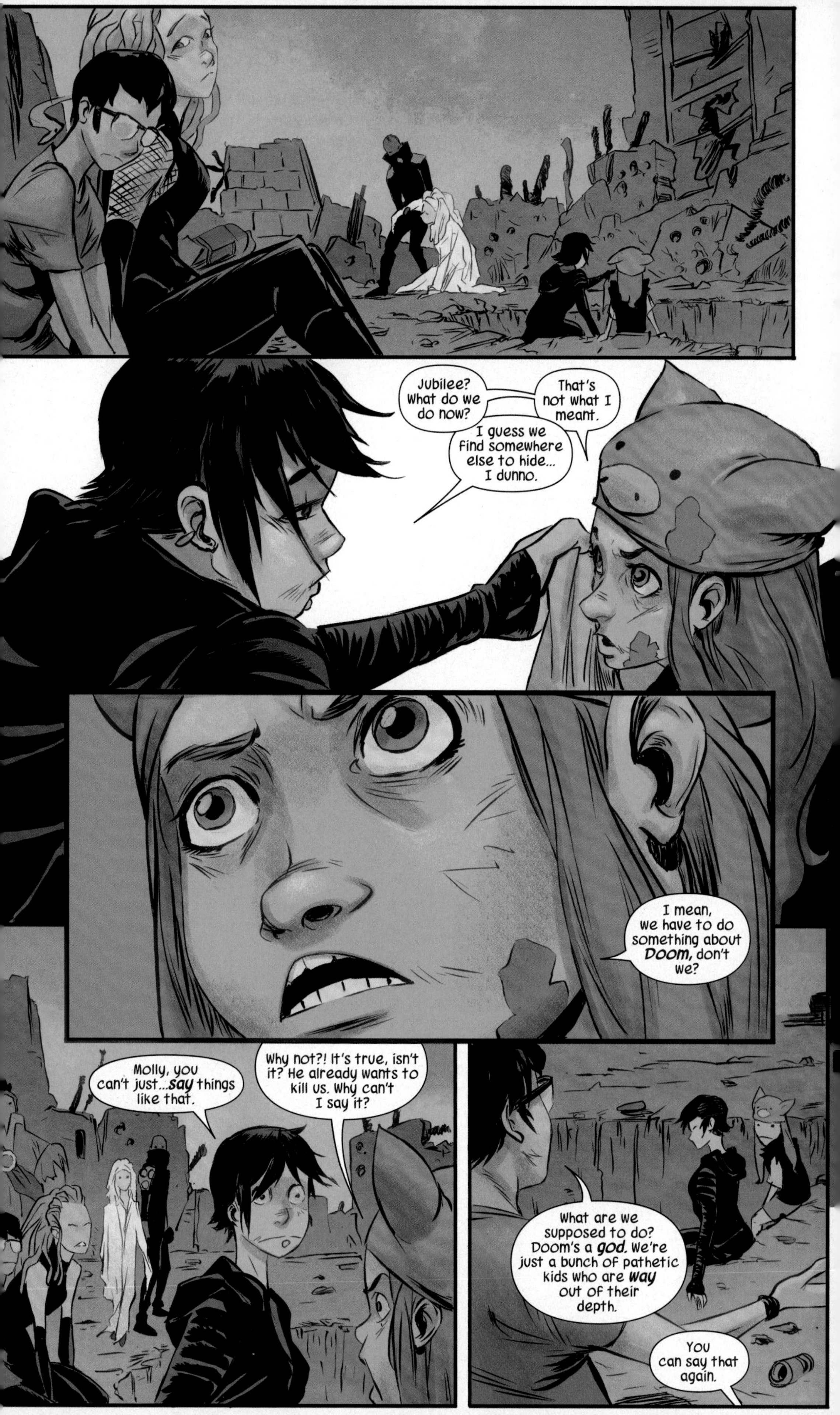

Jubilee? What do we do now?
That's not what I meant.
I guess we find somewhere else to hide... I dunno.
I mean, we have to do something about *Doom,* don't we?
Molly, you can't just...***say*** things like that.
Why not?! It's true, isn't it? He already wants to kill us. Why can't I say it?
What are we supposed to do? Doom's a ***god.*** We're just a bunch of pathetic kids who are ***way*** out of their depth.
You can say that again.

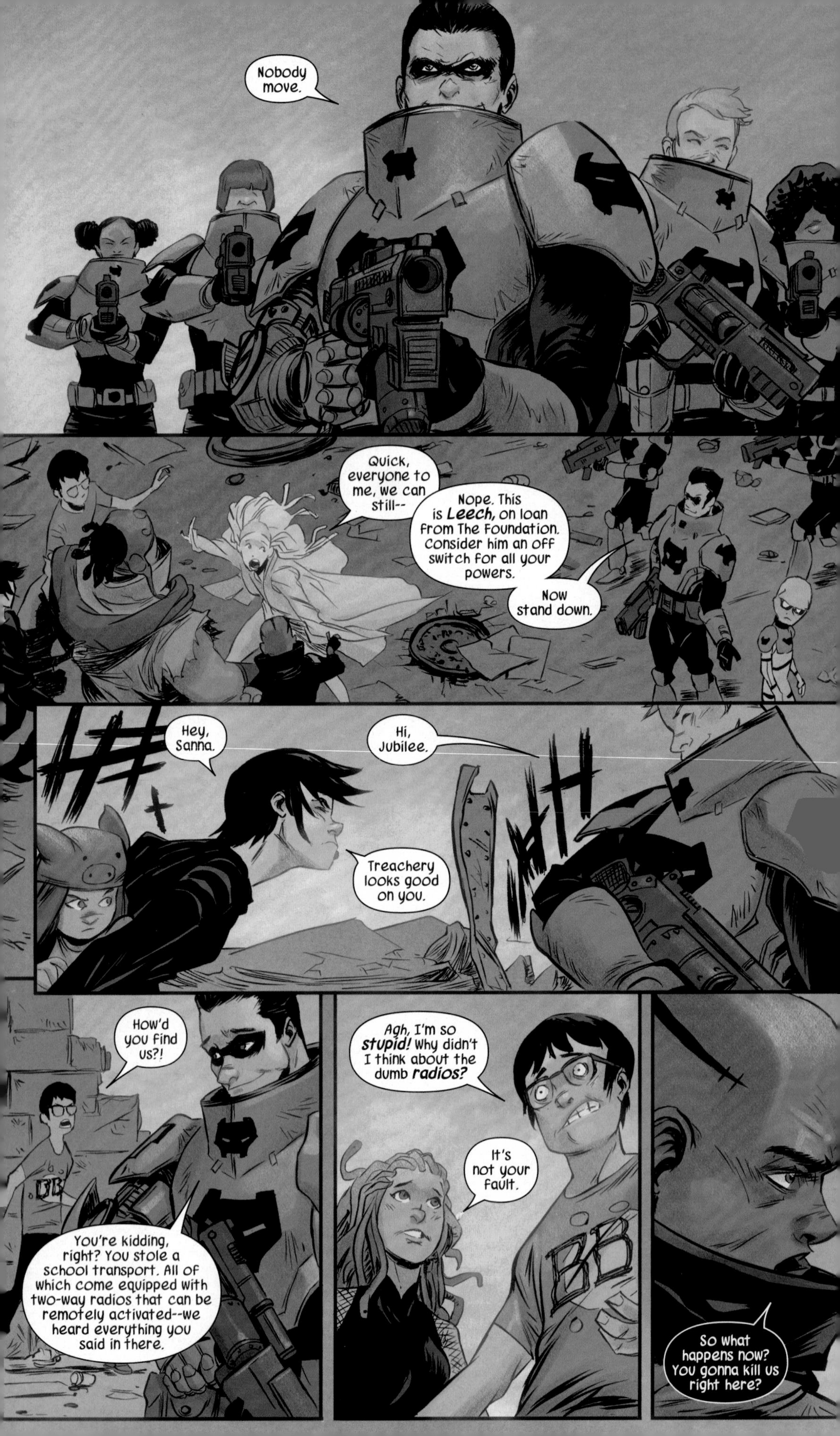
Nobody move.
Quick, everyone to me, we can still--
Nope. This is Leech, on loan from The Foundation. Consider him an off switch for all your powers.
Now stand down.
Hey, Sanna.
Hi, Jubilee.
Treachery looks good on you.
How'd you find us?!
You're kidding, right? You stole a school transport. All of which come equipped with two-way radios that can be remotely activated--we heard everything you said in there.
Agh, I'm so stupid! Why didn't I think about the dumb radios?
It's not your fault.
So what happens now? You gonna kill us right here?

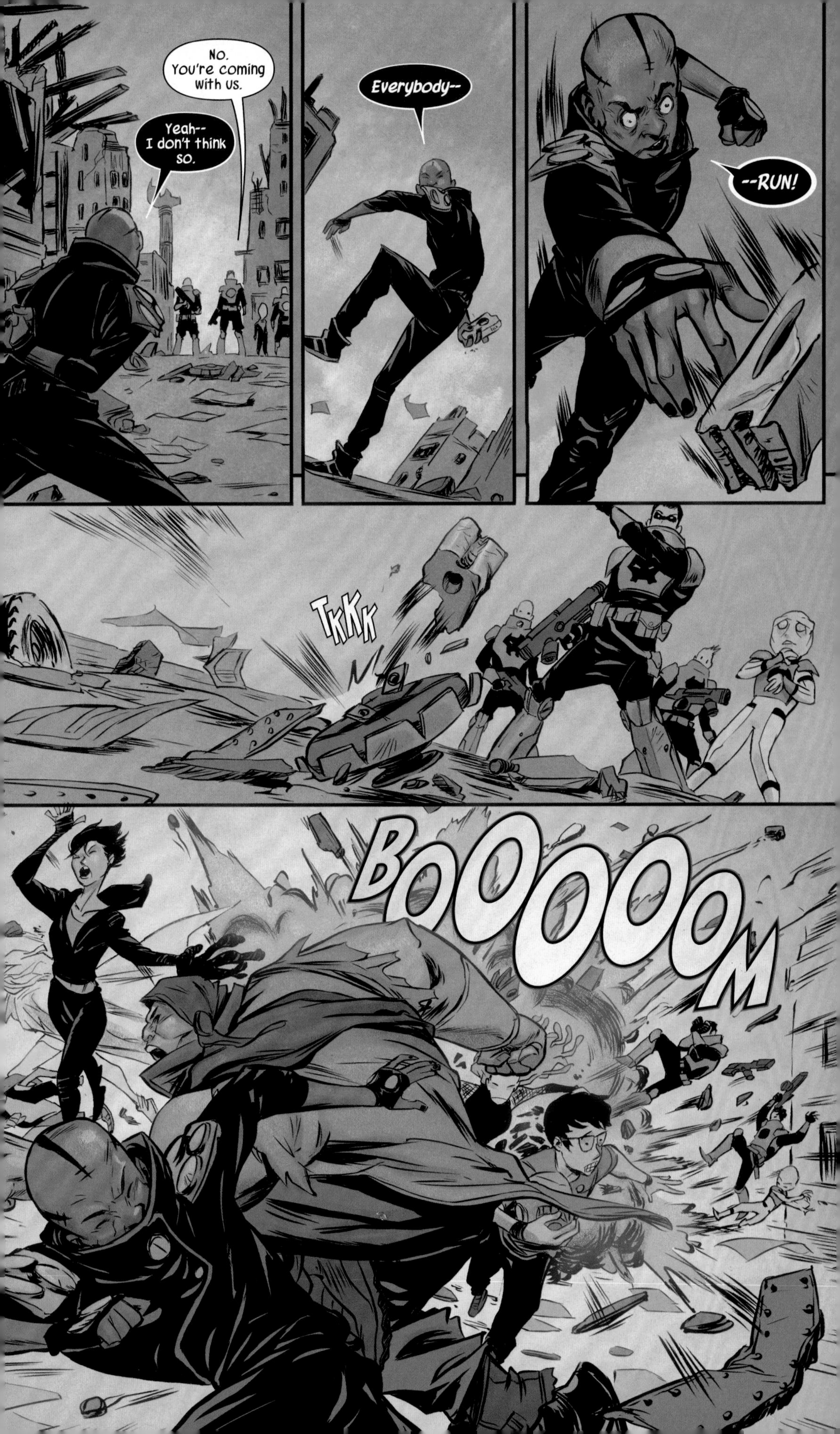
No. You're coming with us.
Yeah-- I don't think so.
Everybody--
--RUN!
TKKK
BOOOOOM

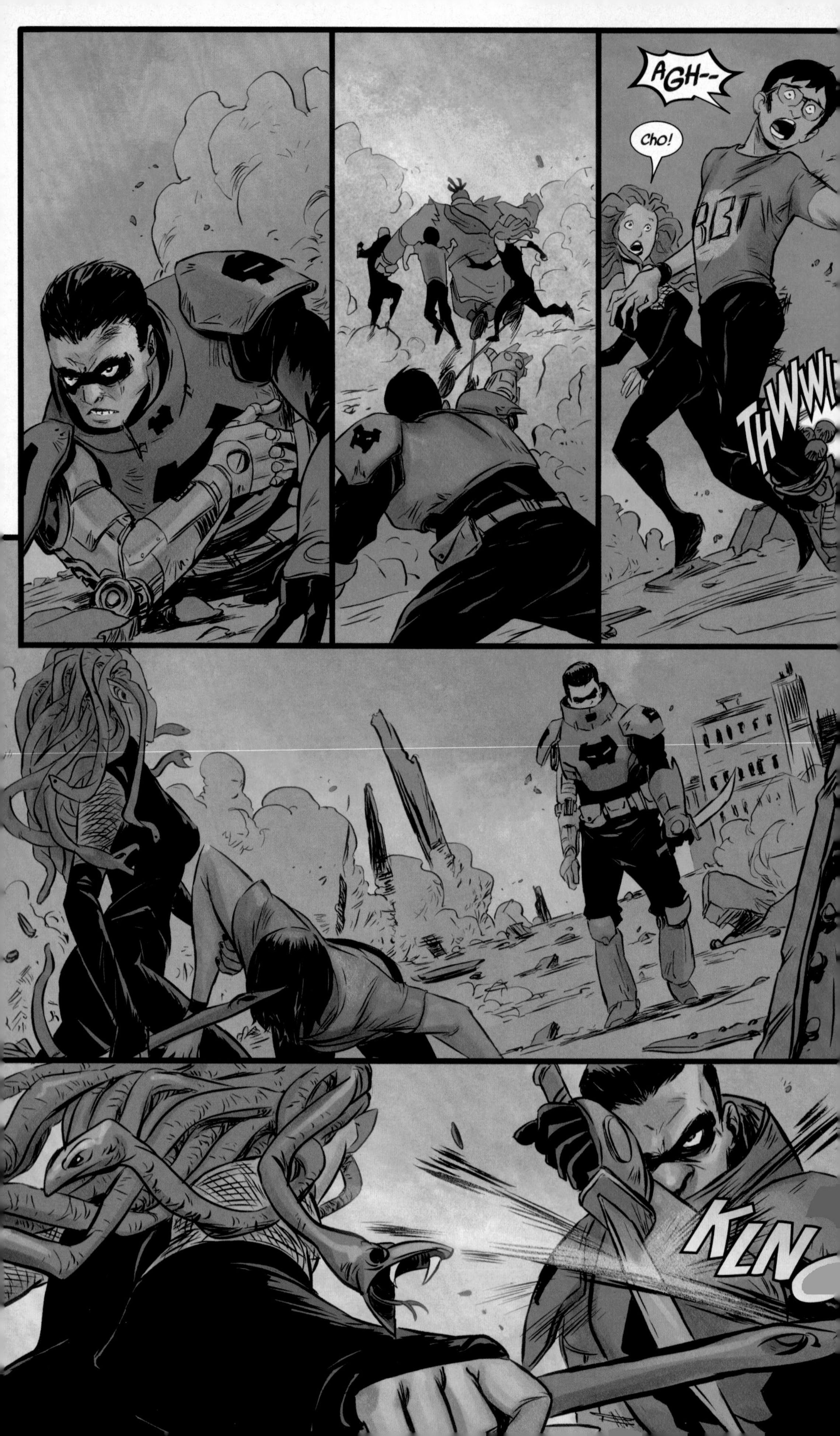
AGH--
Cho!
THWWI
KLN

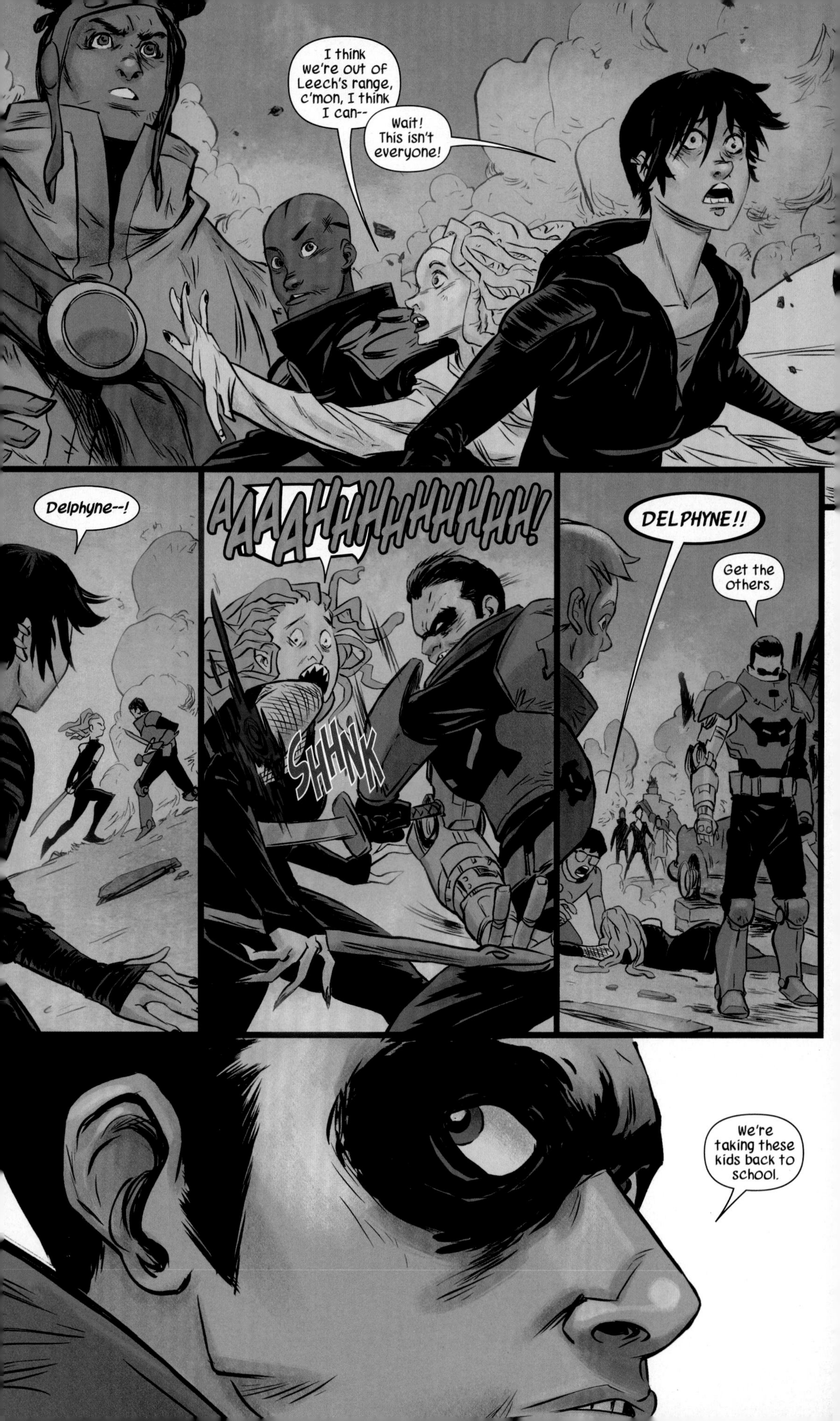
I think we're out of Leech's range, c'mon, I think I can--
Wait! This isn't everyone!
Delphyne--!
AAAAHHHHHHHHHH!
SHHNK
DELPHYNE!!
Get the others.
We're taking these kids back to school.

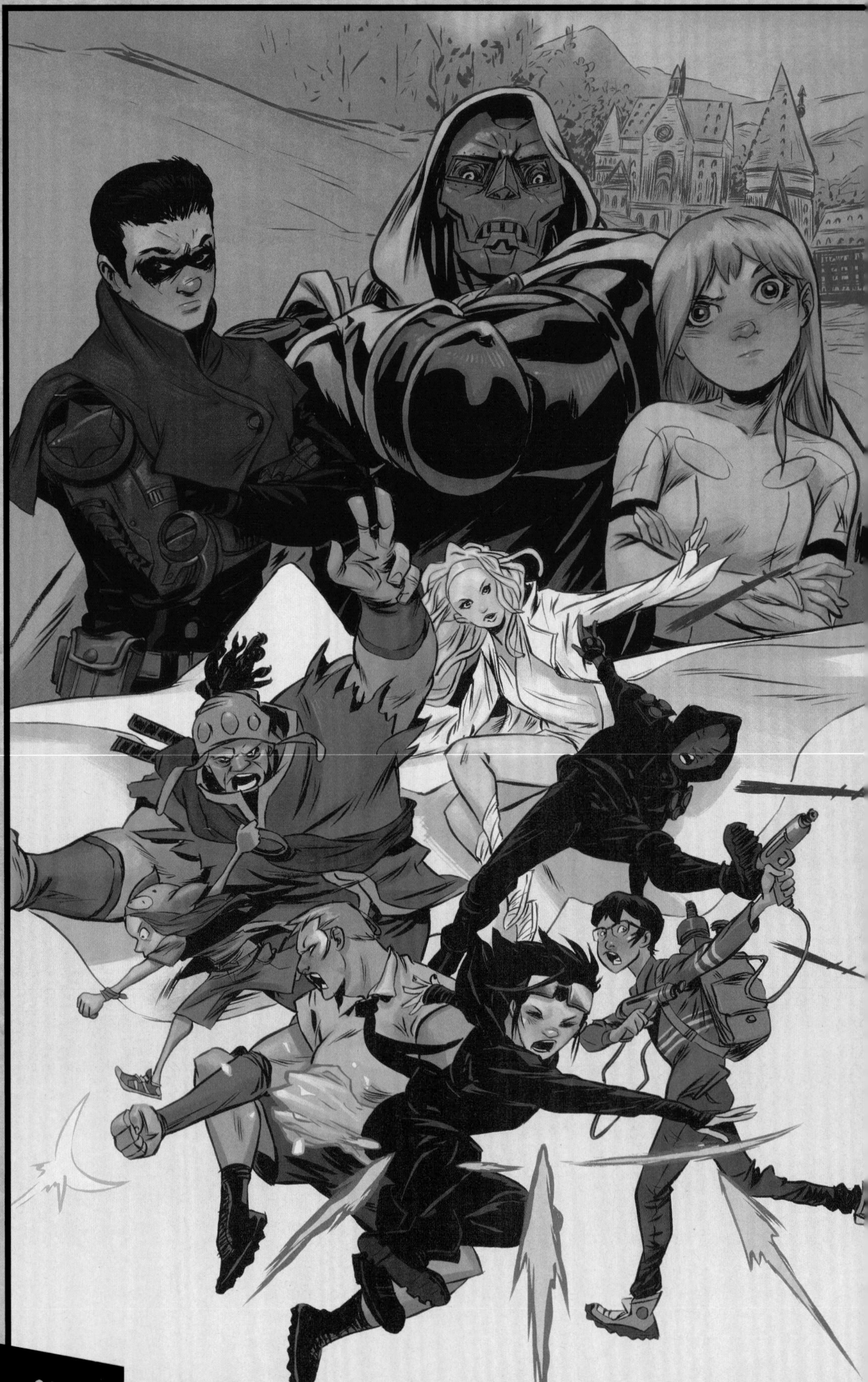

#4

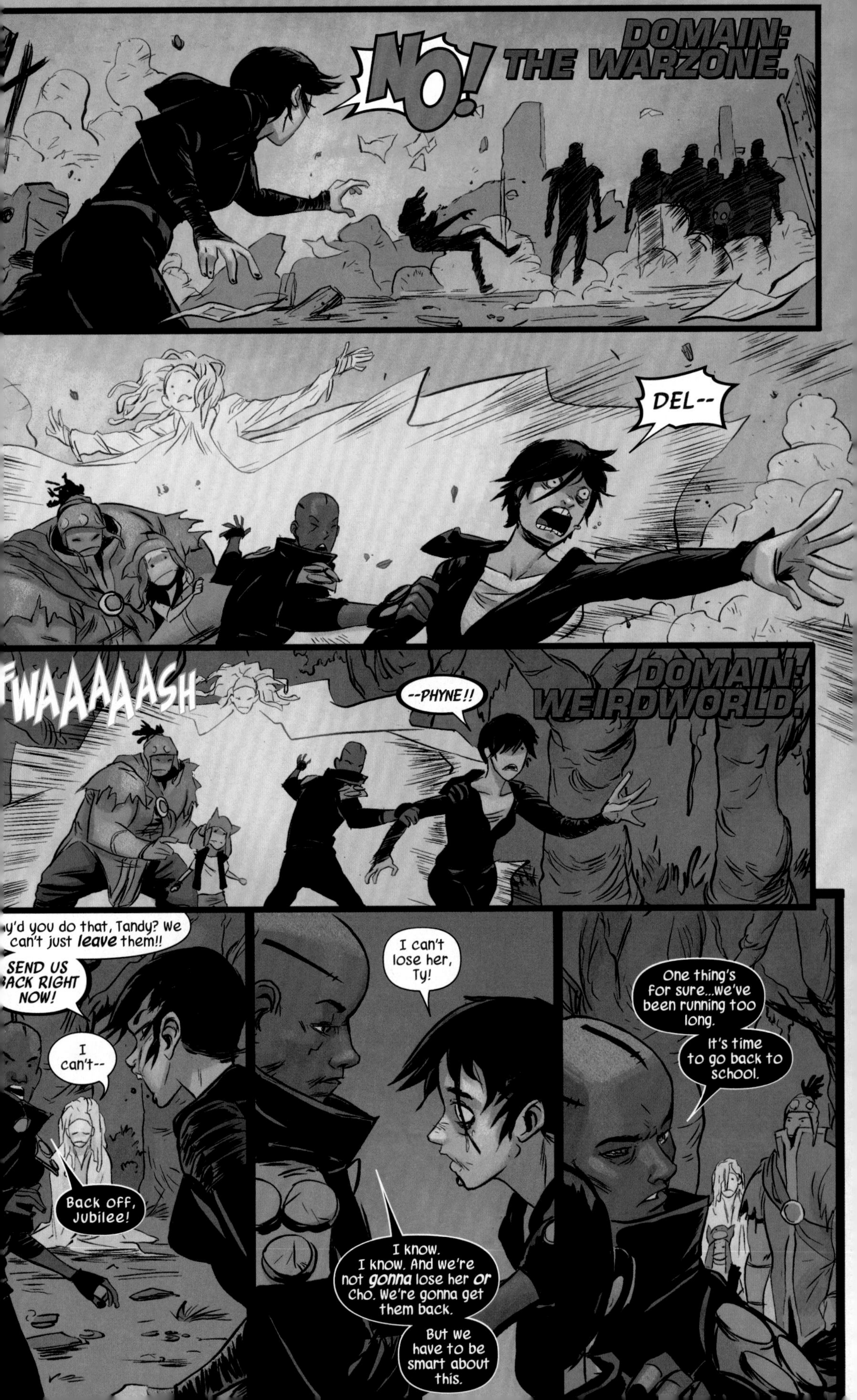
DOMAIN: THE WARZONE.
NO!
DEL--
FWAAAAASH
DOMAIN: WEIRDWORLD.
--PHYNE!!
y'd you do that, Tandy? We can't just leave them!!
SEND US ACK RIGHT NOW!
I can't--
Back off, Jubilee!
I can't lose her, Ty!
I know. I know. And we're not gonna lose her or Cho. We're gonna get them back.
But we have to be smart about this.
One thing's for sure...we've been running too long.
It's time to go back to school.

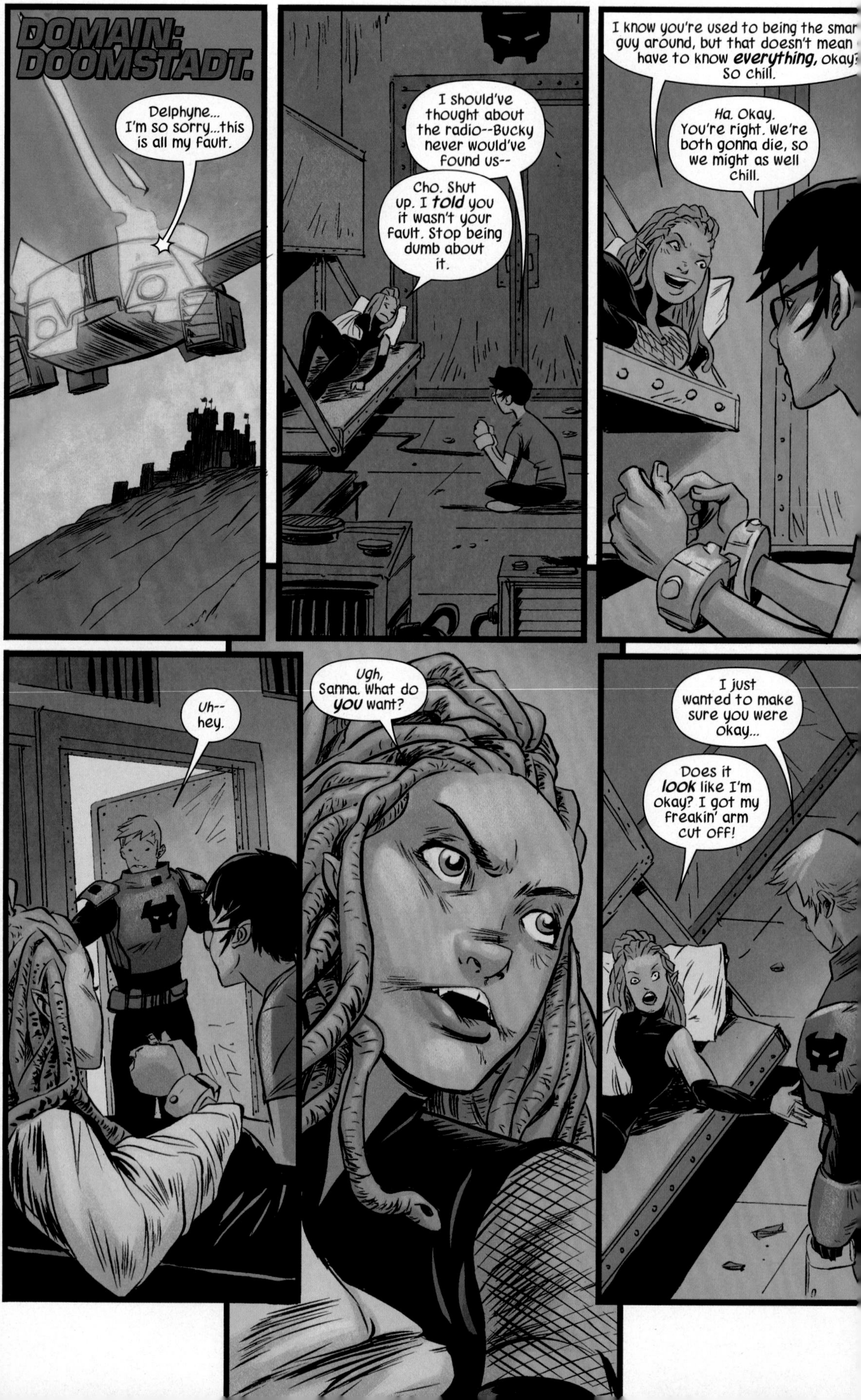

DOMAIN: DOOMSTADT.
Delphyne... I'm so sorry...this is all my fault.
I should've thought about the radio--Bucky never would've found us--
Cho. Shut up. I told you it wasn't your fault. Stop being dumb about it.
I know you're used to being the smar guy around, but that doesn't mean have to know everything, okay? So chill.
Ha. Okay. You're right. We're both gonna die, so we might as well chill.
Uh-- hey.
Ugh, Sanna. What do you want?
I just wanted to make sure you were okay...
Does it look like I'm okay? I got my freakin' arm cut off!

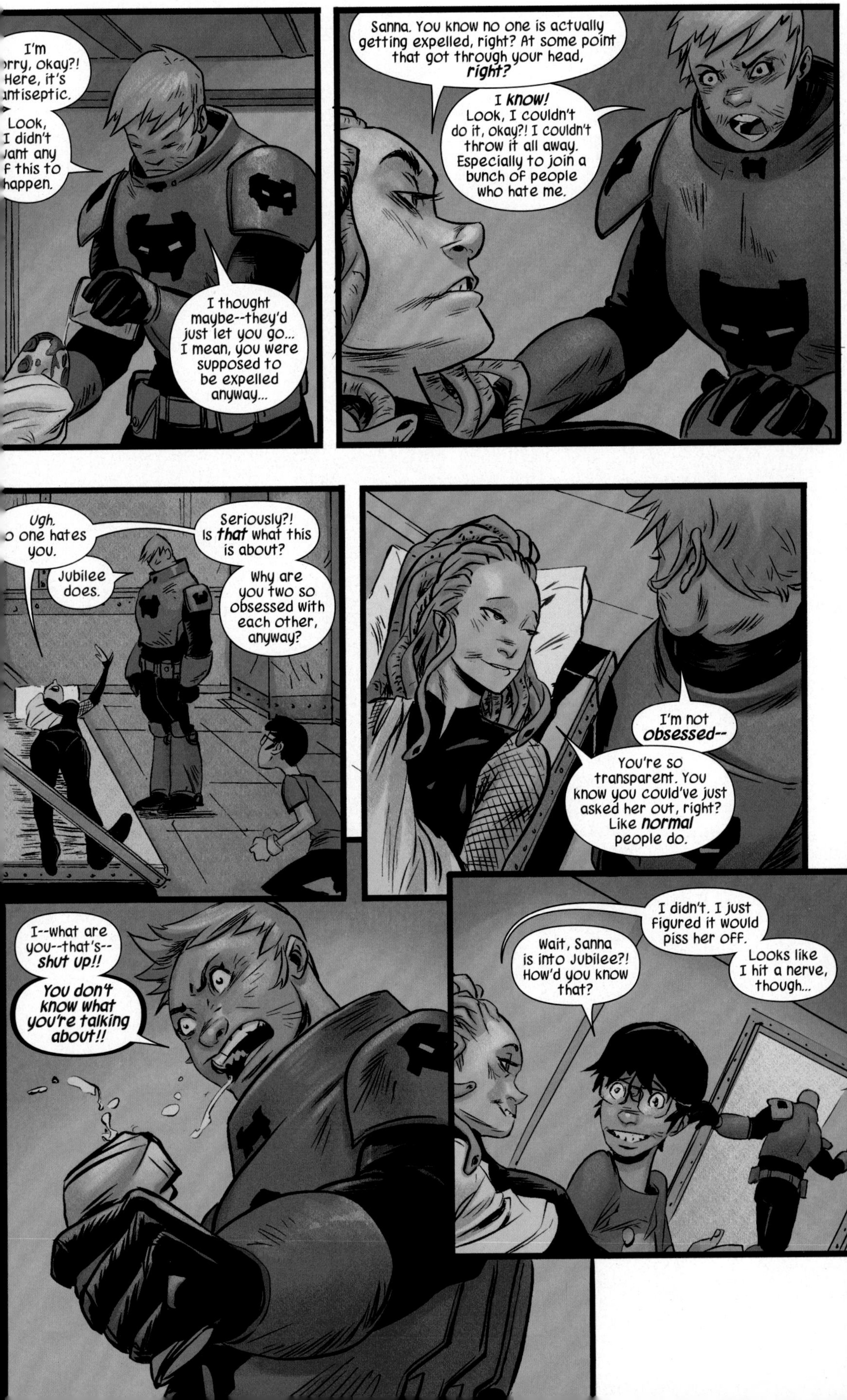

I'm
orry, okay?!
Here, it's
antiseptic.
Look,
I didn't
want any
f this to
happen.
I thought maybe--they'd just let you go... I mean, you were supposed to be expelled anyway...
Sanna. You know no one is actually getting expelled, right? At some point that got through your head, *right?*
I *know!* Look, I couldn't do it, okay?! I couldn't throw it all away. Especially to join a bunch of people who hate me.
Ugh.
o one hates
you.
Jubilee does.
Seriously?! Is *that* what this is about?
Why are you two so obsessed with each other, anyway?
I'm not *obsessed--*
You're so transparent. You know you could've just asked her out, right? Like *normal* people do.
I--what are you--that's-- *shut up!!*
You don't know what you're talking about!!
Wait, Sanna is into Jubilee?! How'd you know that?
I didn't. I just figured it would piss her off.
Looks like I hit a nerve, though...

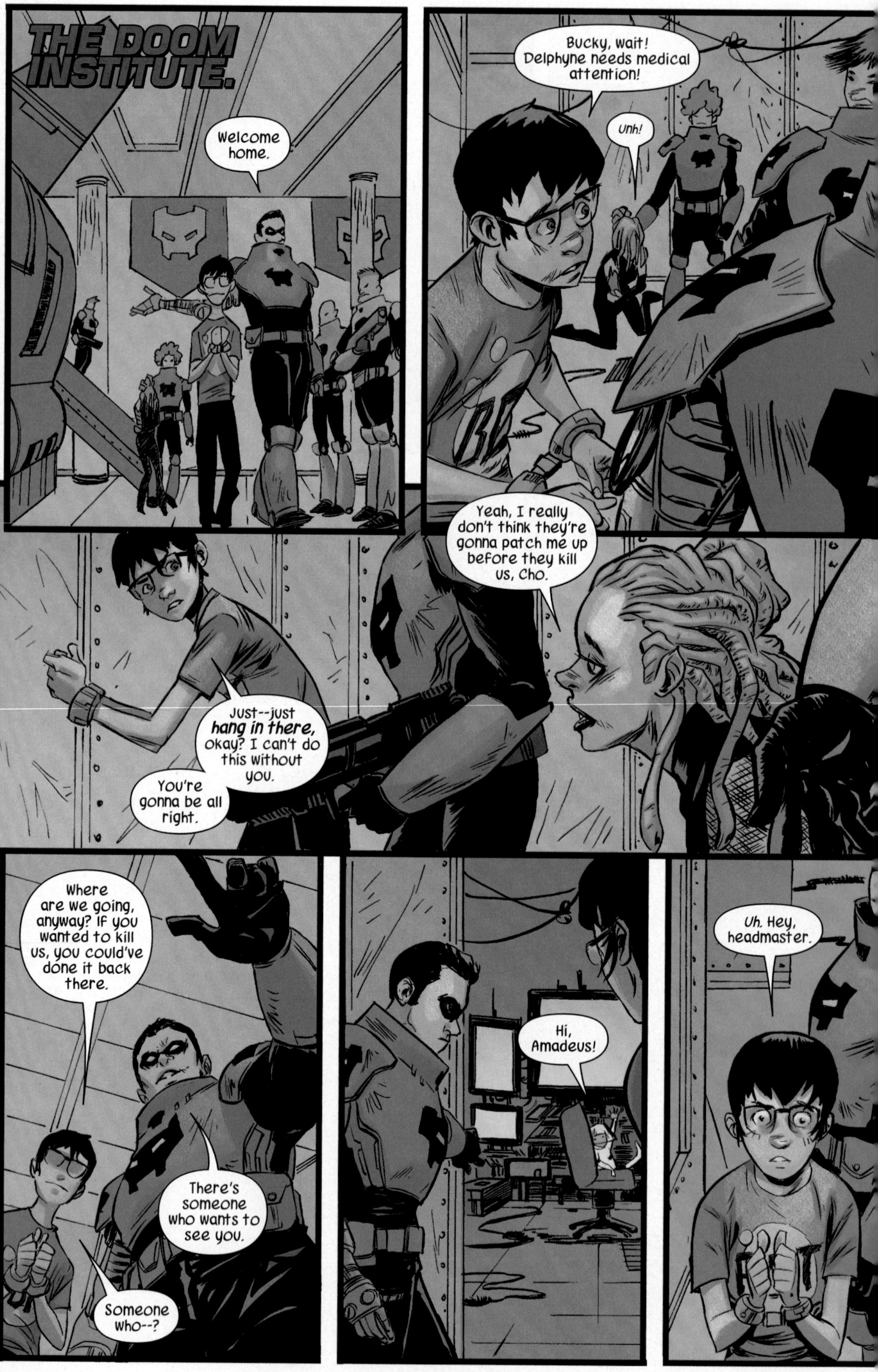
THE DOOM INSTITUTE.
Welcome home.
Bucky, wait! Delphyne needs medical attention!
Unh!
Yeah, I really don't think they're gonna patch me up before they kill us, Cho.
Just--just hang in there, okay? I can't do this without you.
You're gonna be all right.
Where are we going, anyway? If you wanted to kill us, you could've done it back there.
There's someone who wants to see you.
Someone who--?
Hi, Amadeus!
Uh. Hey, headmaster.

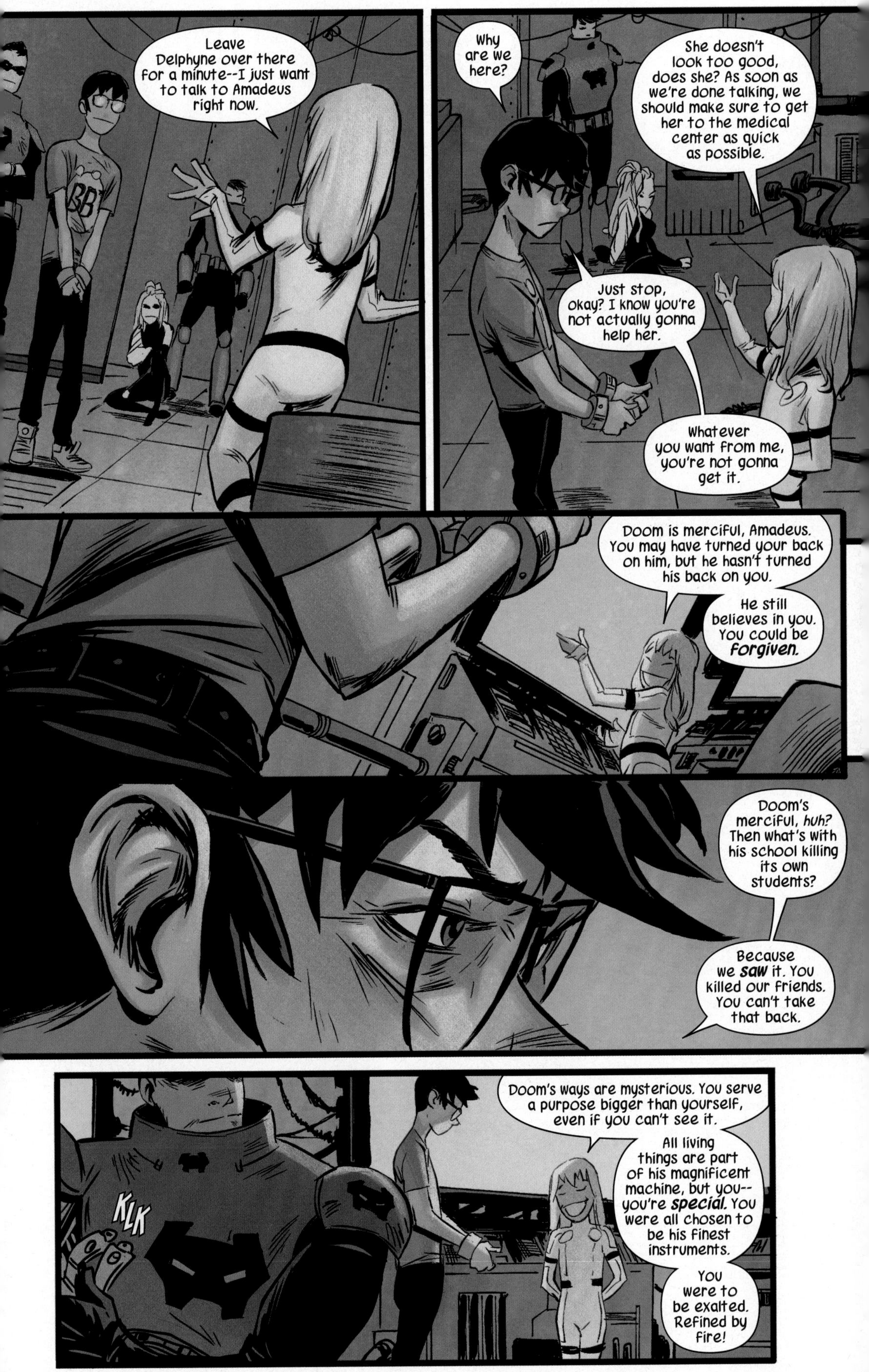
Leave Delphyne over there for a minute--I just want to talk to Amadeus right now.
Why are we here?
She doesn't look too good, does she? As soon as we're done talking, we should make sure to get her to the medical center as quick as possible.
Just stop, okay? I know you're not actually gonna help her.
Whatever you want from me, you're not gonna get it.
Doom is merciful, Amadeus. You may have turned your back on him, but he hasn't turned his back on you.
He still believes in you. You could be *forgiven.*
Doom's merciful, *huh?* Then what's with his school killing its own students?
Because we ***saw*** it. You killed our friends. You can't take that back.
Doom's ways are mysterious. You serve a purpose bigger than yourself, even if you can't see it.
All living things are part of his magnificent machine, but you--you're ***special.*** You were all chosen to be his finest instruments.
You were to be exalted. Refined by fire!
KLK

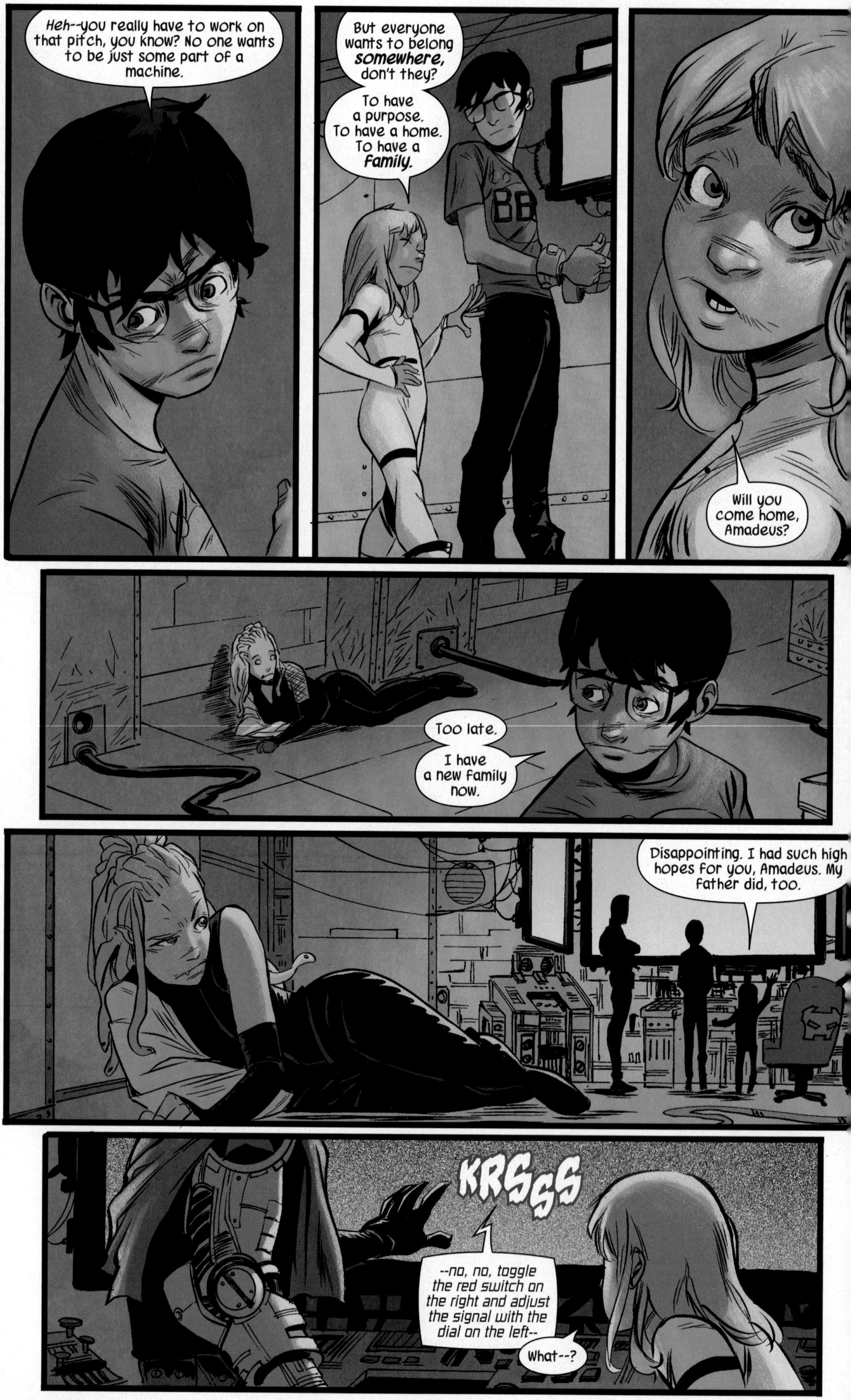
Heh--you really have to work on that pitch, you know? No one wants to be just some part of a machine.
But everyone wants to belong *somewhere,* don't they?
To have a purpose. To have a home. To have a *family.*
Will you come home, Amadeus?
Too late.
I have a new family now.
Disappointing. I had such high hopes for you, Amadeus. My father did, too.
KRSSS
--no, no, toggle the red switch on the right and adjust the signal with the dial on the left--
What--?

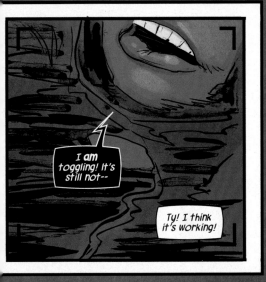

I am toggling! It's still not--

Ty! I think it's working!

Hello? Hello? Oh. Here we go. Awesome.

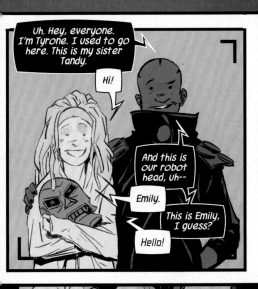

Uh. Hey, everyone. I'm Tyrone. I used to go here. This is my sister Tandy.

Hi!

And this is our robot head, Uh--

Emily.

This is Emily, I guess?

Hello!

You probably didn't expect to see me back here. I failed the Exam, after all. I should be long gone--me and my whole crew.

Funny story--we kind of tried that. We made it pretty far, too. But we had to come back.

Because we can't just let the school get away with what it's doing. We had to come back and warn the rest of you.

They're broadcasting from inside the school--that means the others are here, too. Find them, Bucky, now.

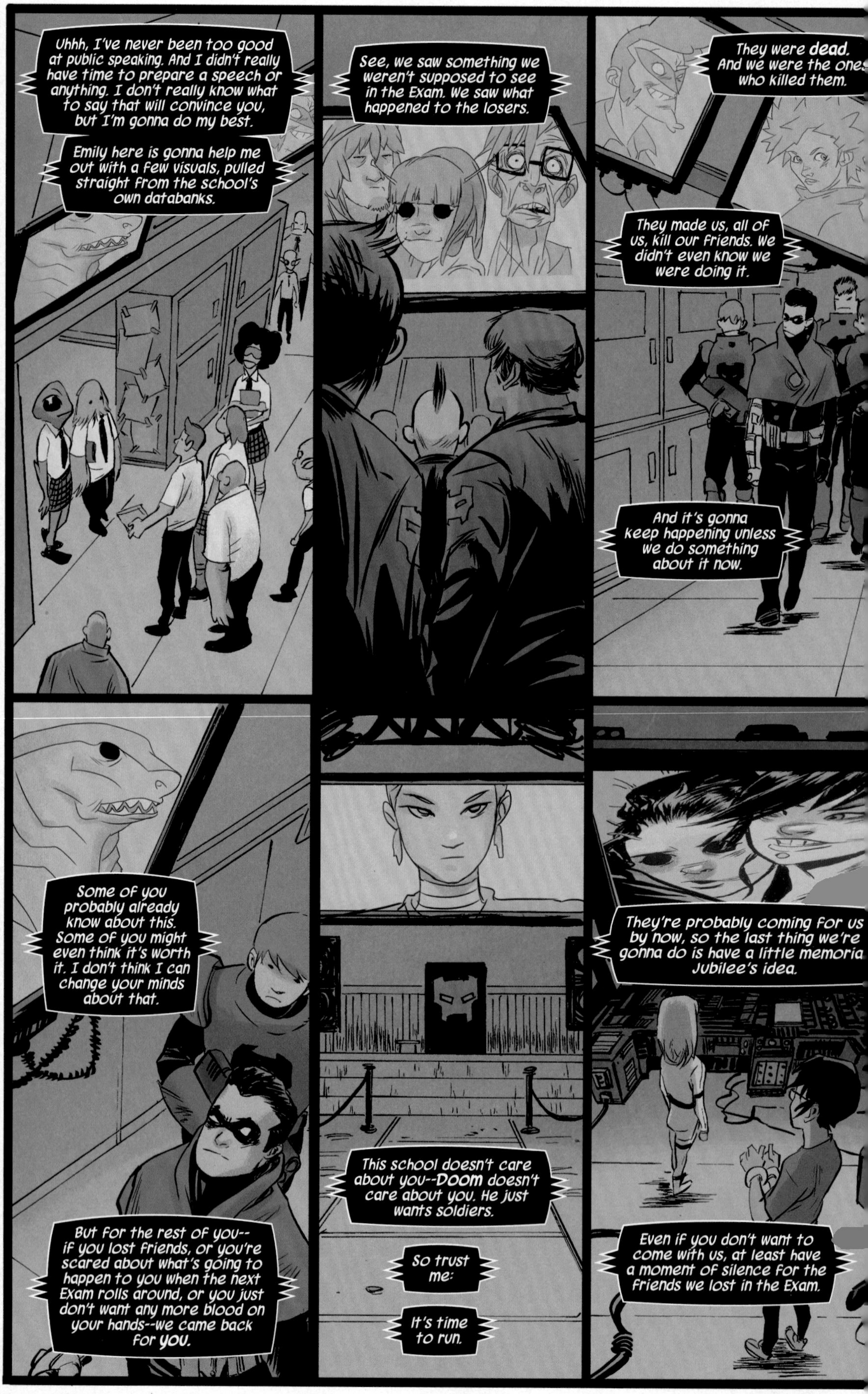
Uhhh, I've never been too good at public speaking. And I didn't really have time to prepare a speech or anything. I don't really know what to say that will convince you, but I'm gonna do my best.
Emily here is gonna help me out with a few visuals, pulled straight from the school's own databanks.
See, we saw something we weren't supposed to see in the Exam. We saw what happened to the losers.
They were **dead.** And we were the ones who killed them.
They made us, all of us, kill our friends. We didn't even know we were doing it.
And it's gonna keep happening unless we do something about it now.
Some of you probably already know about this. Some of you might even think it's worth it. I don't think I can change your minds about that.
But for the rest of you-- if you lost friends, or you're scared about what's going to happen to you when the next Exam rolls around, or you just don't want any more blood on your hands--we came back for **you.**
This school doesn't care about you--**Doom** doesn't care about you. He just wants soldiers.
So trust me:
It's time to run.
They're probably coming for us by now, so the last thing we're gonna do is have a little memoria Jubilee's idea.
Even if you don't want to come with us, at least have a moment of silence for the friends we lost in the Exam.

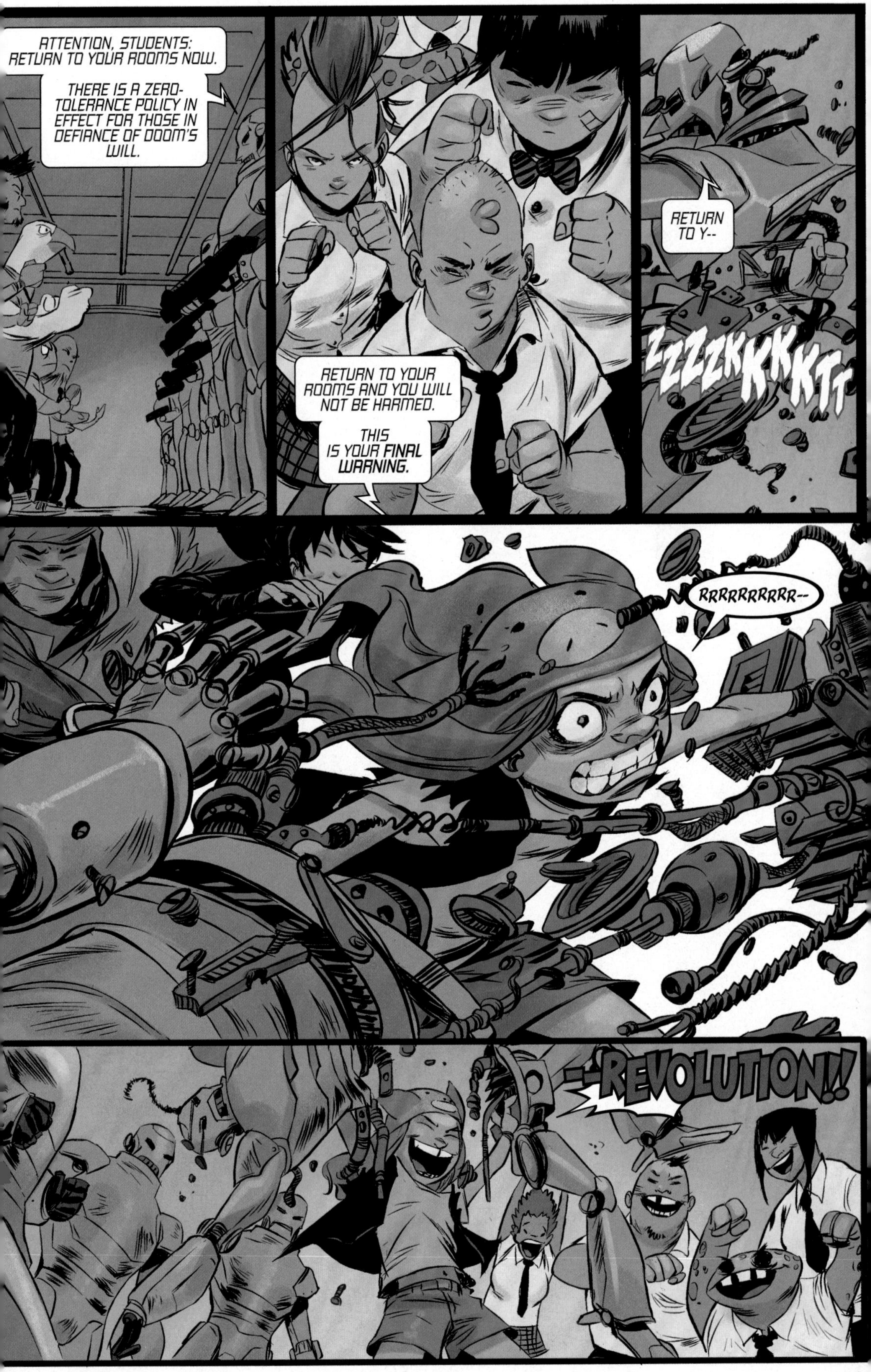
ATTENTION, STUDENTS: RETURN TO YOUR ROOMS NOW.
THERE IS A ZERO-TOLERANCE POLICY IN EFFECT FOR THOSE IN DEFIANCE OF DOOM'S WILL.
RETURN TO YOUR ROOMS AND YOU WILL NOT BE HARMED.
THIS IS YOUR FINAL WARNING.
RETURN TO Y--
ZZZZKKKKTT
RRRRRRRRRR--
--REVOLUTION!!

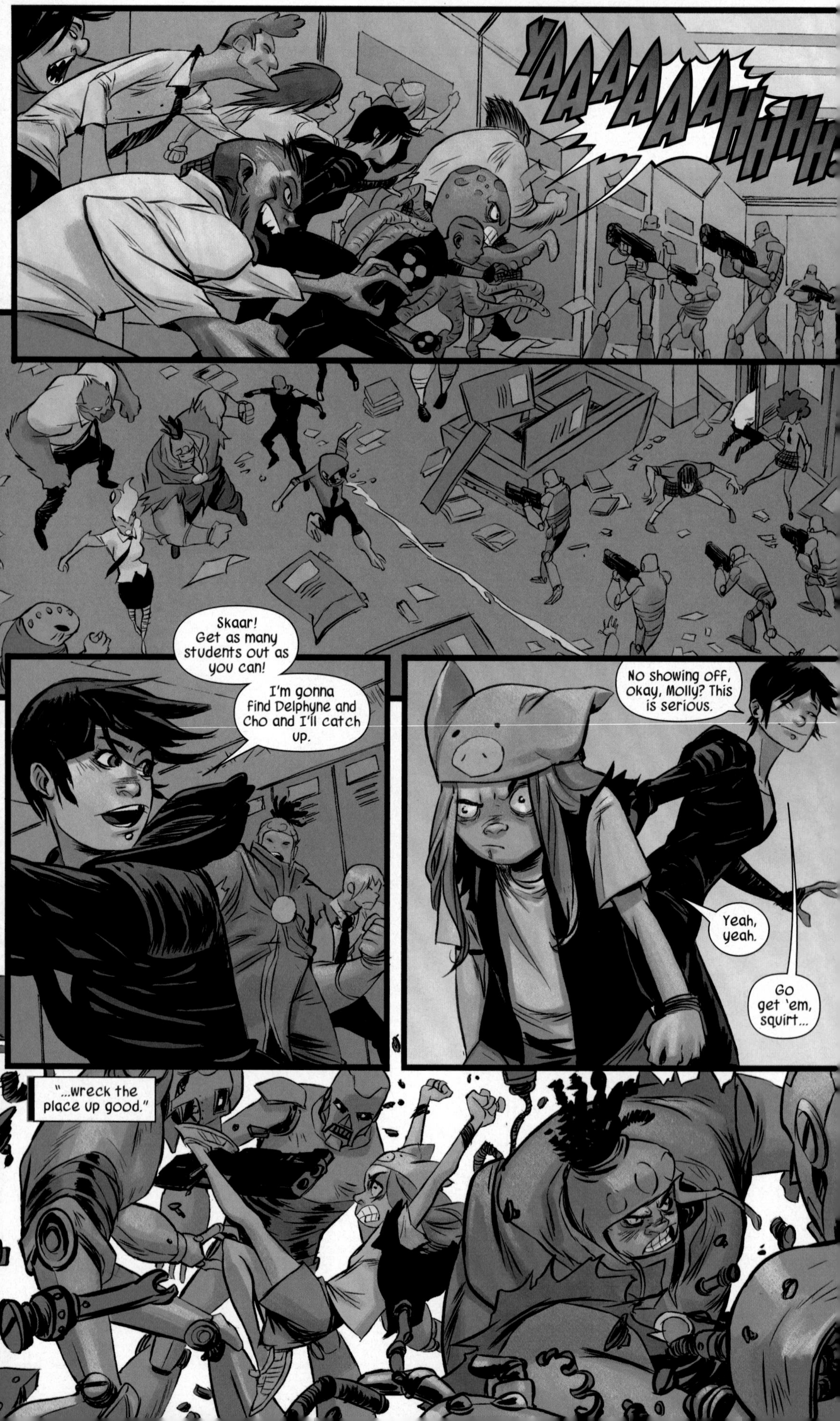
YAAAAAAHHHH!
Skaar! Get as many students out as you can!
I'm gonna find Delphyne and Cho and I'll catch up.
No showing off, okay, Molly? This is serious.
Yeah, yeah.
Go get 'em, squirt...
"...wreck the place up good."

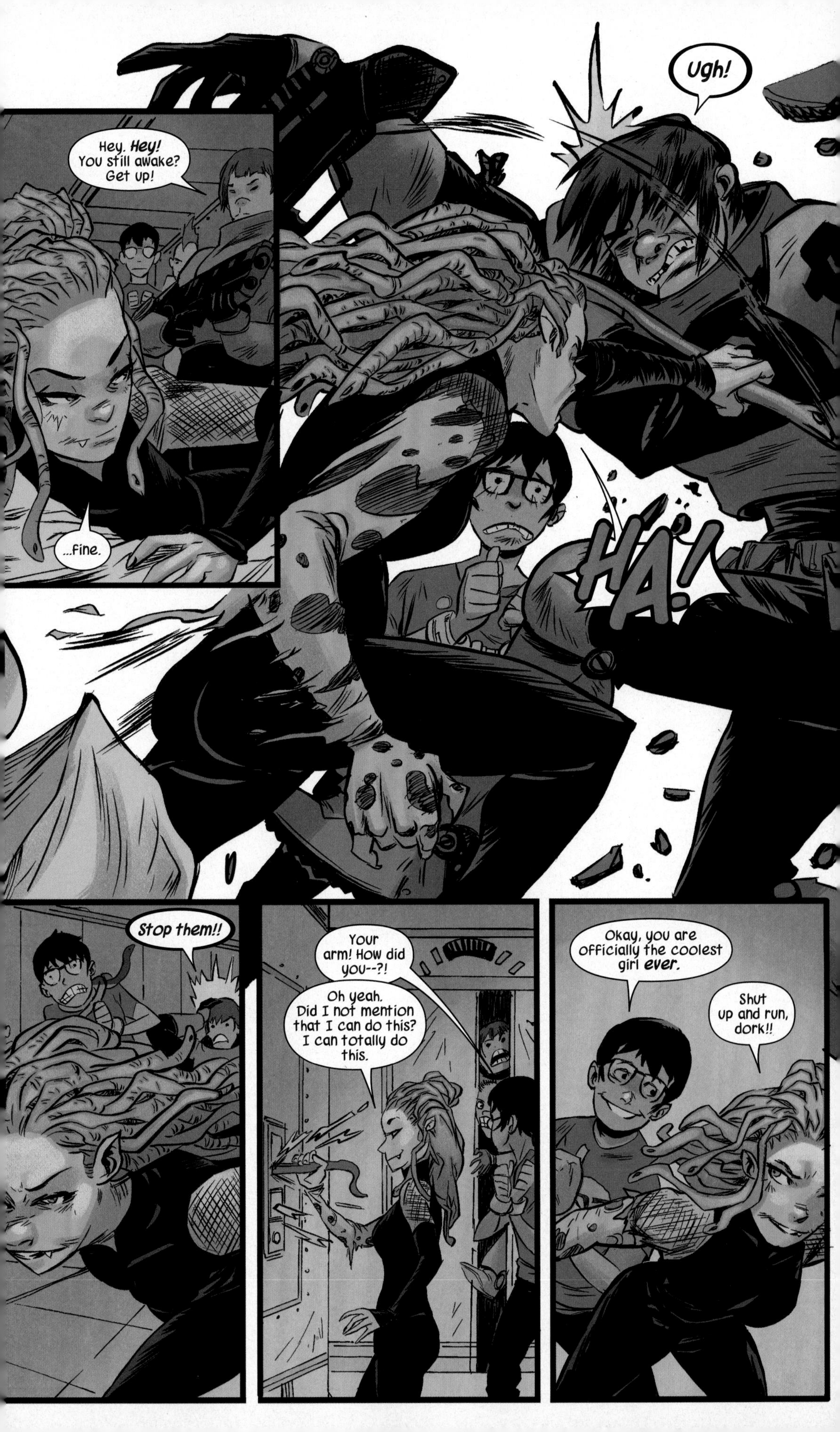
Hey. **Hey!** You still awake? Get up!
...fine.
Ugh!
HA!
Stop them!!
Your arm! How did you--?!
Oh yeah. Did I not mention that I can do this? I can totally do this.
Okay, you are officially the coolest girl **ever**.
Shut up and run, dork!!

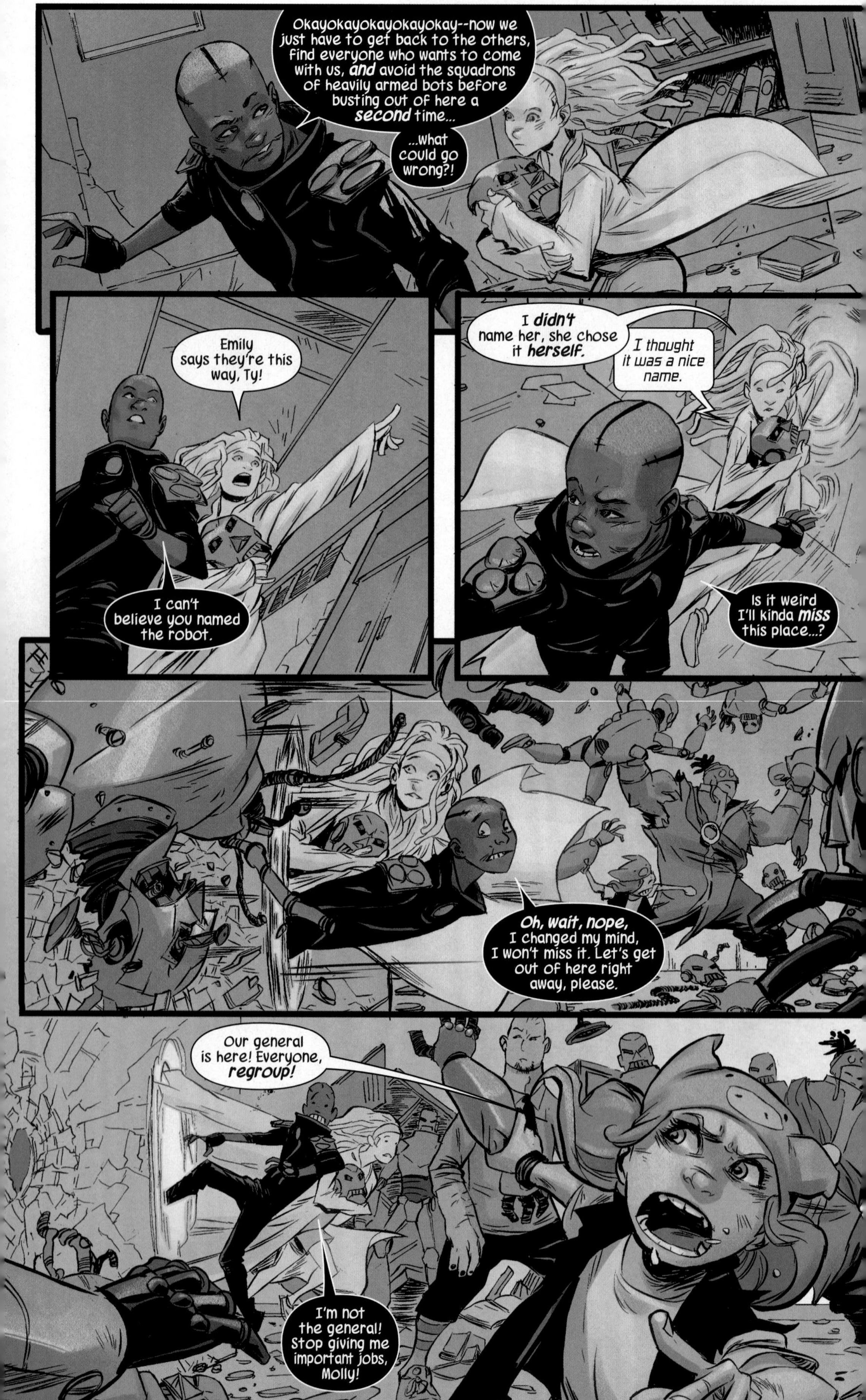
Okayokayokayokayokayokay--now we just have to get back to the others, find everyone who wants to come with us, and avoid the squadrons of heavily armed bots before busting out of here a second time...
...what could go wrong?!
Emily says they're this way, Ty!
I can't believe you named the robot.
I didn't name her, she chose it herself.
I thought it was a nice name.
Is it weird I'll kinda miss this place...?
Oh, wait, nope, I changed my mind, I won't miss it. Let's get out of here right away, please.
Our general is here! Everyone, regroup!
I'm not the general! Stop giving me important jobs, Molly!

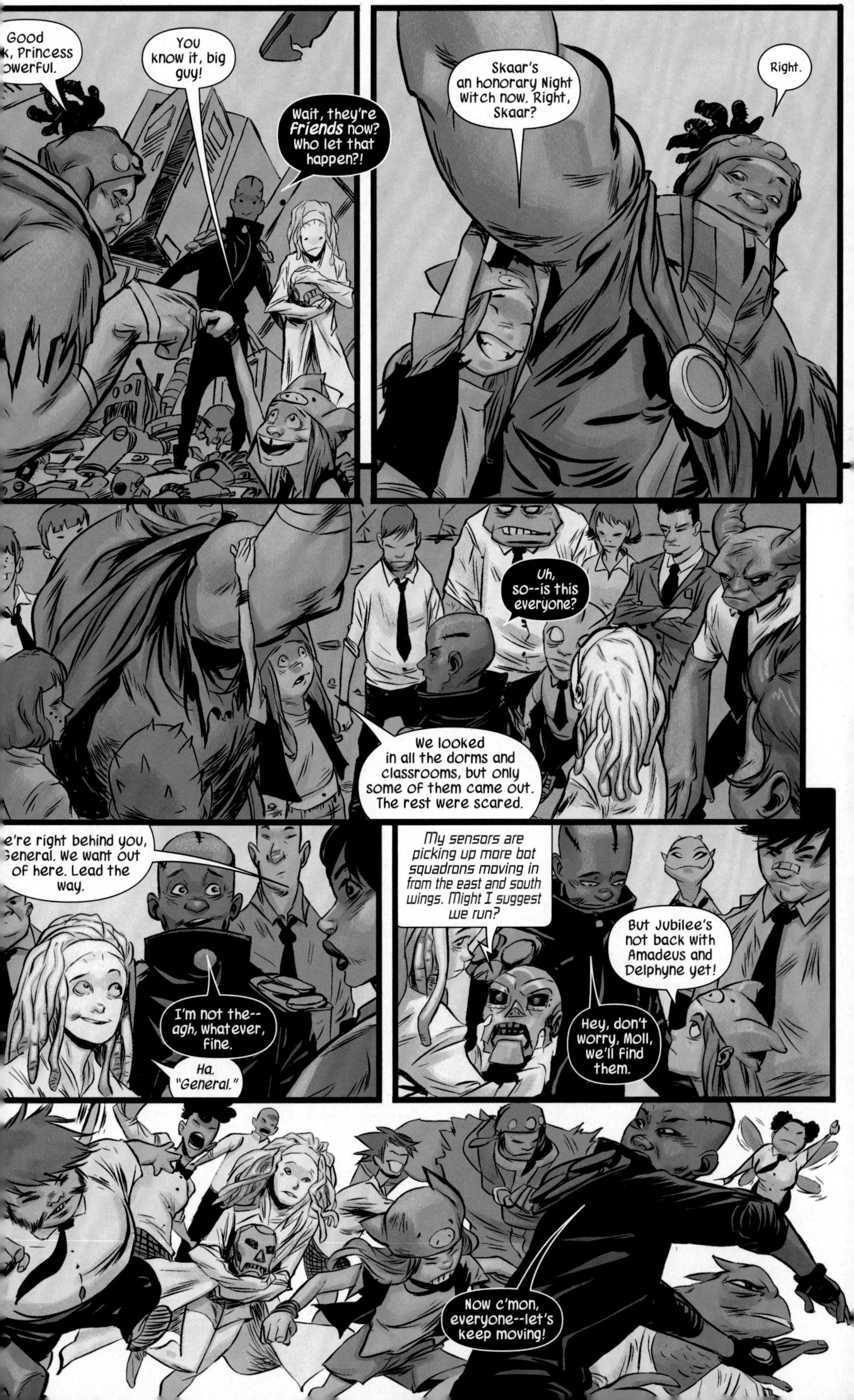
Good
k, Princess
owerful.
You know it, big guy!
Wait, they're *friends* now? Who let that happen?!
Skaar's an honorary Night Witch now. Right, Skaar?
Right.
Uh, so--is this everyone?
We looked in all the dorms and classrooms, but only some of them came out. The rest were scared.
e're right behind you,
General. We want out of here. Lead the way.
I'm not the--agh, whatever, fine.
Ha. "General."
My sensors are picking up more bot squadrons moving in from the east and south wings. Might I suggest we run?
But Jubilee's not back with Amadeus and Delphyne yet!
Hey, don't worry, Moll, we'll find them.
Now c'mon, everyone--let's keep moving!

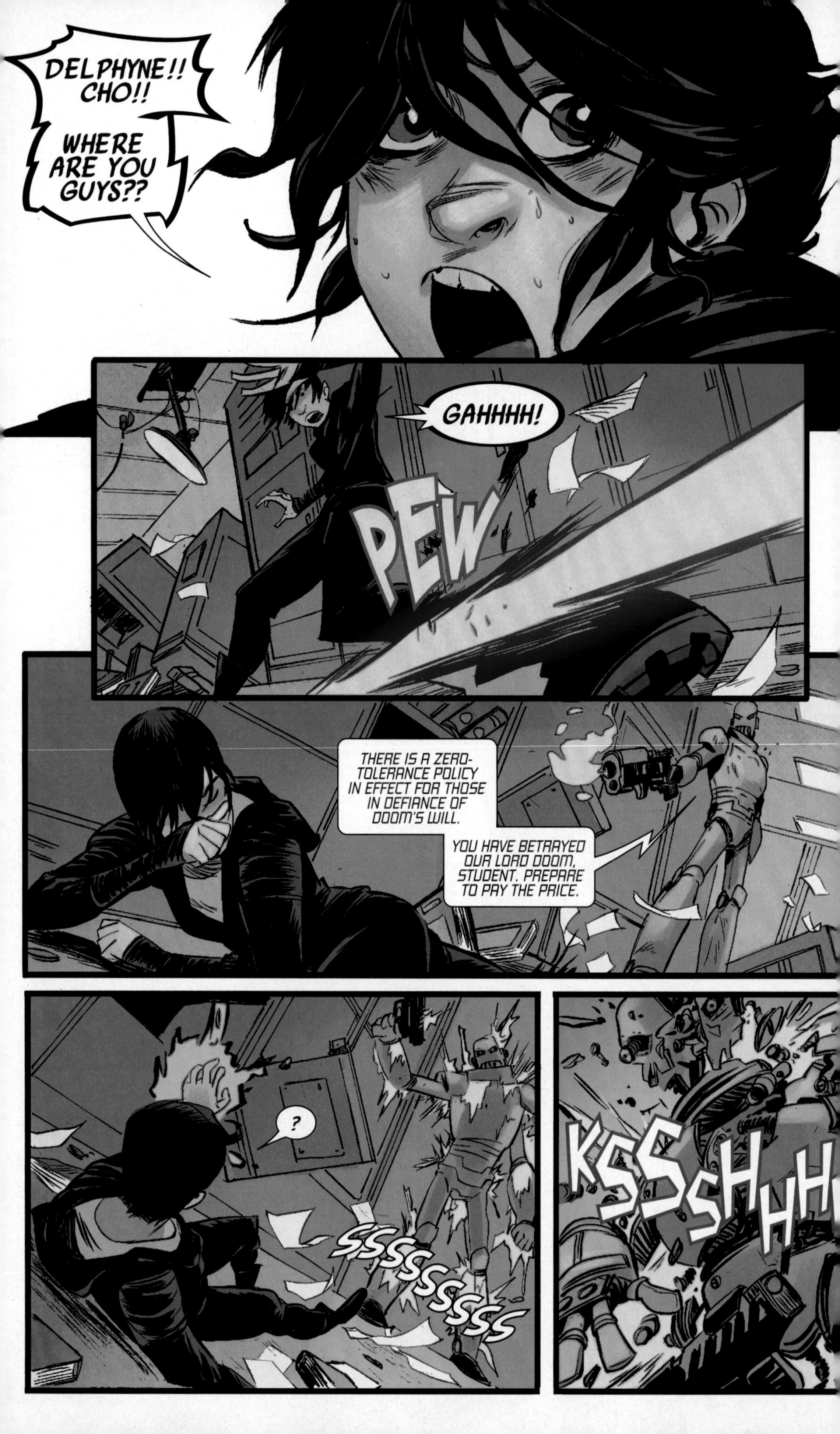
DELPHYNE!! CHO!!
WHERE ARE YOU GUYS??
GAHHHH!
PEW
THERE IS A ZERO-TOLERANCE POLICY IN EFFECT FOR THOSE IN DEFIANCE OF DOOM'S WILL.
YOU HAVE BETRAYED OUR LORD DOOM, STUDENT. PREPARE TO PAY THE PRICE.
?
SSSSSSSSS
KSSSHHH

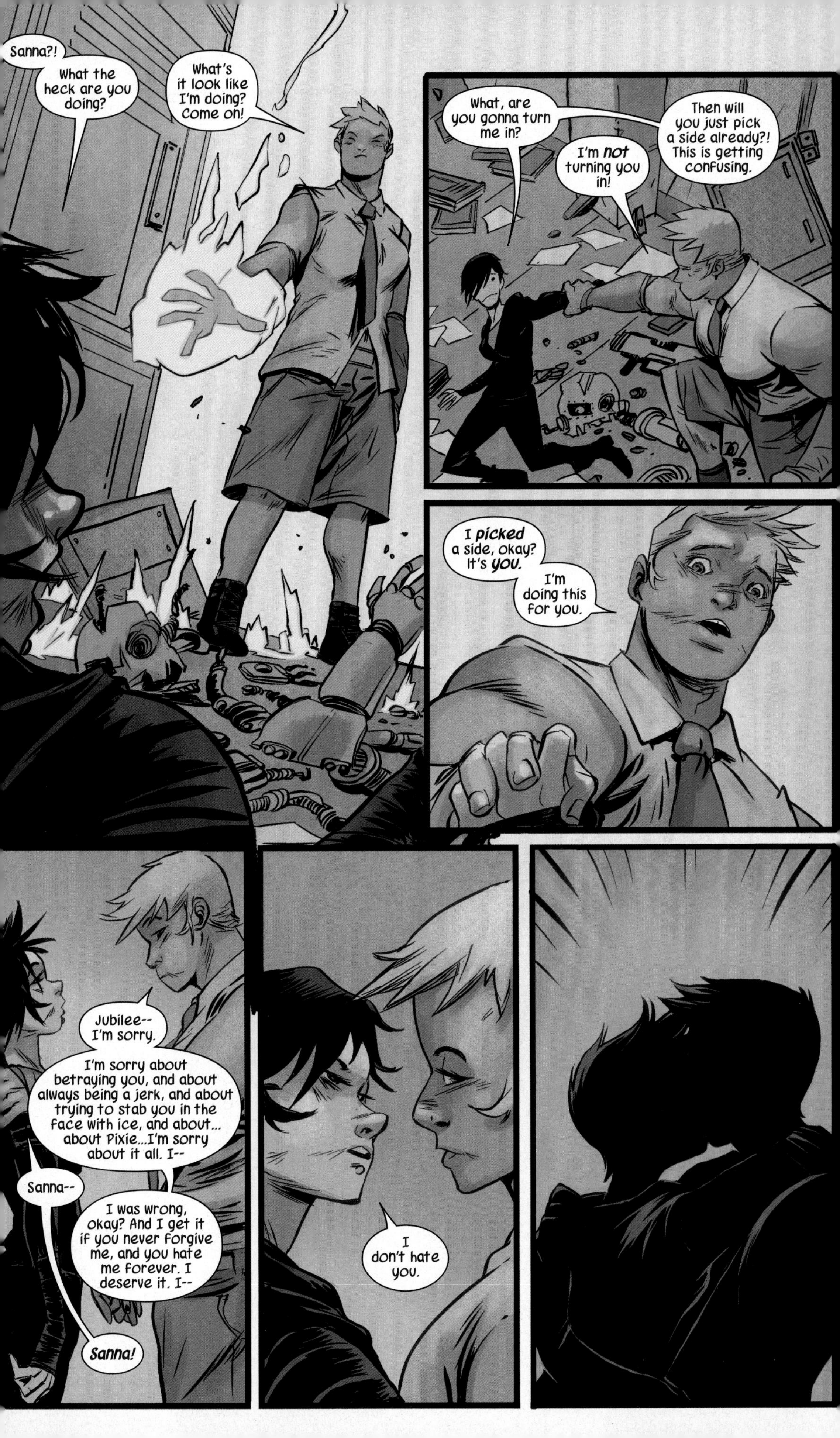
Sanna?!
What the heck are you doing?
What's it look like I'm doing? Come on!
What, are you gonna turn me in?
I'm **not** turning you in!
Then will you just pick a side already?! This is getting confusing.
I **picked** a side, okay? It's **you.**
I'm doing this for you.
Jubilee-- I'm sorry.
I'm sorry about betraying you, and about always being a jerk, and about trying to stab you in the face with ice, and about... about Pixie...I'm sorry about it all. I--
Sanna--
I was wrong, okay? And I get it if you never forgive me, and you hate me forever. I deserve it. I--
Sanna!
I don't hate you.

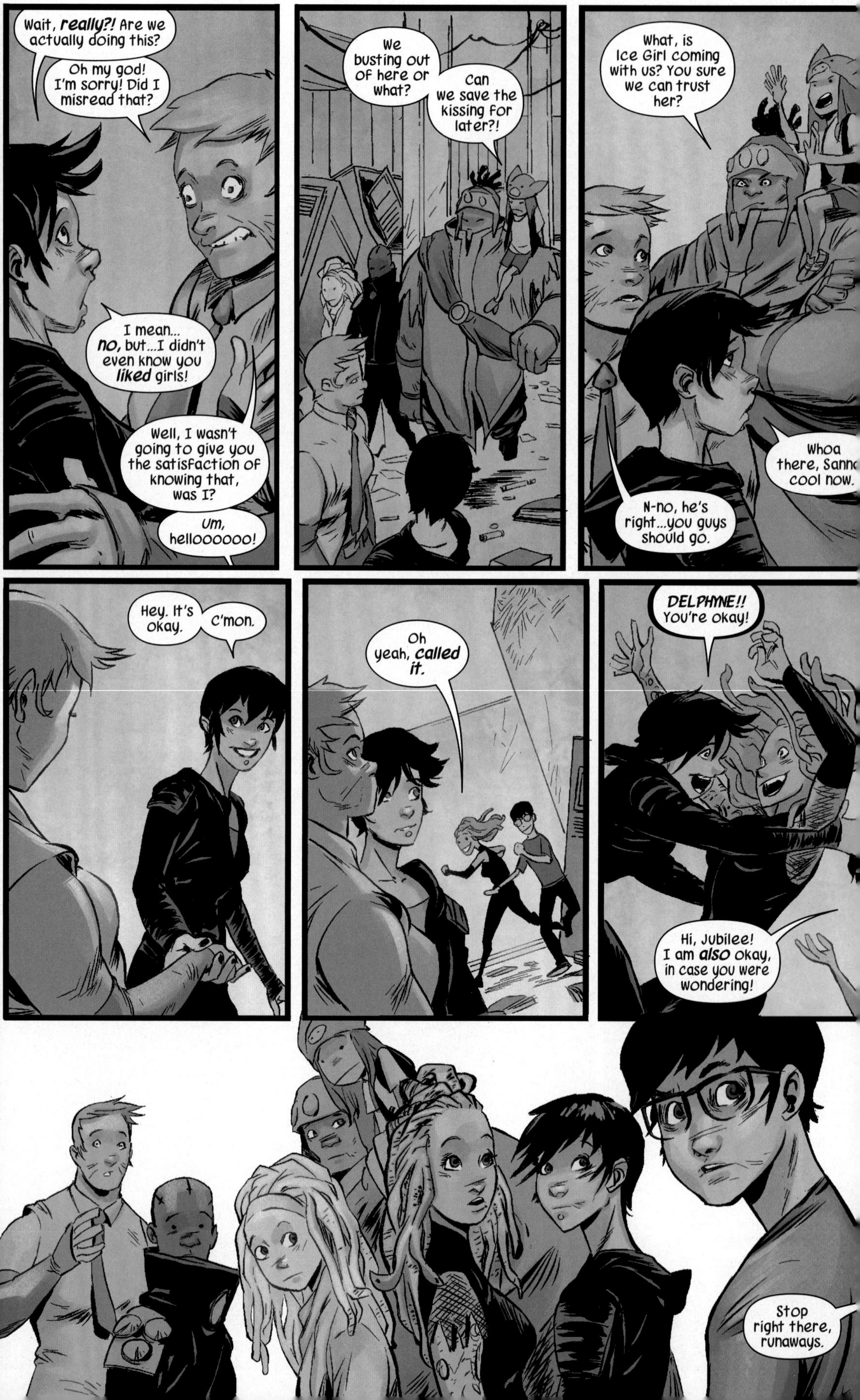
Wait, *really?!* Are we actually doing this?
Oh my god! I'm sorry! Did I misread that?
I mean... *no,* but...I didn't even know you *liked* girls!
Well, I wasn't going to give you the satisfaction of knowing that, was I?
Um, hellooooooo!
We busting out of here or what?
Can we save the kissing for later?!
What, is Ice Girl coming with us? You sure we can trust her?
N-no, he's right...you guys should go.
Hey. It's okay.
C'mon.
Oh yeah, *called it.*
DELPHYNE!! You're okay!
Hi, Jubilee! I am *also* okay, in case you were wondering!
Stop right there, runaways.

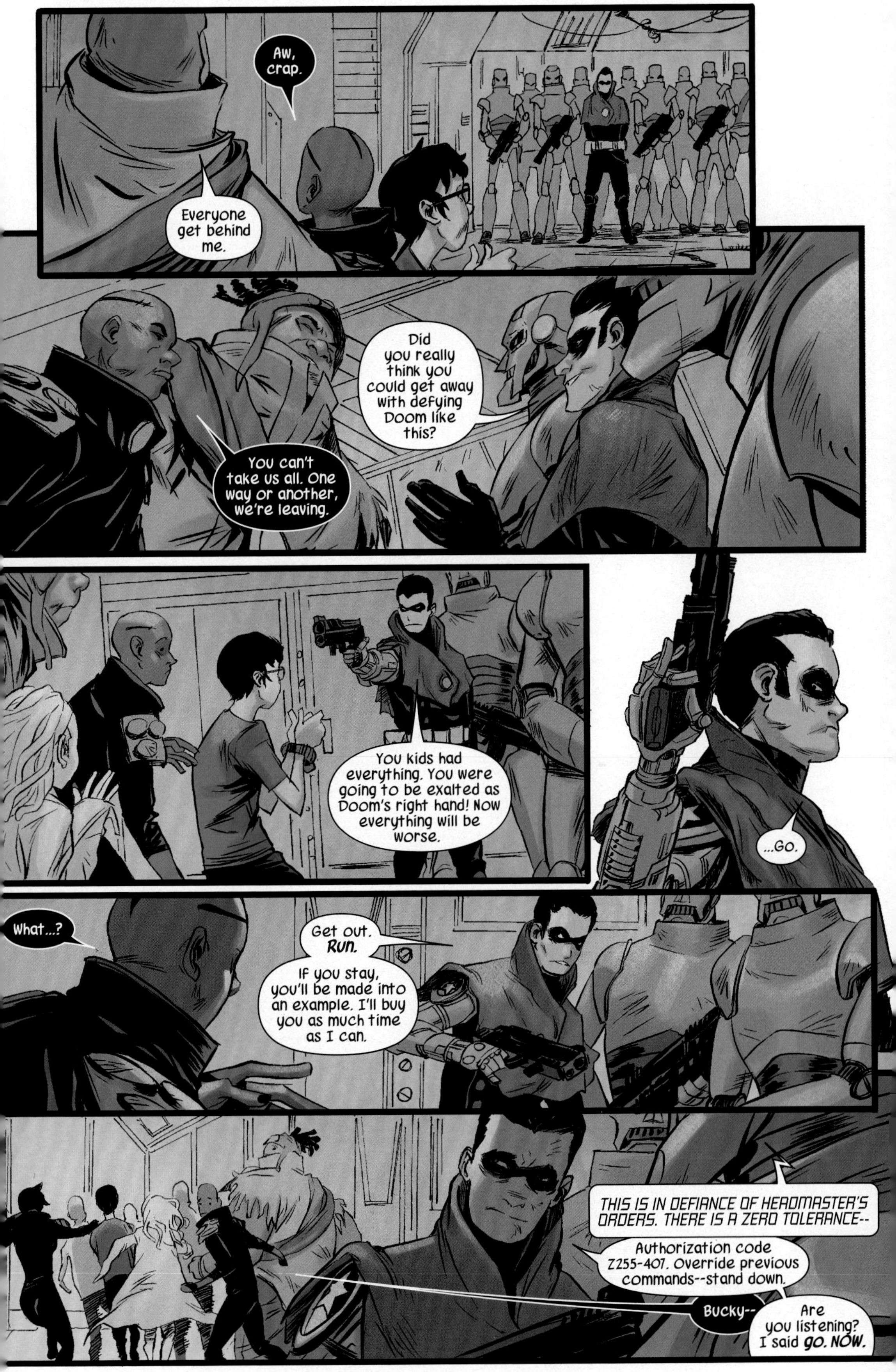
Aw, crap.
Everyone get behind me.
Did you really think you could get away with defying Doom like this?
You can't take us all. One way or another, we're leaving.
You kids had everything. You were going to be exalted as Doom's right hand! Now everything will be worse.
...Go.
What...?
Get out. **RUN.**
If you stay, you'll be made into an example. I'll buy you as much time as I can.
THIS IS IN DEFIANCE OF HEADMASTER'S ORDERS. THERE IS A ZERO TOLERANCE--
Authorization code Z255-407. Override previous commands--stand down.
Bucky--
Are you listening? I said **GO. NOW.**

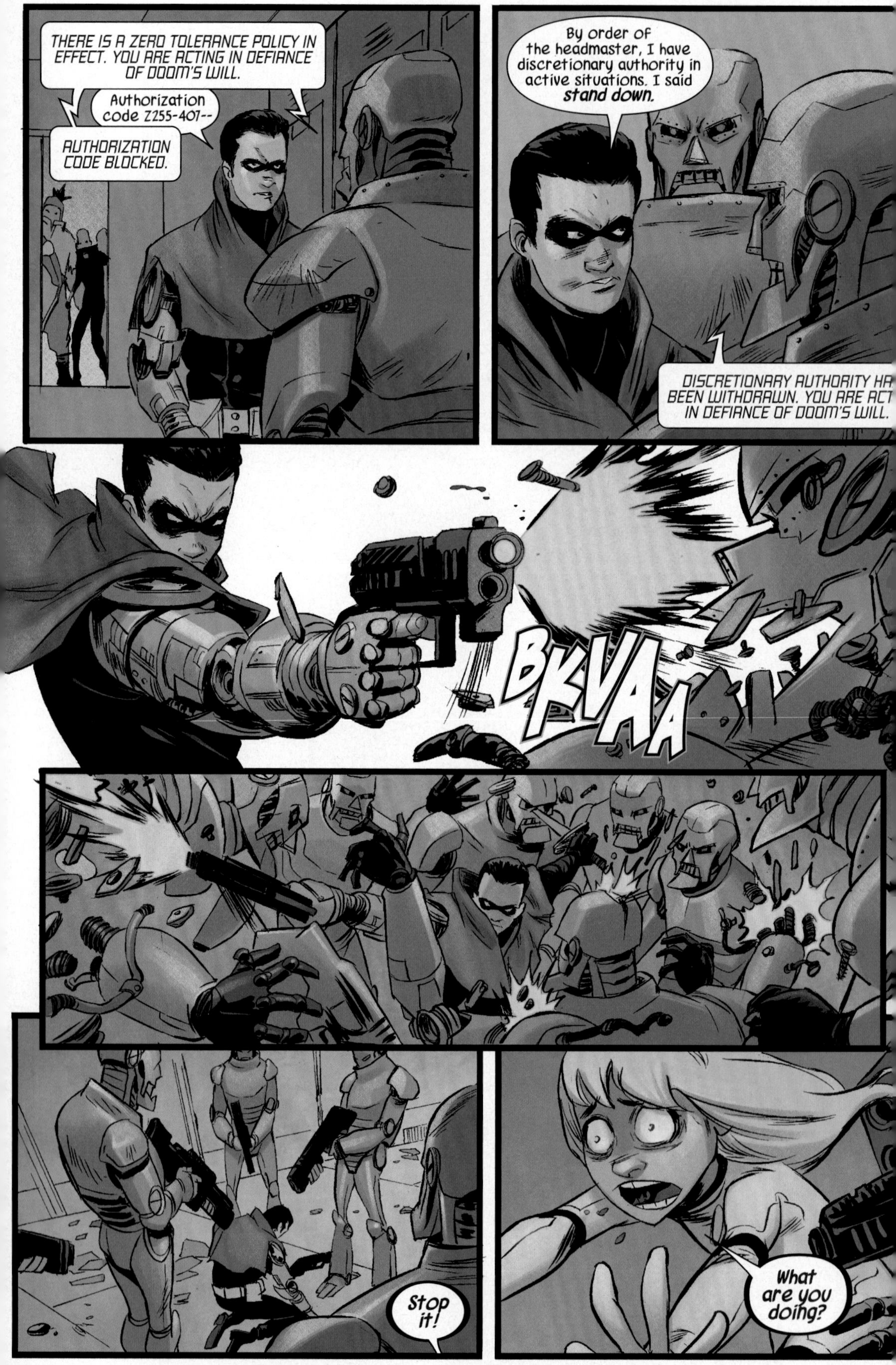
THERE IS A ZERO TOLERANCE POLICY IN EFFECT. YOU ARE ACTING IN DEFIANCE OF DOOM'S WILL.
Authorization code Z255-407--
AUTHORIZATION CODE BLOCKED.
By order of the headmaster, I have discretionary authority in active situations. I said stand down.
DISCRETIONARY AUTHORITY HA BEEN WITHDRAWN. YOU ARE ACT IN DEFIANCE OF DOOM'S WILL.
BKVAAA
Stop it!
What are you doing?

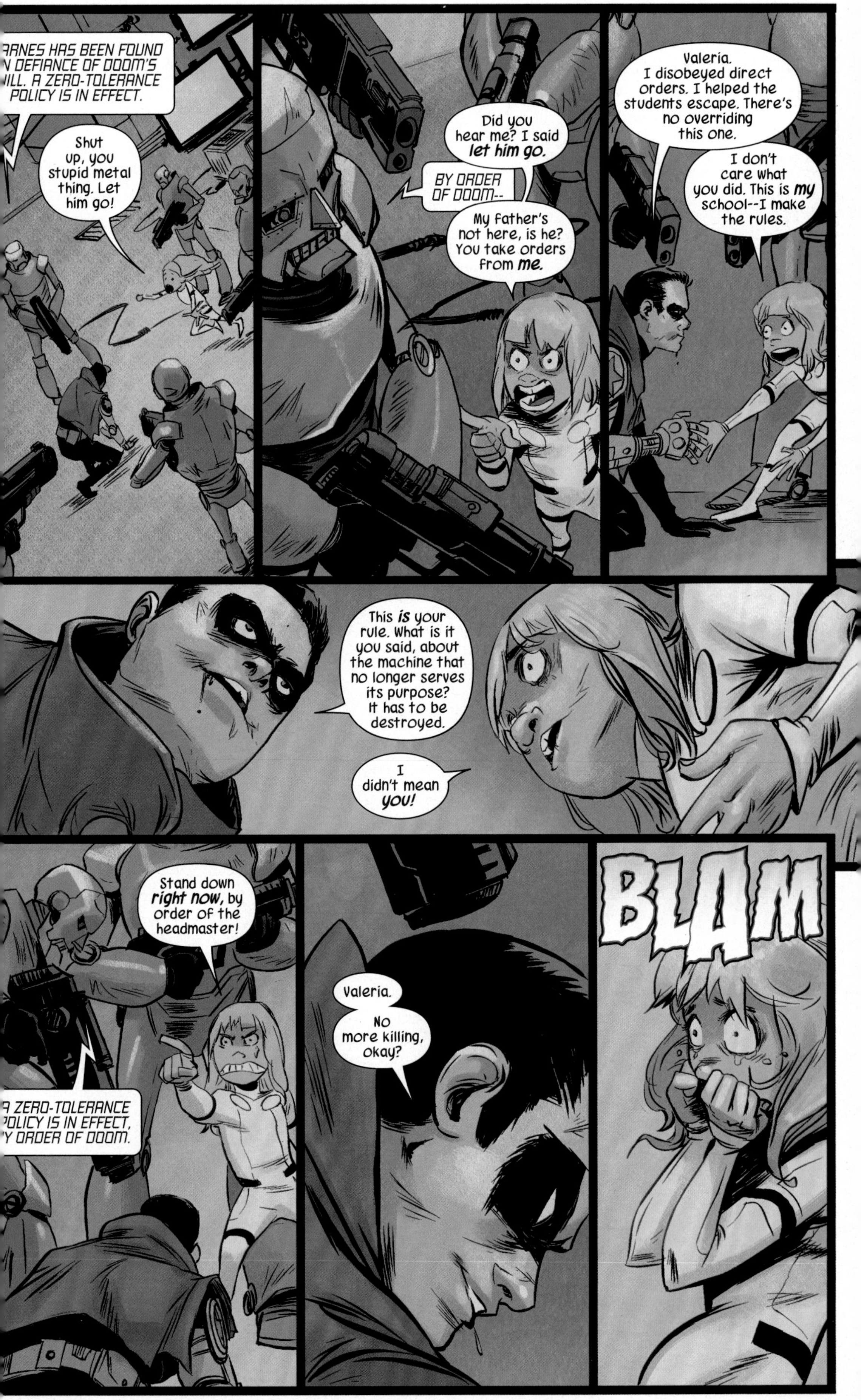
ARNES HAS BEEN FOUND
N DEFIANCE OF DOOM'S
ILL. A ZERO-TOLERANCE
POLICY IS IN EFFECT.
Shut up, you stupid metal thing. Let him go!
Did you hear me? I said let him go.
BY ORDER OF DOOM--
My father's not here, is he? You take orders from me.
Valeria. I disobeyed direct orders. I helped the students escape. There's no overriding this one.
I don't care what you did. This is my school--I make the rules.
This is your rule. What is it you said, about the machine that no longer serves its purpose? It has to be destroyed.
I didn't mean you!
Stand down right now, by order of the headmaster!
A ZERO-TOLERANCE
POLICY IS IN EFFECT,
Y ORDER OF DOOM.
Valeria.
No more killing, okay?
BLAM

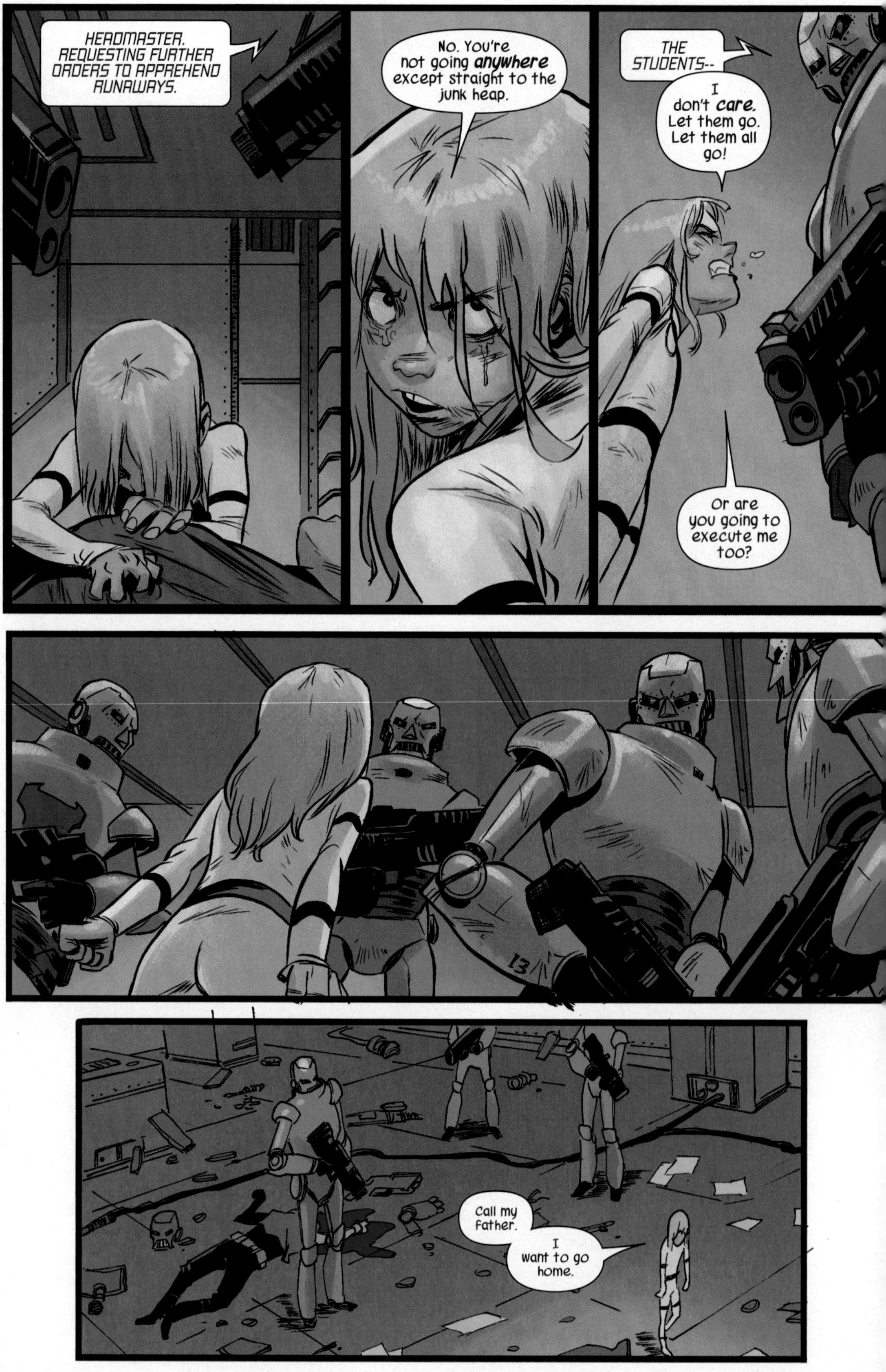
HEADMASTER. REQUESTING FURTHER ORDERS TO APPREHEND RUNAWAYS.
No. You're not going **anywhere** except straight to the junk heap.
THE STUDENTS--
I don't **care.** Let them go. Let them all go!
Or are you going to execute me too?
Call my father.
I want to go home.

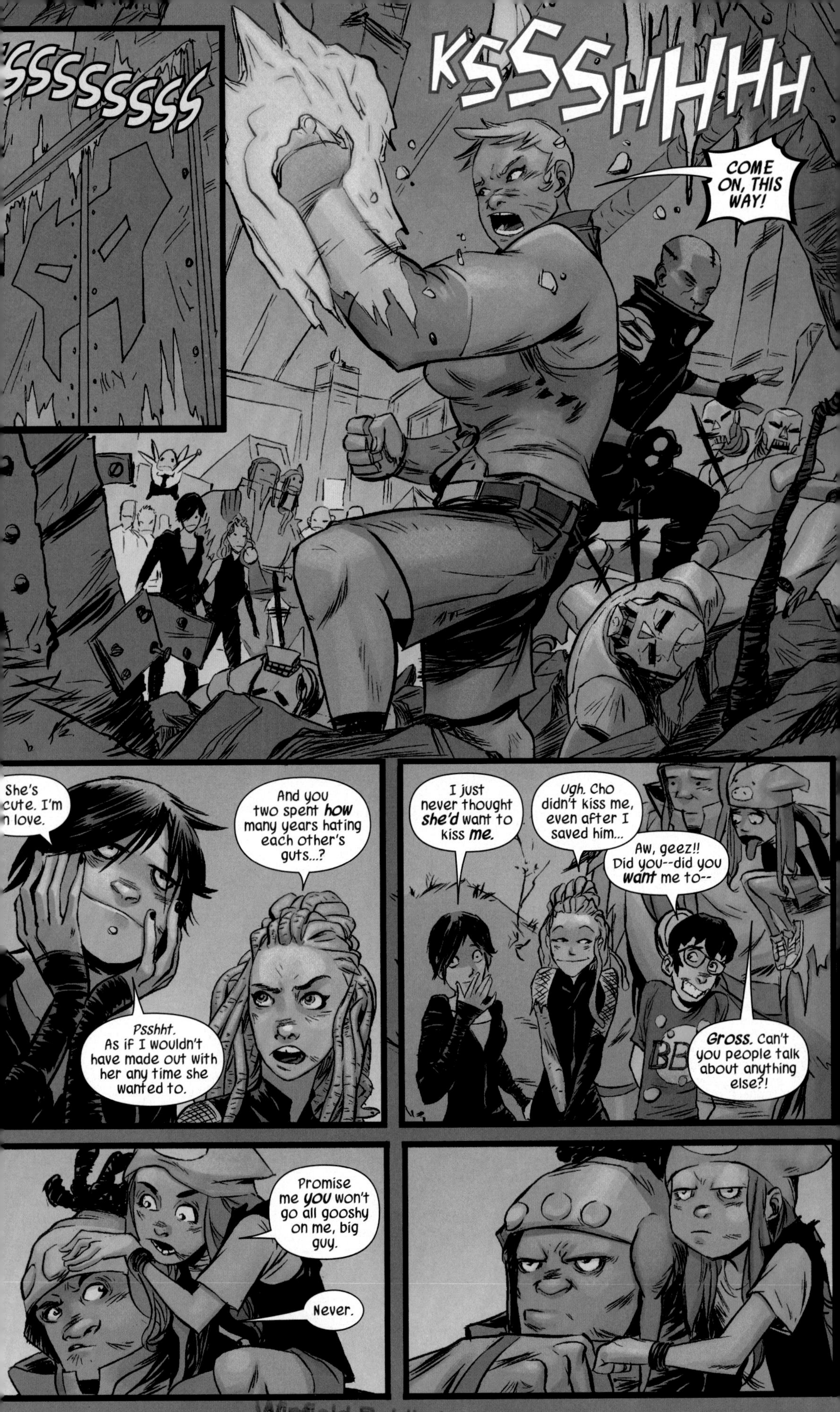
SSSSSSSS
KSSSHHHH
COME ON, THIS WAY!
She's cute. I'm n love.
And you two spent how many years hating each other's guts...?
Psshht. As if I wouldn't have made out with her any time she wanted to.
I just never thought she'd want to kiss me.
Ugh. Cho didn't kiss me, even after I saved him...
Aw, geez!! Did you--did you want me to--
Gross. Can't you people talk about anything else?!
Promise me you won't go all gooshy on me, big guy.
Never.

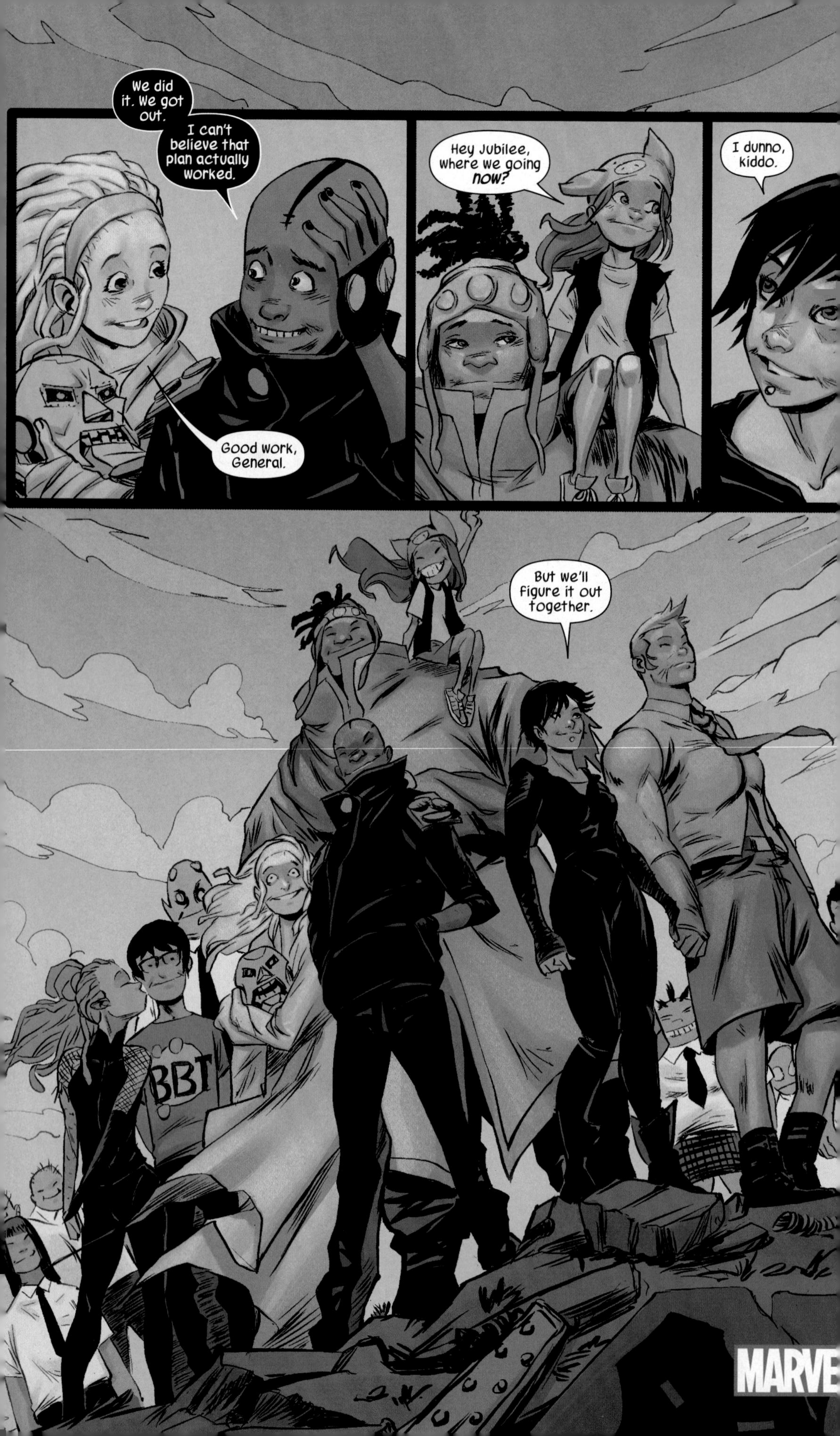
We did it. We got out.
I can't believe that plan actually worked.
Good work, General.
Hey Jubilee, where we going now?
I dunno, kiddo.
But we'll figure it out together.
MARVEL

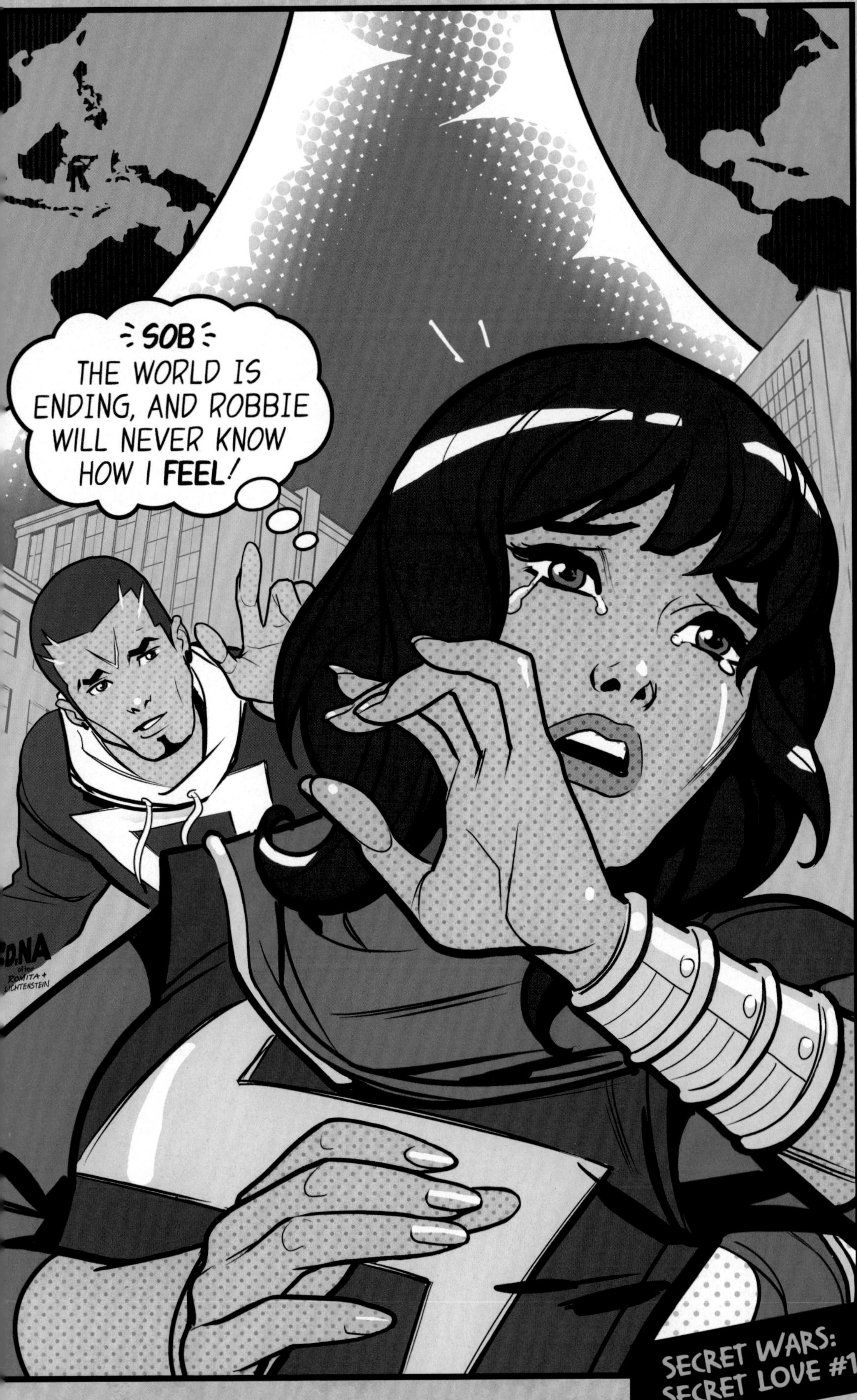
SOB
THE WORLD IS ENDING, AND ROBBIE WILL NEVER KNOW HOW I FEEL!
SECRET WARS: SECRET LOVE #1

secret wars:

Secret Love

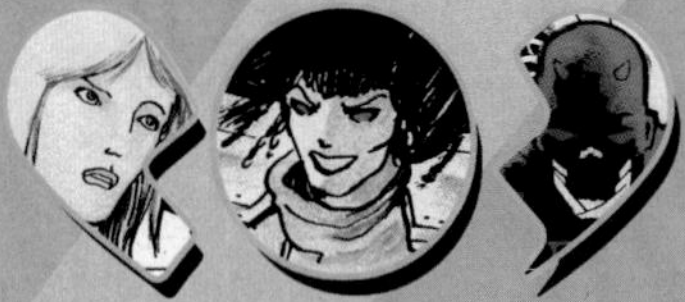

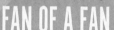

GUILTY PLEASURE
words and art by MICHEL FIFFE
letters by VC'S CLAYTON COWLES

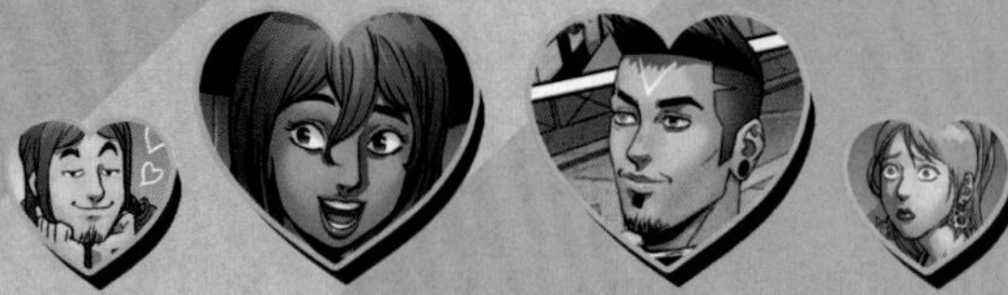

FAN OF A FAN
words and art by FELIPE SMITH
color by VAL STAPLES
letters by VC'S CLAYTON COWLES

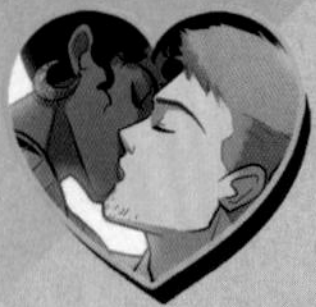

MISTY AND DANNY FOREVER
words by JEREMY WHITLEY
art by GURIHIRU
letters by VC'S CLAYTON COWLES

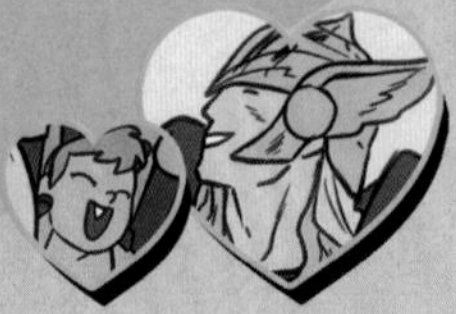

SQUIRREL GIRL WINS A DATE WITH THO
words by MARGUERITE BENNETT
art by KRIS ANKA
letters by VC'S CLAYTON COWLES

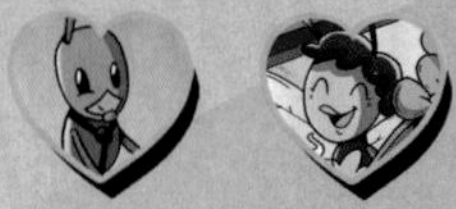

HAPPY ANT-IVERSARY
words and art by KATIE COOK

SECRET WARS

COVER:
DAVID NAKAYAMA

VARIANT COVER:
PASQUAL CAMPION

PRODUCTION DESIGN:
IDETTE WINECOOR

EDITOR:
EMILY SHAW

SENIOR EDITOR:
MARK PANICCIA

EDITOR IN CHIEF:
AXEL ALONSO

CHIEF CREATIVE OFFICER:
JOE QUESADA

PUBLISHER:
DAN BUCKLEY

EXECUTIVE PRODUCER:
ALAN FINE

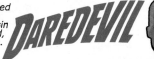

Matt Murdock, blind attorney turned super hero, has led a varied lifestyle in his time as Daredevil. He's fought Nazi hippies in San Francisco, he's been an amnesiac amateur boxer, and his assassin ex-lover came back from the dead (maybe). He's been disbarred, unmasked, armored, and homeless. He even flipped burgers once. Through it all, he's always been Hell's Kitchen's protector:

DAREDEVIL

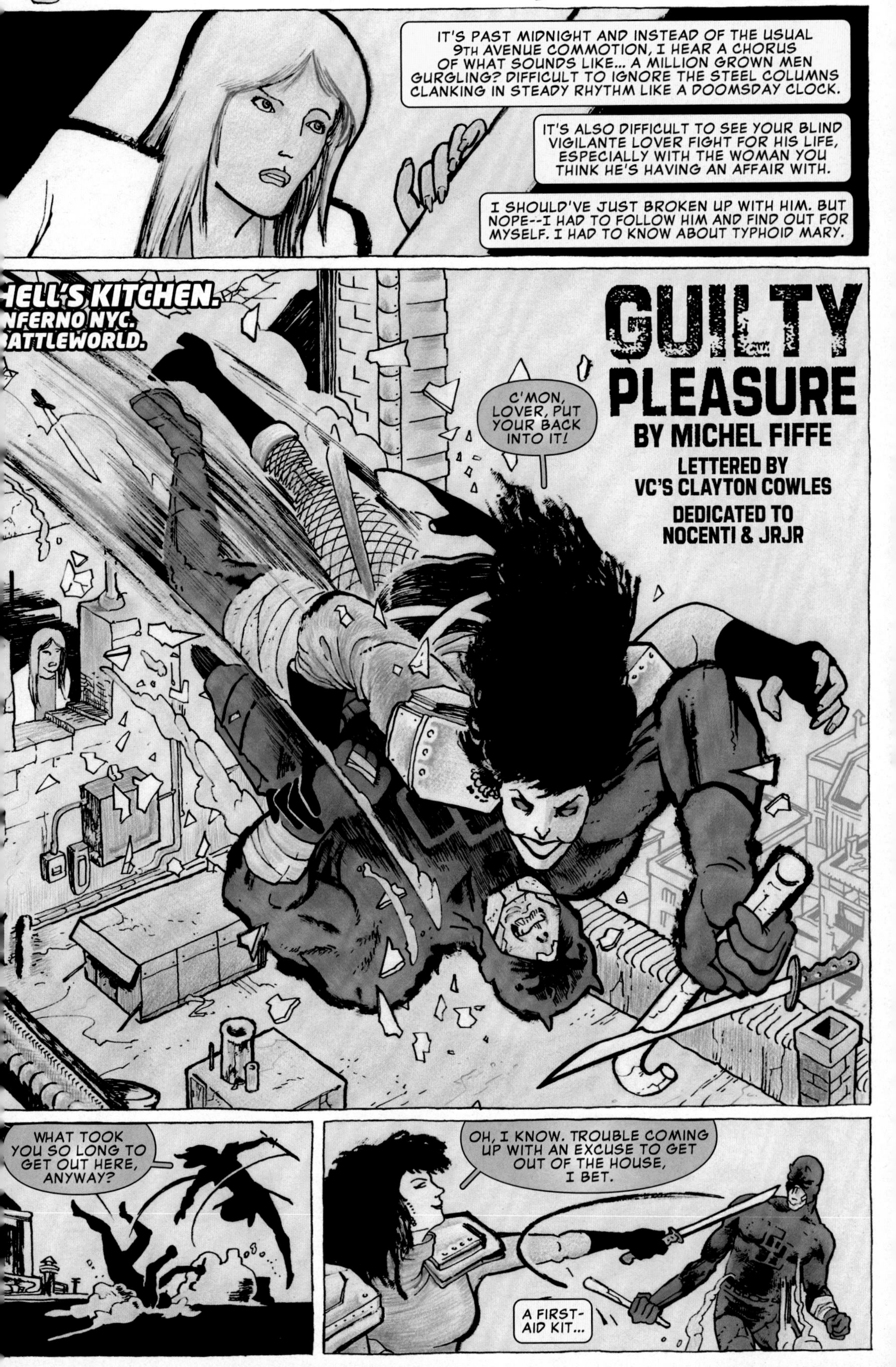

IT'S PAST MIDNIGHT AND INSTEAD OF THE USUAL 9TH AVENUE COMMOTION, I HEAR A CHORUS OF WHAT SOUNDS LIKE... A MILLION GROWN MEN GURGLING? DIFFICULT TO IGNORE THE STEEL COLUMNS CLANKING IN STEADY RHYTHM LIKE A DOOMSDAY CLOCK.
IT'S ALSO DIFFICULT TO SEE YOUR BLIND VIGILANTE LOVER FIGHT FOR HIS LIFE, ESPECIALLY WITH THE WOMAN YOU THINK HE'S HAVING AN AFFAIR WITH.
I SHOULD'VE JUST BROKEN UP WITH HIM. BUT NOPE--I HAD TO FOLLOW HIM AND FIND OUT FOR MYSELF. I HAD TO KNOW ABOUT TYPHOID MARY.
HELL'S KITCHEN.
INFERNO NYC.
BATTLEWORLD.
GUILTY PLEASURE
BY MICHEL FIFFE
LETTERED BY VC'S CLAYTON COWLES
DEDICATED TO NOCENTI & JRJR
C'MON, LOVER, PUT YOUR BACK INTO IT!
WHAT TOOK YOU SO LONG TO GET OUT HERE, ANYWAY?
OH, I KNOW. TROUBLE COMING UP WITH AN EXCUSE TO GET OUT OF THE HOUSE, I BET.
A FIRST-AID KIT...

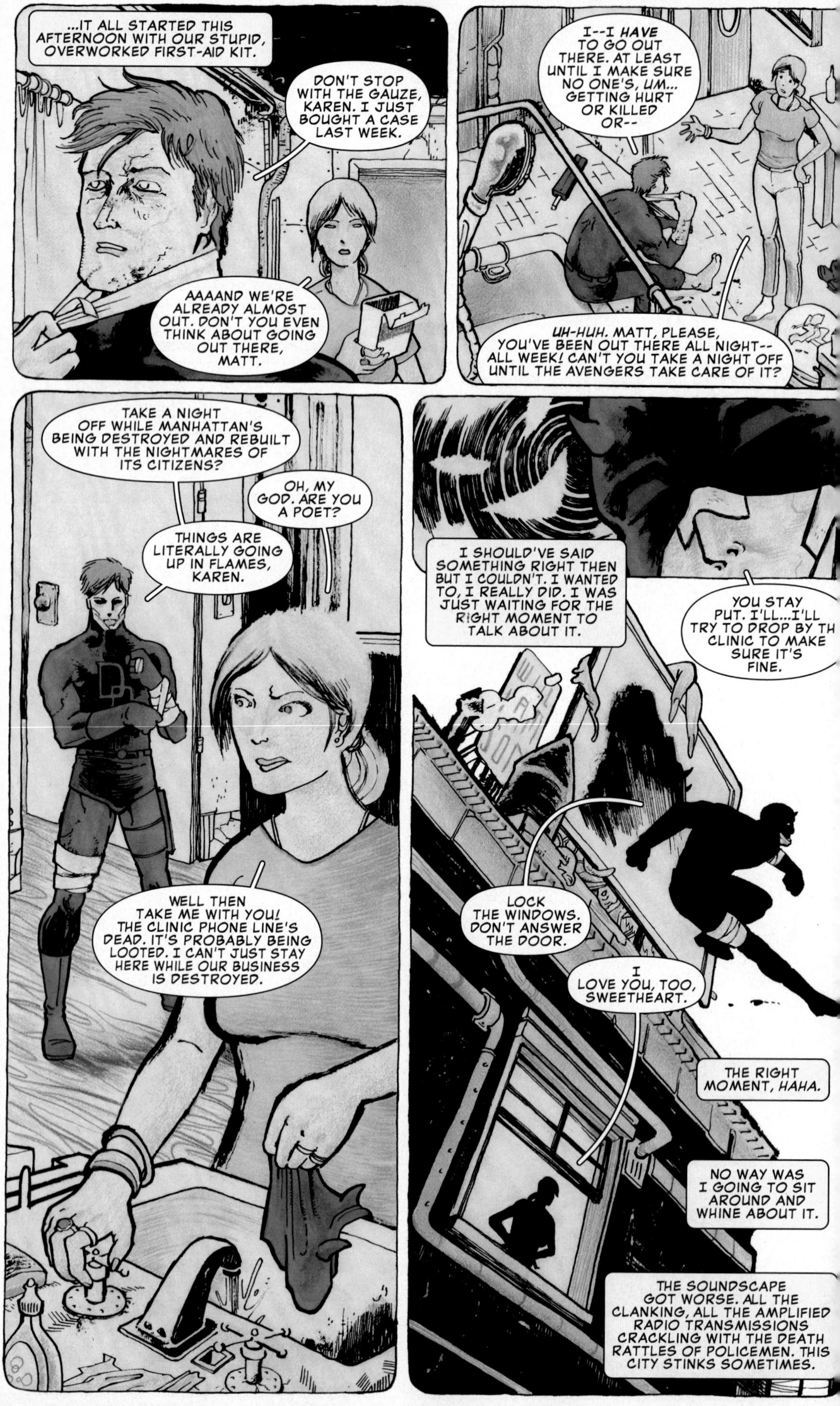
...IT ALL STARTED THIS AFTERNOON WITH OUR STUPID, OVERWORKED FIRST-AID KIT.
DON'T STOP WITH THE GAUZE, KAREN. I JUST BOUGHT A CASE LAST WEEK.
AAAAND WE'RE ALREADY ALMOST OUT. DON'T YOU EVEN THINK ABOUT GOING OUT THERE, MATT.
I--I *HAVE* TO GO OUT THERE. AT LEAST UNTIL I MAKE SURE NO ONE'S, *UM*... GETTING HURT OR KILLED OR--
UH-HUH. MATT, PLEASE, YOU'VE BEEN OUT THERE ALL NIGHT-- ALL WEEK! CAN'T YOU TAKE A NIGHT OFF UNTIL THE AVENGERS TAKE CARE OF IT?
TAKE A NIGHT OFF WHILE MANHATTAN'S BEING DESTROYED AND REBUILT WITH THE NIGHTMARES OF ITS CITIZENS?
OH, MY GOD. ARE YOU A POET?
THINGS ARE LITERALLY GOING UP IN FLAMES, KAREN.
WELL THEN TAKE ME WITH YOU! THE CLINIC PHONE LINE'S DEAD. IT'S PROBABLY BEING LOOTED. I CAN'T JUST STAY HERE WHILE OUR BUSINESS IS DESTROYED.
I SHOULD'VE SAID SOMETHING RIGHT THEN BUT I COULDN'T. I WANTED TO, I REALLY DID. I WAS JUST WAITING FOR THE RIGHT MOMENT TO TALK ABOUT IT.
YOU STAY PUT. I'LL...I'LL TRY TO DROP BY TH CLINIC TO MAKE SURE IT'S FINE.
LOCK THE WINDOWS. DON'T ANSWER THE DOOR.
I LOVE YOU, TOO, SWEETHEART.
THE RIGHT MOMENT, *HAHA.*
NO WAY WAS I GOING TO SIT AROUND AND WHINE ABOUT IT.
THE SOUNDSCAPE GOT WORSE. ALL THE CLANKING, ALL THE AMPLIFIED RADIO TRANSMISSIONS CRACKLING WITH THE DEATH RATTLES OF POLICEMEN. THIS CITY STINKS SOMETIMES.

I DID THE SENSIBLE THING. I FOLLOWED HIM--AND GOT AWAY WITH IT! MATT MUST'VE REALLY BEEN OFF. HIS RADAR SENSE WOULD'VE PICKED OUT MY HEARTBEAT A MILE AWAY.

I ALMOST FELT BAD SPYING ON HIM BECAUSE...WELL, HE DID WHAT HE SAID HE'D DO, TRUE TO HIS WORD. HE PROTECTED HELL'S KITCHEN.

MAYBE I WAS OVERREACTING. AS IF I'VE BEEN AN ANGEL. SHOOT, SOMETIMES I FEEL GUILTY FOR HAVING SUCH A GREAT GUY WITH ME. THAT'S *MY DUDE*.

MATT'S KIND, BUT NOT A PUSHOVER. EXCELLENT WITH BIRTHDAYS. HE'S A GREAT COOK, TOO. PLUS, HE'S HOT.

HE'S FIT, WELL GROOMED, AND SOMETIMES A LITTLE *TOO* CHARMING. I LOVE IT ALL. THOSE LIPS, THAT SHARP NOSE, THAT RHINO TOENAIL THAT ALWAYS CUTS ME, THAT LITTLE MOLE ON HIS BACK THAT I ASK HIM TO GET CHECKED OUT ALL THE TIME.

MATT'S THE ONLY MAN WHO I LIKED SLEEPING NEXT TO, EVEN WHEN I'D WAKE UP IN THE MIDDLE OF THE NIGHT BECAUSE HIS HEAVY LEG WAS CRUSHING ME.

JUST LAST WEEK HE STARTED TALKING IN HIS SLEEP. IT WASN'T CREEPY OR ANYTHING, JUST DIFFERENT. HE'D NEVER DONE THAT BEFORE. IT WAS FUNNY AT FIRST, BUT THEN HE SAID A NAME.

HER NAME.

MARY.

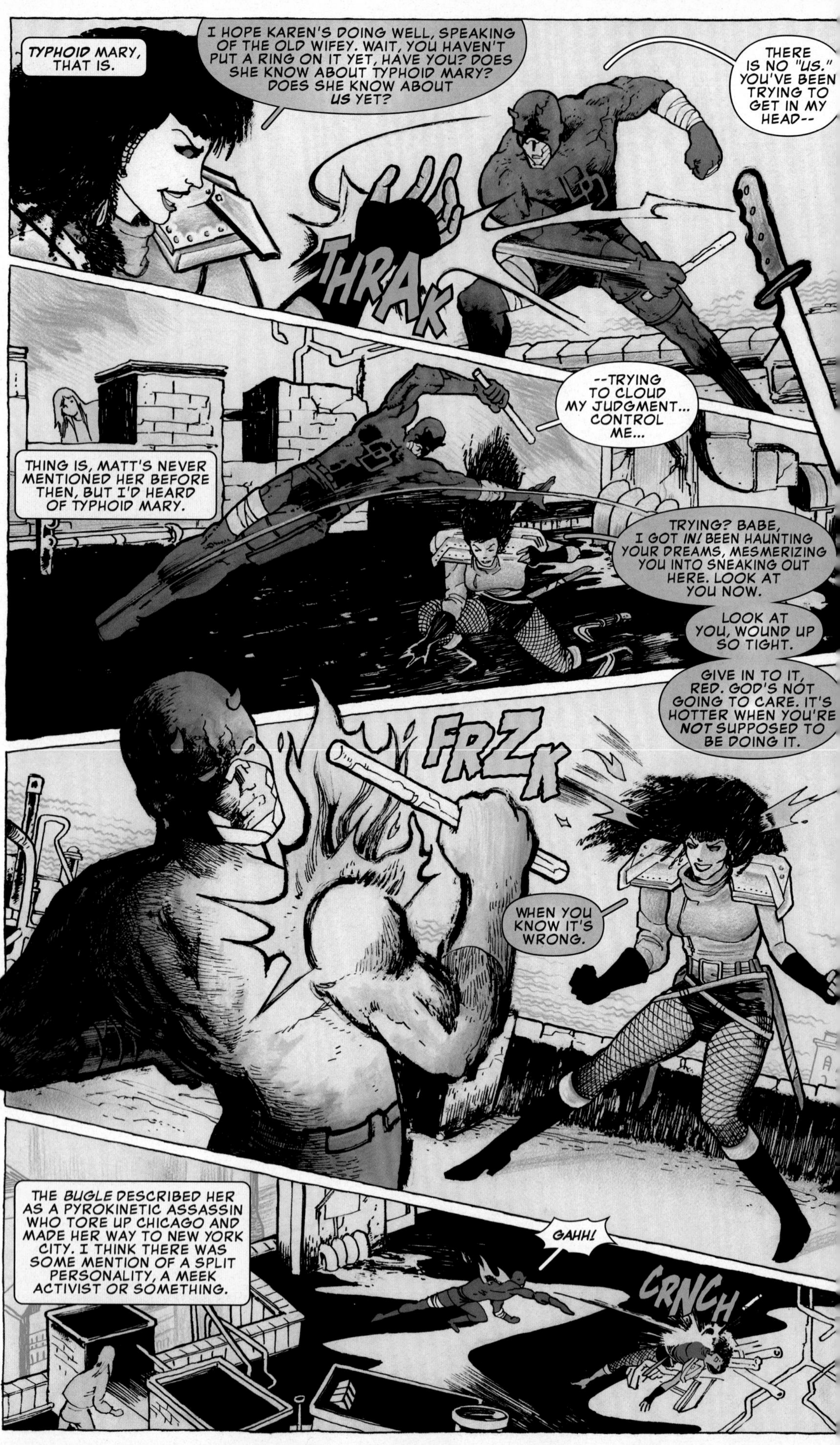

TYPHOID MARY, THAT IS.
I HOPE KAREN'S DOING WELL, SPEAKING OF THE OLD WIFEY. WAIT, YOU HAVEN'T PUT A RING ON IT YET, HAVE YOU? DOES SHE KNOW ABOUT TYPHOID MARY? DOES SHE KNOW ABOUT US YET?
THERE IS NO "US." YOU'VE BEEN TRYING TO GET IN MY HEAD--
THRAK
--TRYING TO CLOUD MY JUDGMENT... CONTROL ME...
THING IS, MATT'S NEVER MENTIONED HER BEFORE THEN, BUT I'D HEARD OF TYPHOID MARY.
TRYING? BABE, I GOT IN! BEEN HAUNTING YOUR DREAMS, MESMERIZING YOU INTO SNEAKING OUT HERE. LOOK AT YOU NOW.
LOOK AT YOU, WOUND UP SO TIGHT.
GIVE IN TO IT, RED. GOD'S NOT GOING TO CARE. IT'S HOTTER WHEN YOU'RE NOT SUPPOSED TO BE DOING IT.
FRZK
WHEN YOU KNOW IT'S WRONG.
THE BUGLE DESCRIBED HER AS A PYROKINETIC ASSASSIN WHO TORE UP CHICAGO AND MADE HER WAY TO NEW YORK CITY. I THINK THERE WAS SOME MENTION OF A SPLIT PERSONALITY, A MEEK ACTIVIST OR SOMETHING.
GAHH!
CRNCH

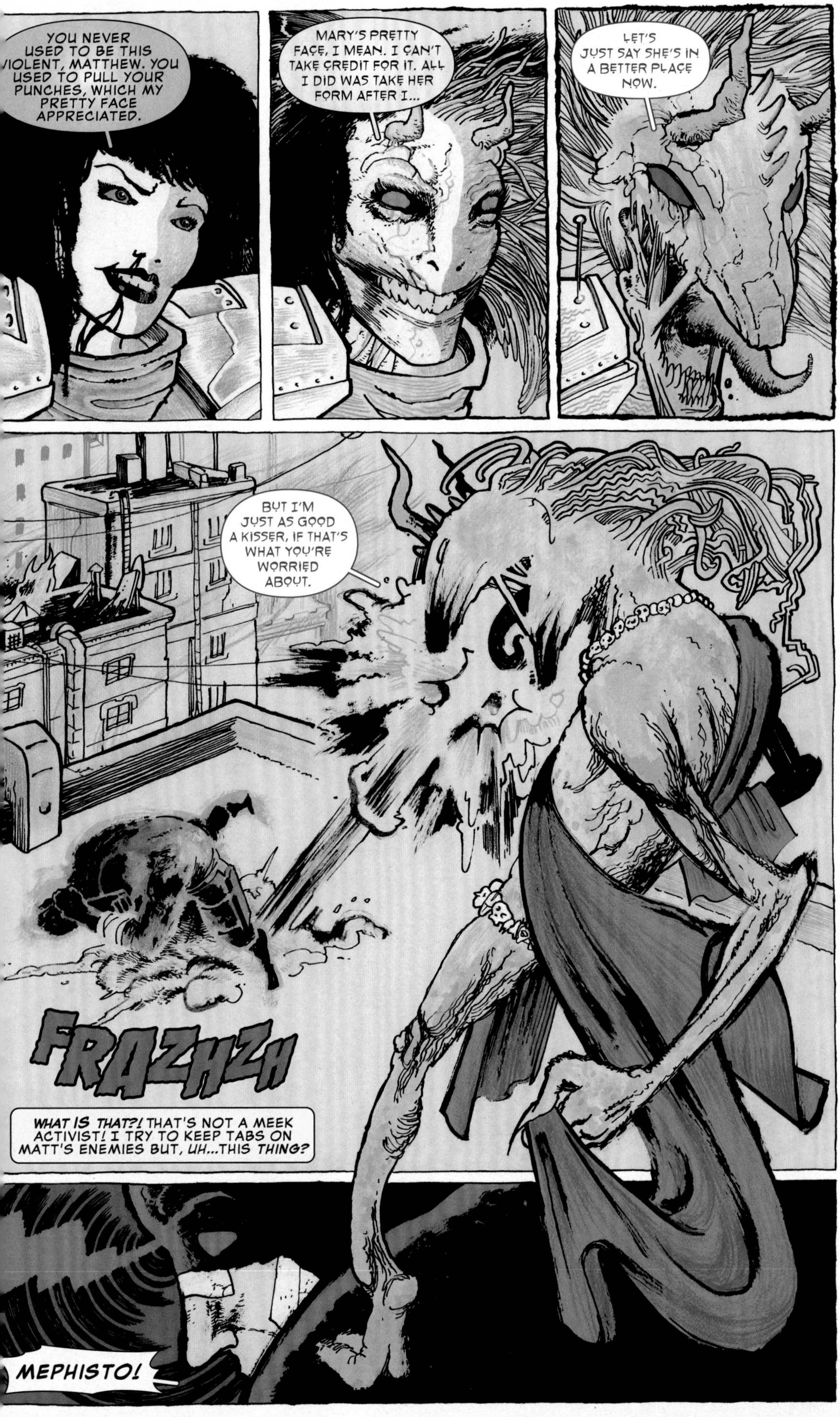

YOU NEVER USED TO BE THIS VIOLENT, MATTHEW. YOU USED TO PULL YOUR PUNCHES, WHICH MY PRETTY FACE APPRECIATED.
MARY'S PRETTY FACE, I MEAN. I CAN'T TAKE CREDIT FOR IT. ALL I DID WAS TAKE HER FORM AFTER I...
LET'S JUST SAY SHE'S IN A BETTER PLACE NOW.
BUT I'M JUST AS GOOD A KISSER, IF THAT'S WHAT YOU'RE WORRIED ABOUT.
FRAZHZH
WHAT IS THAT?! THAT'S NOT A MEEK ACTIVIST! I TRY TO KEEP TABS ON MATT'S ENEMIES BUT, UH...THIS THING?
MEPHISTO!

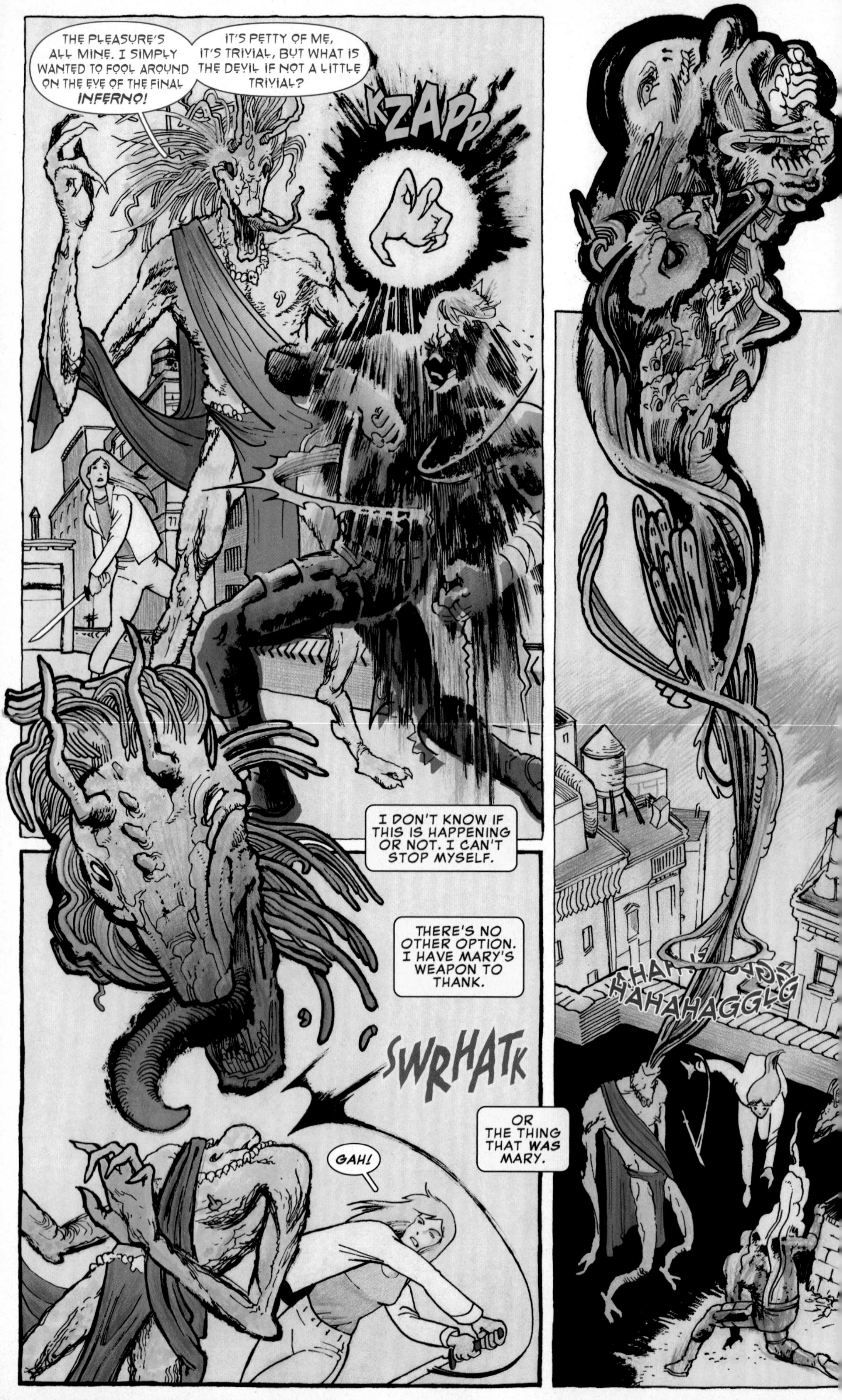
THE PLEASURE'S ALL MINE. I SIMPLY WANTED TO FOOL AROUND ON THE EVE OF THE FINAL INFERNO!
IT'S PETTY OF ME, IT'S TRIVIAL, BUT WHAT IS THE DEVIL IF NOT A LITTLE TRIVIAL?
KZAPP
I DON'T KNOW IF THIS IS HAPPENING OR NOT. I CAN'T STOP MYSELF.
THERE'S NO OTHER OPTION. I HAVE MARY'S WEAPON TO THANK.
SWRHATK
GAH!
OR THE THING THAT WAS MARY.
HAHAHAGGLG

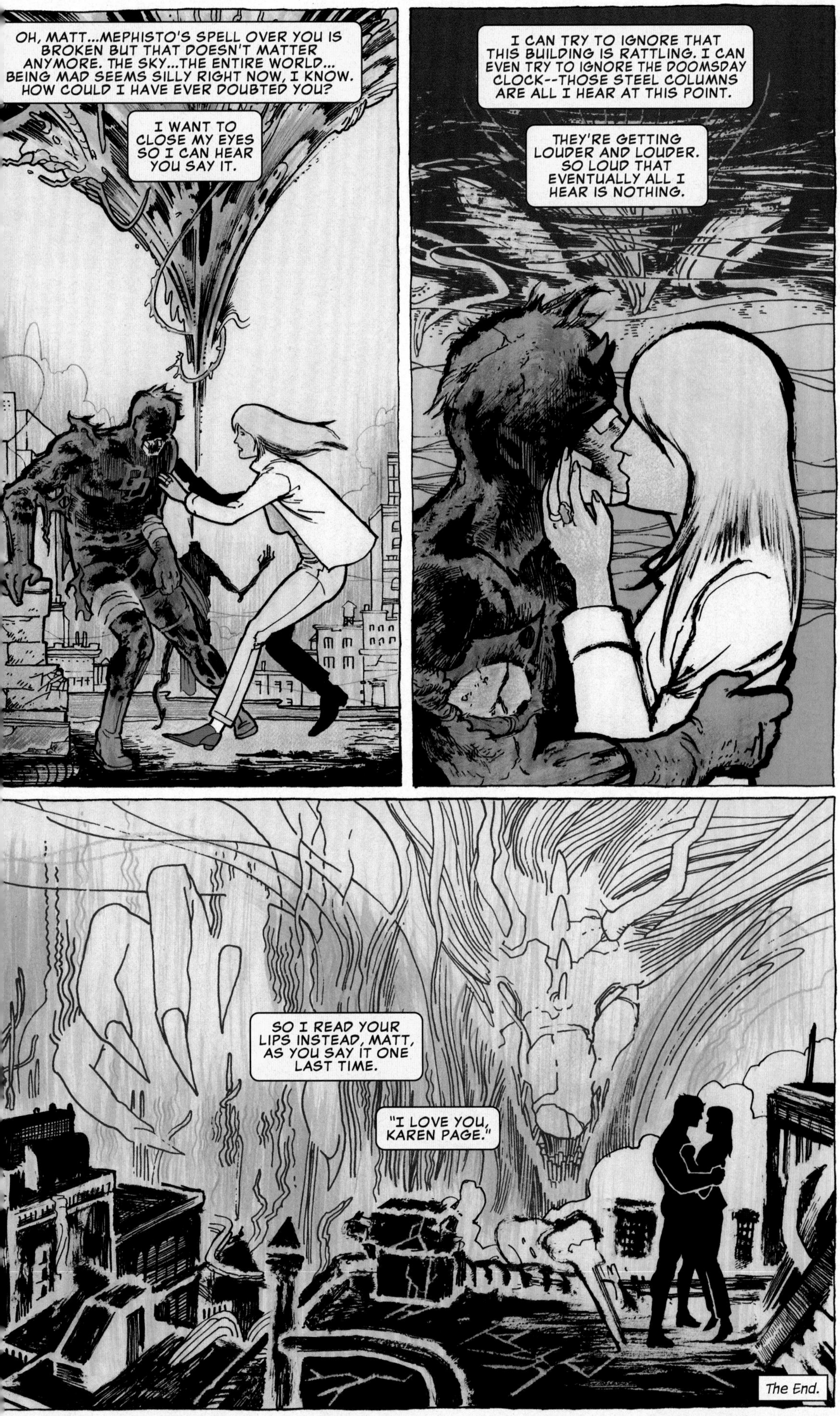
OH, MATT...MEPHISTO'S SPELL OVER YOU IS BROKEN BUT THAT DOESN'T MATTER ANYMORE. THE SKY...THE ENTIRE WORLD... BEING MAD SEEMS SILLY RIGHT NOW, I KNOW. HOW COULD I HAVE EVER DOUBTED YOU?
I WANT TO CLOSE MY EYES SO I CAN HEAR YOU SAY IT.
I CAN TRY TO IGNORE THAT THIS BUILDING IS RATTLING. I CAN EVEN TRY TO IGNORE THE DOOMSDAY CLOCK--THOSE STEEL COLUMNS ARE ALL I HEAR AT THIS POINT.
THEY'RE GETTING LOUDER AND LOUDER. SO LOUD THAT EVENTUALLY ALL I HEAR IS NOTHING.
SO I READ YOUR LIPS INSTEAD, MATT, AS YOU SAY IT ONE LAST TIME.
"I LOVE YOU, KAREN PAGE."
The End.

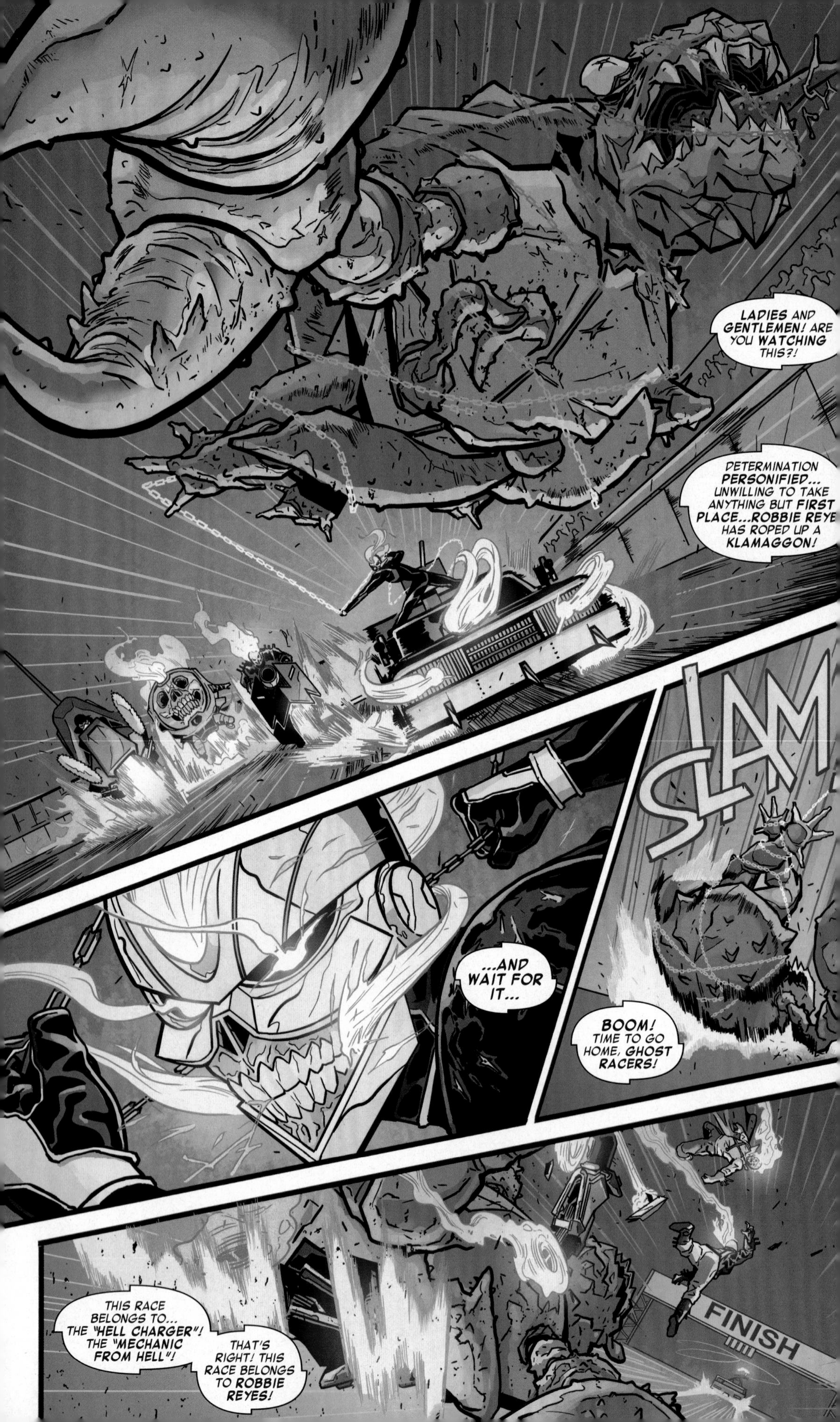
LADIES AND GENTLEMEN! ARE YOU WATCHING THIS?!
DETERMINATION PERSONIFIED... UNWILLING TO TAKE ANYTHING BUT FIRST PLACE...ROBBIE REYES HAS ROPED UP A KLAMAGGON!
SLAM
...AND WAIT FOR IT...
BOOM! TIME TO GO HOME, GHOST RACERS!
THIS RACE BELONGS TO... THE "HELL CHARGER"! THE "MECHANIC FROM HELL"!
THAT'S RIGHT! THIS RACE BELONGS TO ROBBIE REYES!
FINISH

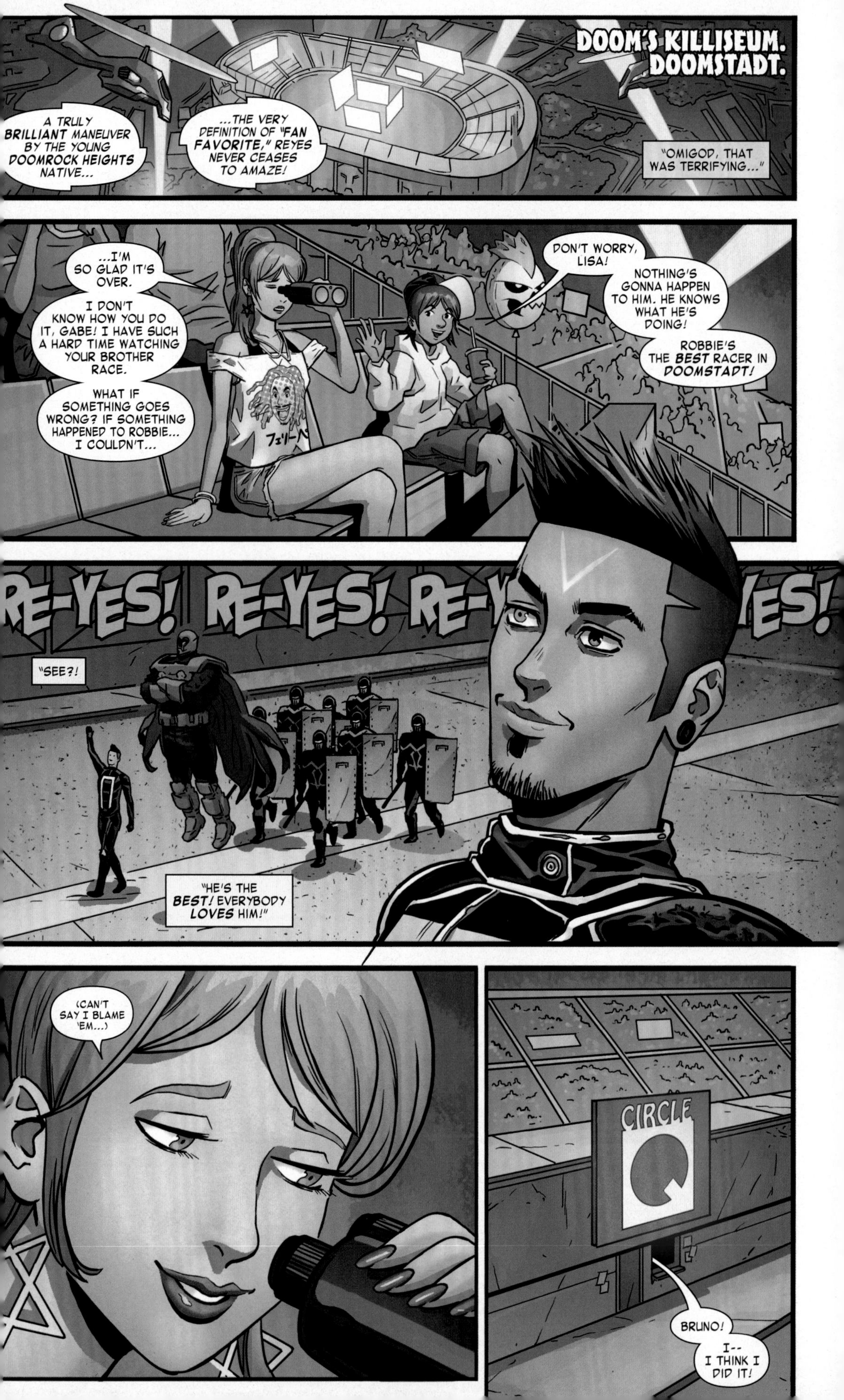
DOOM'S KILLISEUM. DOOMSTADT.
A TRULY BRILLIANT MANEUVER BY THE YOUNG DOOMROCK HEIGHTS NATIVE...
...THE VERY DEFINITION OF "FAN FAVORITE," REYES NEVER CEASES TO AMAZE!
"OMIGOD, THAT WAS TERRIFYING..."
...I'M SO GLAD IT'S OVER.
I DON'T KNOW HOW YOU DO IT, GABE! I HAVE SUCH A HARD TIME WATCHING YOUR BROTHER RACE.
WHAT IF SOMETHING GOES WRONG? IF SOMETHING HAPPENED TO ROBBIE... I COULDN'T...
DON'T WORRY, LISA!
NOTHING'S GONNA HAPPEN TO HIM. HE KNOWS WHAT HE'S DOING!
ROBBIE'S THE BEST RACER IN DOOMSTADT!
RE-YES! RE-YES! RE-Y YES!
"SEE?!
"HE'S THE BEST! EVERYBODY LOVES HIM!"
(CAN'T SAY I BLAME 'EM...)
CIRCLE Q
BRUNO!
I-- I THINK I DID IT!

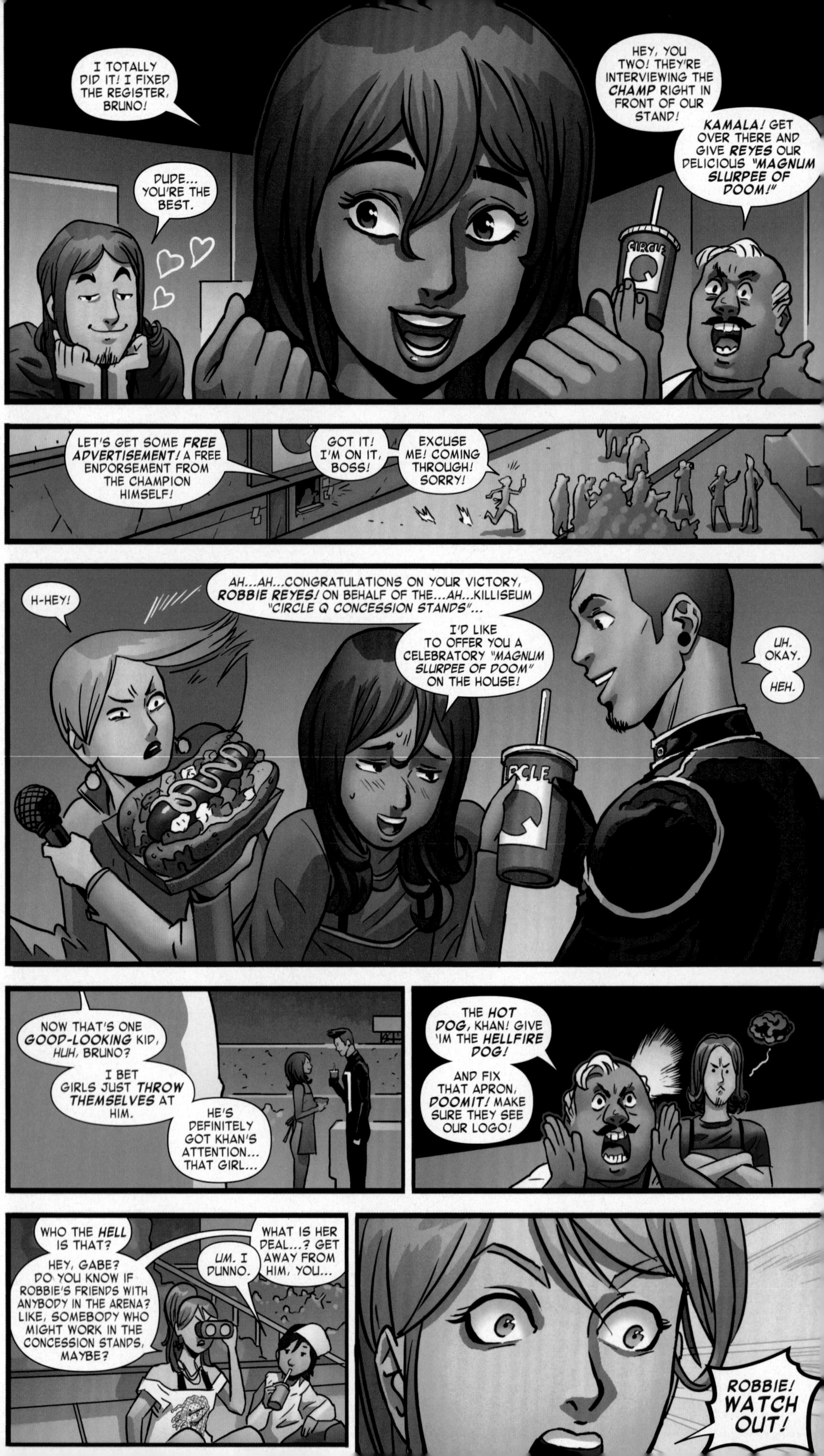

I TOTALLY DID IT! I FIXED THE REGISTER, BRUNO!
DUDE... YOU'RE THE BEST.
HEY, YOU TWO! THEY'RE INTERVIEWING THE CHAMP RIGHT IN FRONT OF OUR STAND!
KAMALA! GET OVER THERE AND GIVE REYES OUR DELICIOUS "MAGNUM SLURPEE OF DOOM!"
LET'S GET SOME FREE ADVERTISEMENT! A FREE ENDORSEMENT FROM THE CHAMPION HIMSELF!
GOT IT! I'M ON IT, BOSS!
EXCUSE ME! COMING THROUGH! SORRY!
H-HEY!
AH...AH...CONGRATULATIONS ON YOUR VICTORY, ROBBIE REYES! ON BEHALF OF THE...AH...KILLISEUM "CIRCLE Q CONCESSION STANDS"...
I'D LIKE TO OFFER YOU A CELEBRATORY "MAGNUM SLURPEE OF DOOM" ON THE HOUSE!
UH. OKAY.
HEH.
NOW THAT'S ONE GOOD-LOOKING KID, HUH, BRUNO?
I BET GIRLS JUST THROW THEMSELVES AT HIM.
HE'S DEFINITELY GOT KHAN'S ATTENTION... THAT GIRL...
THE HOT DOG, KHAN! GIVE 'IM THE HELLFIRE DOG!
AND FIX THAT APRON, DOOMIT! MAKE SURE THEY SEE OUR LOGO!
WHO THE HELL IS THAT?
HEY, GABE? DO YOU KNOW IF ROBBIE'S FRIENDS WITH ANYBODY IN THE ARENA? LIKE, SOMEBODY WHO MIGHT WORK IN THE CONCESSION STANDS, MAYBE?
UM. I DUNNO.
WHAT IS HER DEAL...? GET AWAY FROM HIM, YOU...
ROBBIE! WATCH OUT!

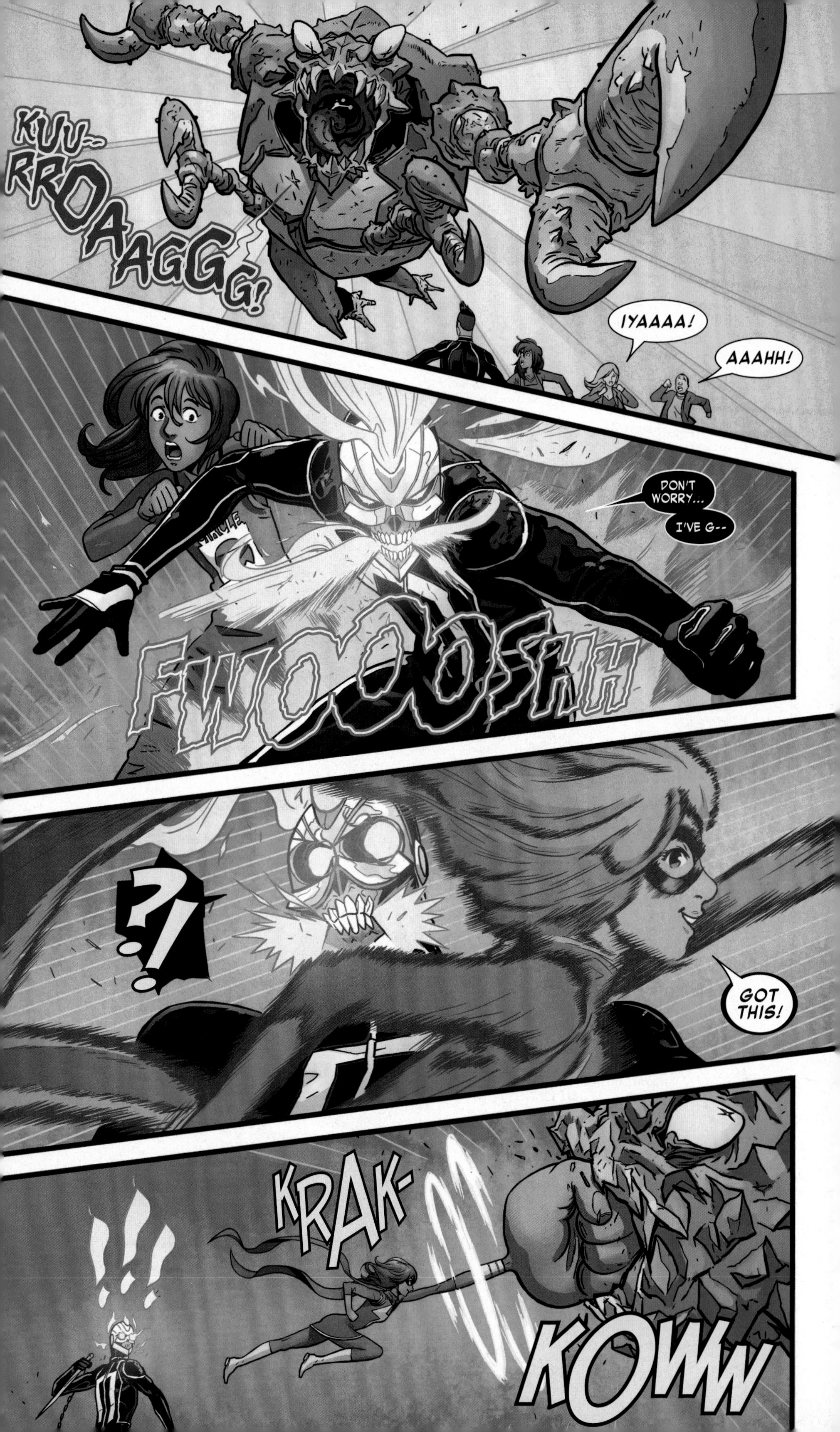

KUU--RROAAGGG!
IYAAAA!
AAAHH!
DON'T WORRY...
I'VE G--
FWOOOSHH
?!
GOT THIS!
!!!
KRAK-
KOWW

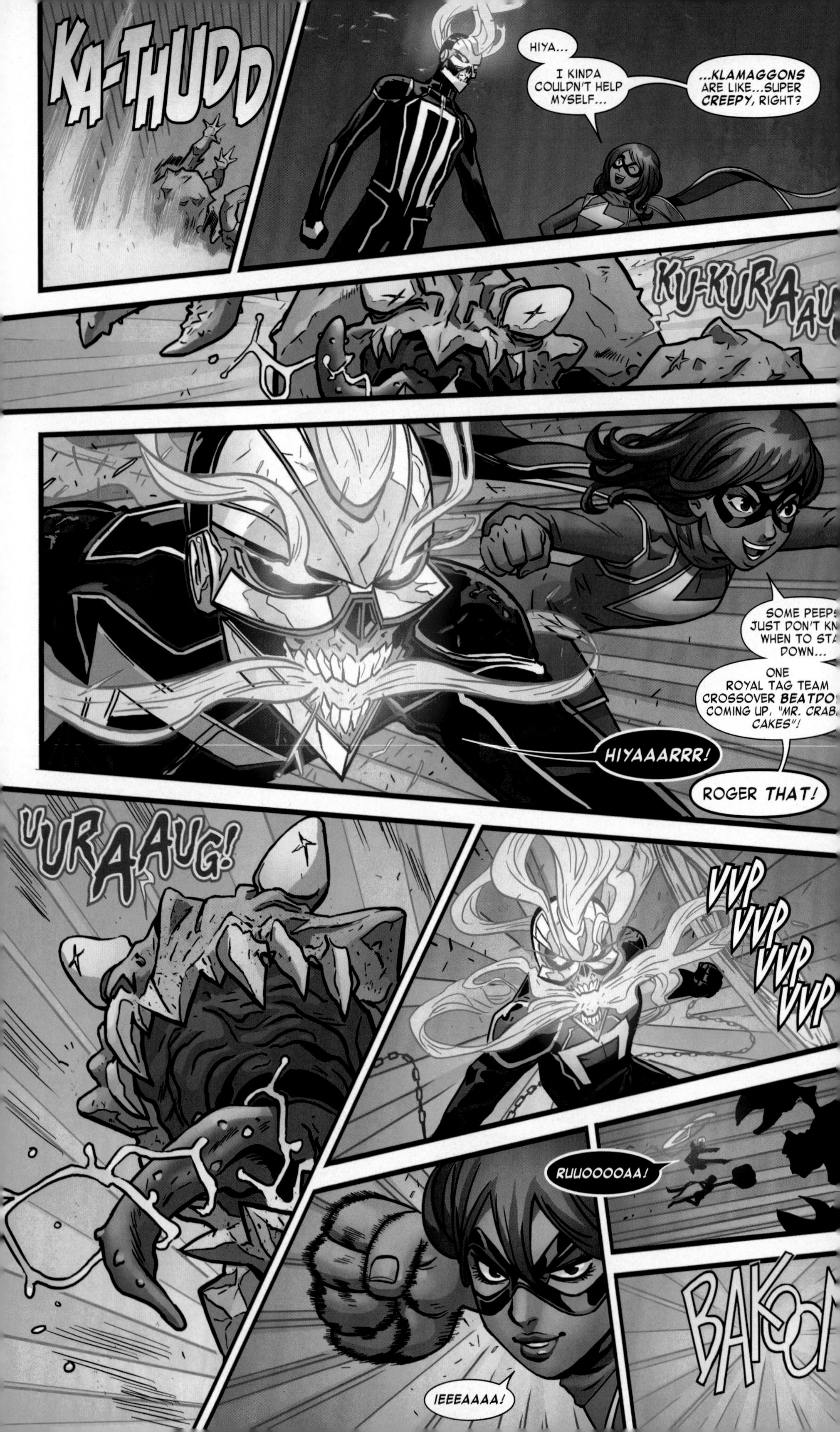
KA-THUDD
HIYA...
I KINDA COULDN'T HELP MYSELF...
...KLAMAGGONS ARE LIKE...SUPER CREEPY, RIGHT?
KU-KURAAAU
SOME PEEPS JUST DON'T KN WHEN TO STA DOWN...
ONE ROYAL TAG TEAM CROSSOVER BEATDO COMING UP, "MR. CRAB CAKES"!
HIYAAARRR!
ROGER THAT!
UURAAUG!
VVP VVP VVP VVP
RUUOOOOAA!
BAKOO
IEEEAAAA!

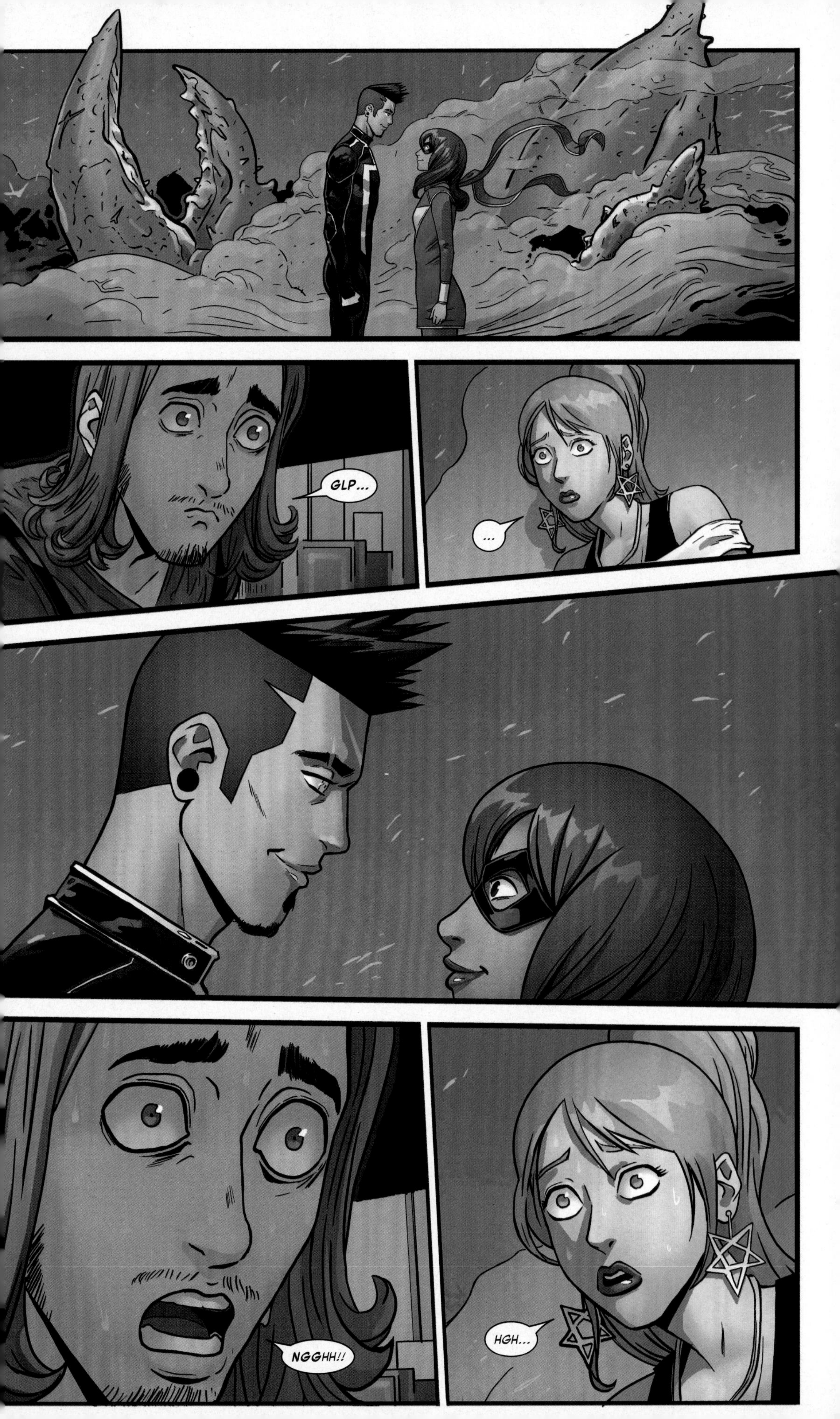
GLP...
...
NGGHH!!
HGH...

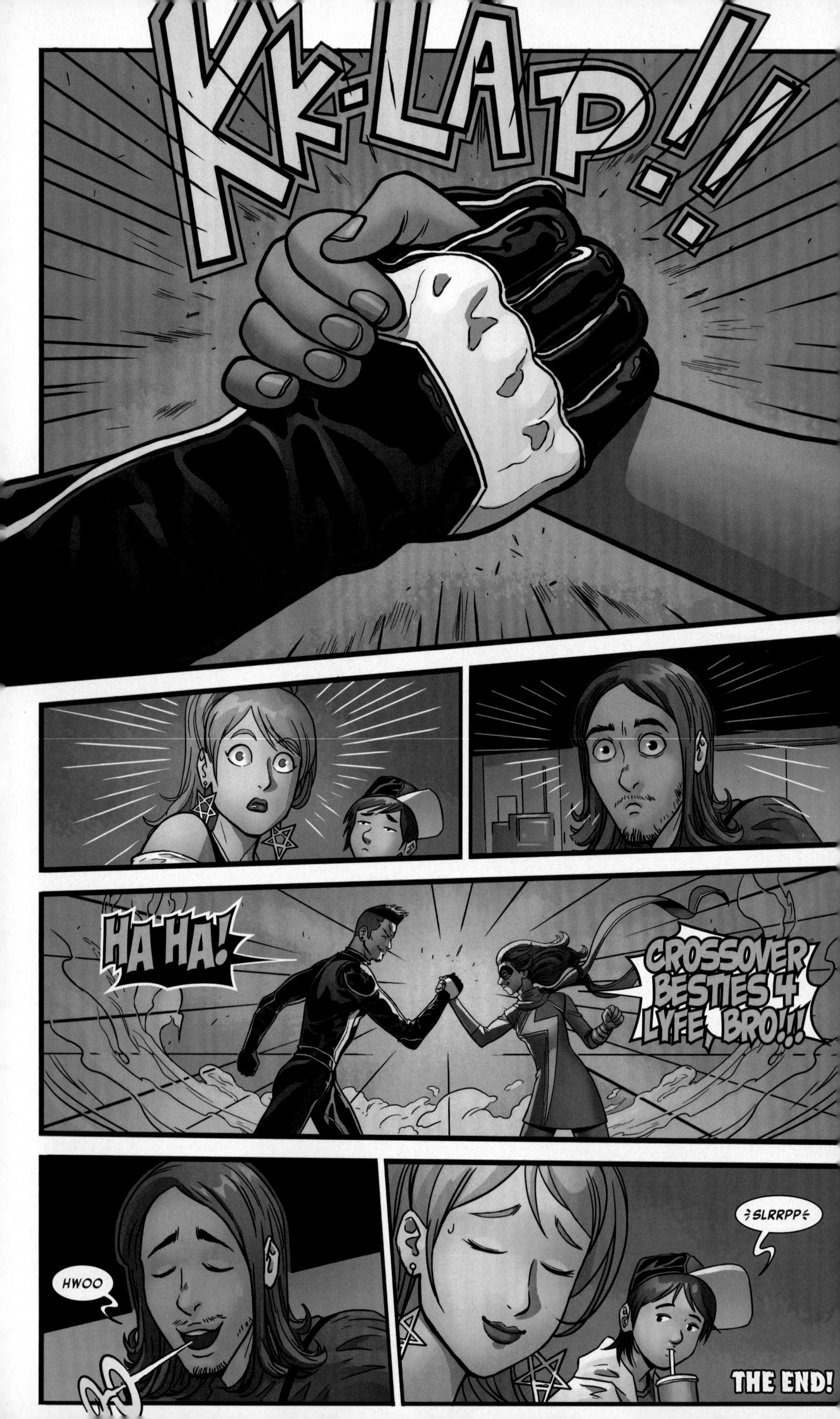
KK-LAP!!
HA HA!
CROSSOVER BESTIES 4 LYFE, BRO!!!
HWOO
SLRRPP
THE END!

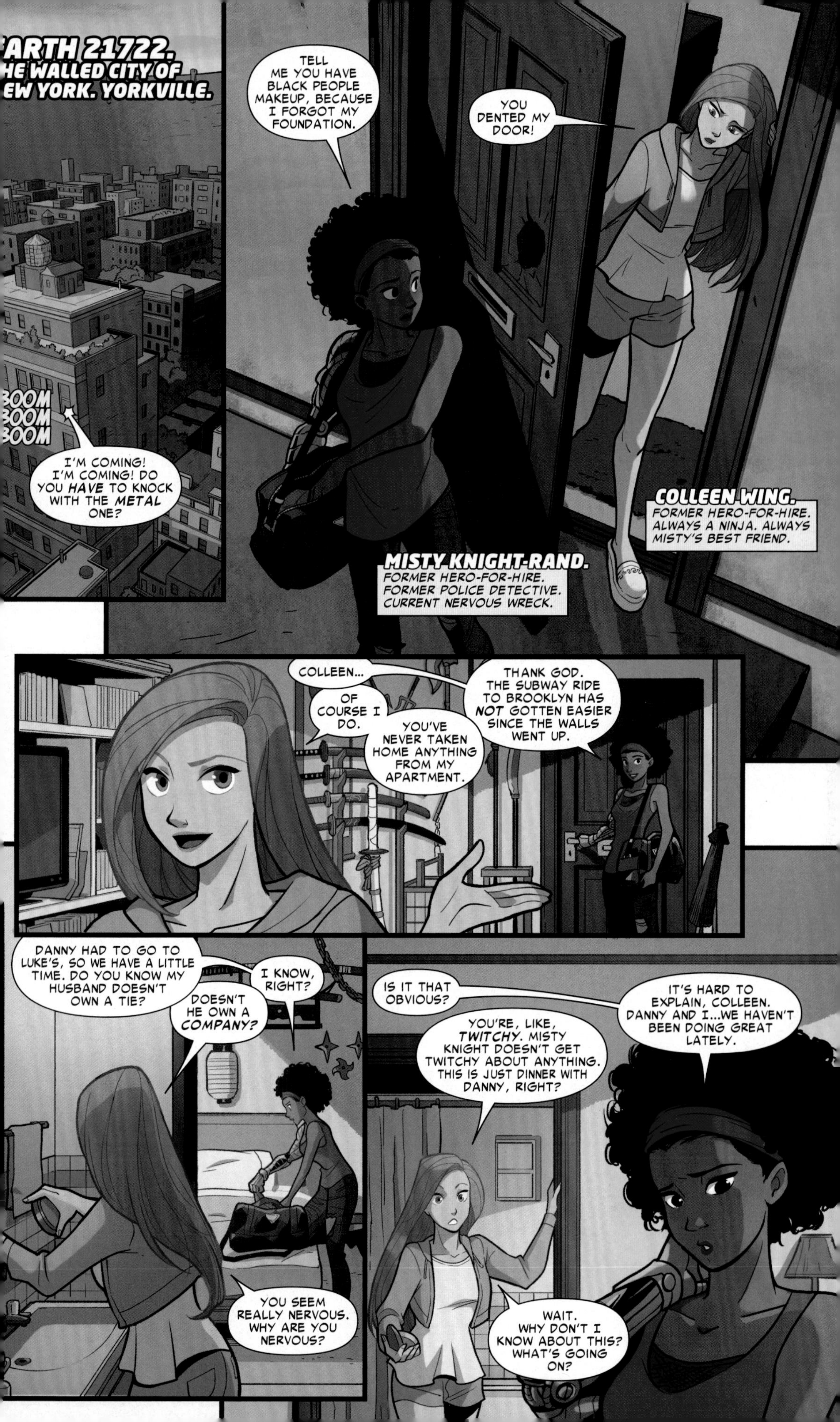

ARTH 21722.
HE WALLED CITY OF
EW YORK. YORKVILLE.
OOM
OOM
OOM
I'M COMING! I'M COMING! DO YOU *HAVE* TO KNOCK WITH THE *METAL* ONE?
TELL ME YOU HAVE BLACK PEOPLE MAKEUP, BECAUSE I FORGOT MY FOUNDATION.
YOU DENTED MY DOOR!
COLLEEN WING.
FORMER HERO-FOR-HIRE. ALWAYS A NINJA. ALWAYS MISTY'S BEST FRIEND.
MISTY KNIGHT-RAND.
FORMER HERO-FOR-HIRE. FORMER POLICE DETECTIVE. CURRENT NERVOUS WRECK.
COLLEEN...
THANK GOD. THE SUBWAY RIDE TO BROOKLYN HAS *NOT* GOTTEN EASIER SINCE THE WALLS WENT UP.
OF COURSE I DO.
YOU'VE NEVER TAKEN HOME ANYTHING FROM MY APARTMENT.
DANNY HAD TO GO TO LUKE'S, SO WE HAVE A LITTLE TIME. DO YOU KNOW MY HUSBAND DOESN'T OWN A TIE?
DOESN'T HE OWN A *COMPANY?*
I KNOW, RIGHT?
YOU SEEM REALLY NERVOUS. WHY ARE YOU NERVOUS?
IS IT THAT OBVIOUS?
YOU'RE, LIKE, *TWITCHY*. MISTY KNIGHT DOESN'T GET TWITCHY ABOUT ANYTHING. THIS IS JUST DINNER WITH DANNY, RIGHT?
IT'S HARD TO EXPLAIN, COLLEEN. DANNY AND I...WE HAVEN'T BEEN DOING GREAT LATELY.
WAIT. WHY DON'T I KNOW ABOUT THIS? WHAT'S GOING ON?

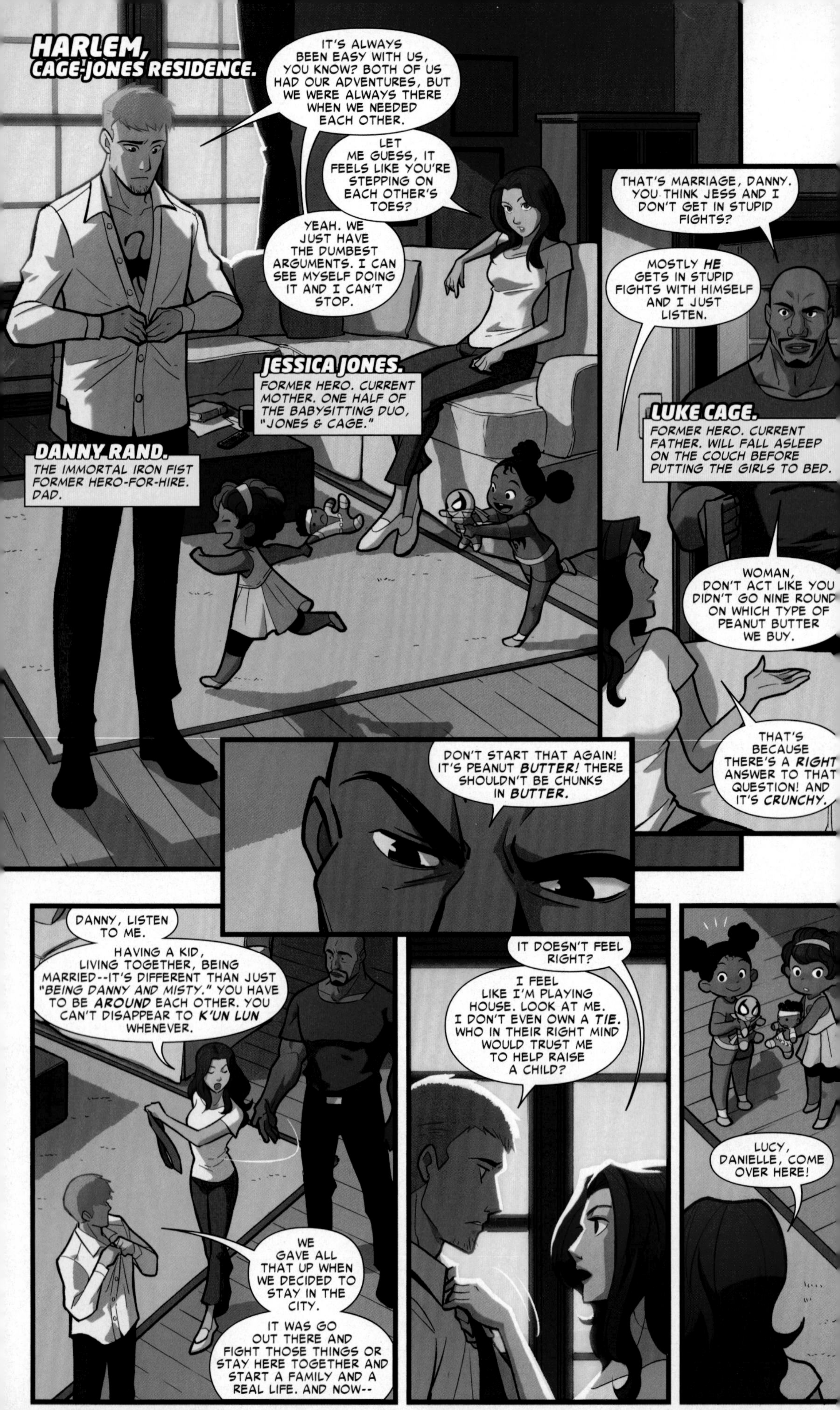

HARLEM, CAGE-JONES RESIDENCE.
IT'S ALWAYS BEEN EASY WITH US, YOU KNOW? BOTH OF US HAD OUR ADVENTURES, BUT WE WERE ALWAYS THERE WHEN WE NEEDED EACH OTHER.
LET ME GUESS, IT FEELS LIKE YOU'RE STEPPING ON EACH OTHER'S TOES?
YEAH. WE JUST HAVE THE DUMBEST ARGUMENTS. I CAN SEE MYSELF DOING IT AND I CAN'T STOP.
JESSICA JONES.
FORMER HERO. CURRENT MOTHER. ONE HALF OF THE BABYSITTING DUO, "JONES & CAGE."
DANNY RAND.
THE IMMORTAL IRON FIST FORMER HERO-FOR-HIRE. DAD.
THAT'S MARRIAGE, DANNY. YOU THINK JESS AND I DON'T GET IN STUPID FIGHTS?
MOSTLY HE GETS IN STUPID FIGHTS WITH HIMSELF AND I JUST LISTEN.
LUKE CAGE.
FORMER HERO. CURRENT FATHER. WILL FALL ASLEEP ON THE COUCH BEFORE PUTTING THE GIRLS TO BED.
WOMAN, DON'T ACT LIKE YOU DIDN'T GO NINE ROUND ON WHICH TYPE OF PEANUT BUTTER WE BUY.
THAT'S BECAUSE THERE'S A RIGHT ANSWER TO THAT QUESTION! AND IT'S CRUNCHY.
DON'T START THAT AGAIN! IT'S PEANUT BUTTER! THERE SHOULDN'T BE CHUNKS IN BUTTER.
DANNY, LISTEN TO ME.
HAVING A KID, LIVING TOGETHER, BEING MARRIED--IT'S DIFFERENT THAN JUST "BEING DANNY AND MISTY." YOU HAVE TO BE AROUND EACH OTHER. YOU CAN'T DISAPPEAR TO K'UN LUN WHENEVER.
WE GAVE ALL THAT UP WHEN WE DECIDED TO STAY IN THE CITY.
IT WAS GO OUT THERE AND FIGHT THOSE THINGS OR STAY HERE TOGETHER AND START A FAMILY AND A REAL LIFE. AND NOW--
IT DOESN'T FEEL RIGHT?
I FEEL LIKE I'M PLAYING HOUSE. LOOK AT ME. I DON'T EVEN OWN A TIE. WHO IN THEIR RIGHT MIND WOULD TRUST ME TO HELP RAISE A CHILD?
LUCY, DANIELLE, COME OVER HERE!

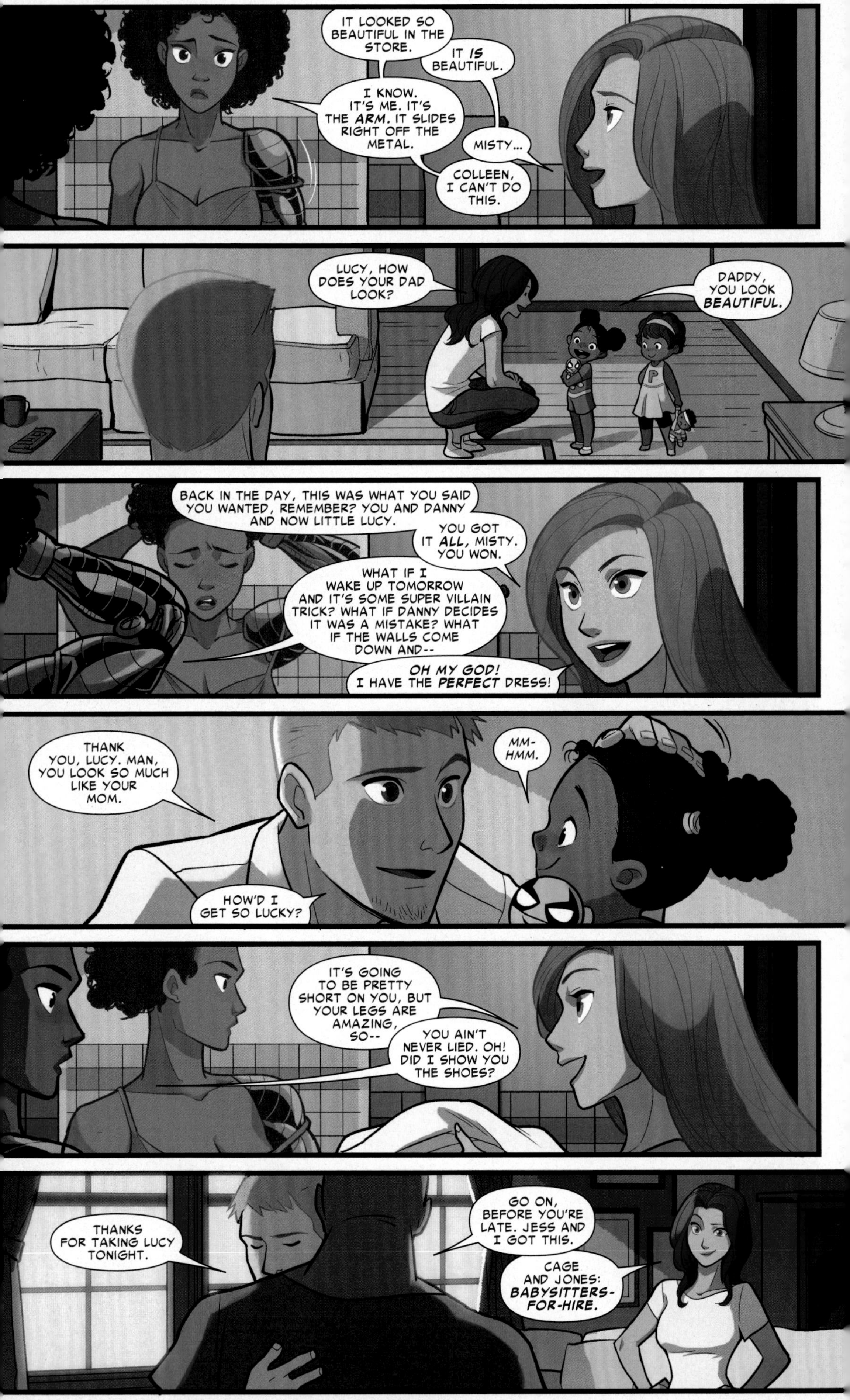
IT LOOKED SO BEAUTIFUL IN THE STORE.
IT IS BEAUTIFUL.
I KNOW. IT'S ME. IT'S THE ARM. IT SLIDES RIGHT OFF THE METAL.
MISTY...
COLLEEN, I CAN'T DO THIS.
LUCY, HOW DOES YOUR DAD LOOK?
DADDY, YOU LOOK BEAUTIFUL.
BACK IN THE DAY, THIS WAS WHAT YOU SAID YOU WANTED, REMEMBER? YOU AND DANNY AND NOW LITTLE LUCY.
YOU GOT IT ALL, MISTY. YOU WON.
WHAT IF I WAKE UP TOMORROW AND IT'S SOME SUPER VILLAIN TRICK? WHAT IF DANNY DECIDES IT WAS A MISTAKE? WHAT IF THE WALLS COME DOWN AND--
OH MY GOD! I HAVE THE PERFECT DRESS!
THANK YOU, LUCY. MAN, YOU LOOK SO MUCH LIKE YOUR MOM.
MM-HMM.
HOW'D I GET SO LUCKY?
IT'S GOING TO BE PRETTY SHORT ON YOU, BUT YOUR LEGS ARE AMAZING, SO--
YOU AIN'T NEVER LIED. OH! DID I SHOW YOU THE SHOES?
THANKS FOR TAKING LUCY TONIGHT.
GO ON, BEFORE YOU'RE LATE. JESS AND I GOT THIS.
CAGE AND JONES: BABYSITTERS-FOR-HIRE.

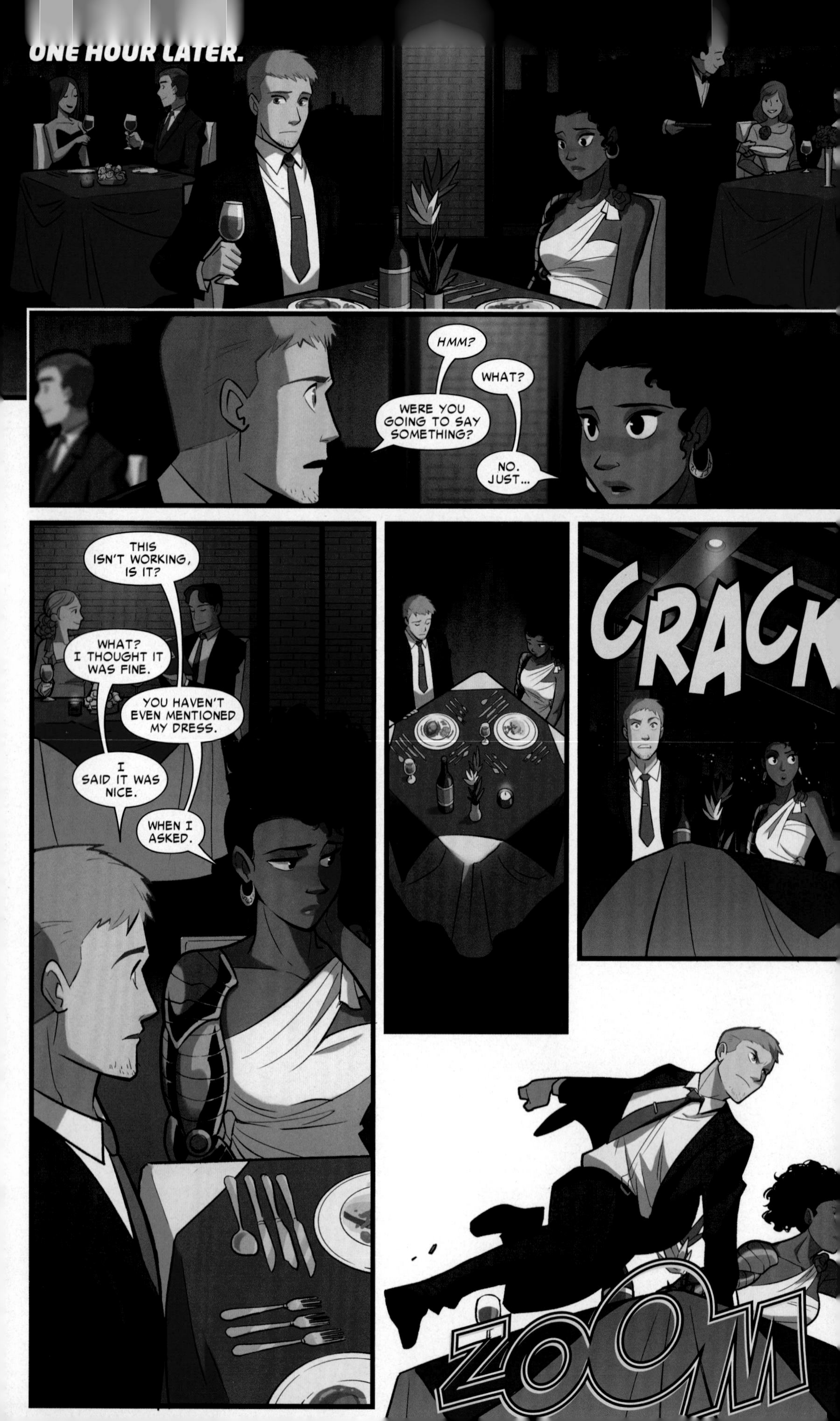
ONE HOUR LATER.
HMM?
WERE YOU GOING TO SAY SOMETHING?
WHAT?
NO. JUST...
THIS ISN'T WORKING, IS IT?
WHAT? I THOUGHT IT WAS FINE.
YOU HAVEN'T EVEN MENTIONED MY DRESS.
I SAID IT WAS NICE.
WHEN I ASKED.
CRACK
ZOOM

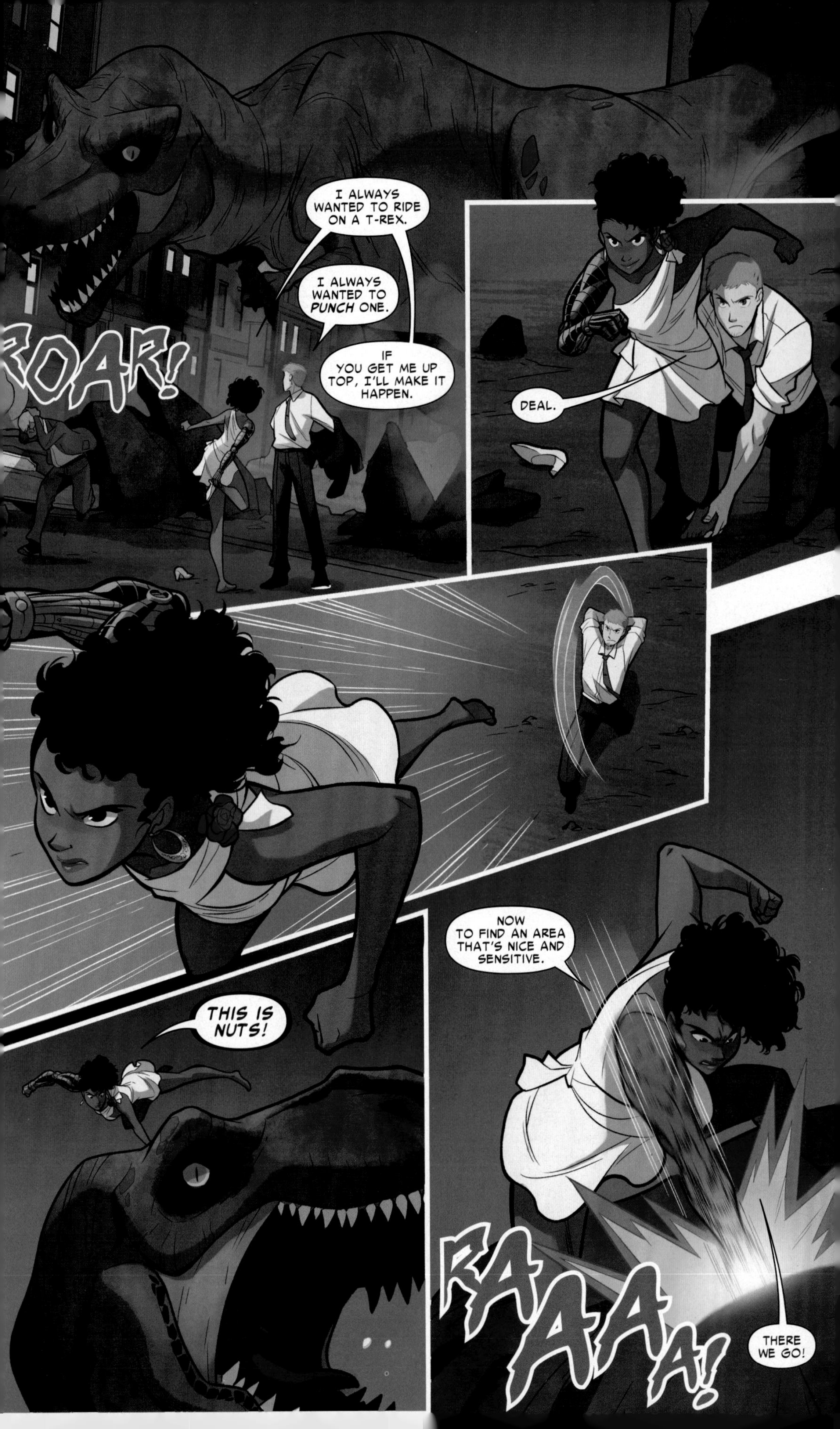
ROAR!
I ALWAYS WANTED TO RIDE ON A T-REX.
I ALWAYS WANTED TO *PUNCH* ONE.
IF YOU GET ME UP TOP, I'LL MAKE IT HAPPEN.
DEAL.
THIS IS NUTS!
NOW TO FIND AN AREA THAT'S NICE AND SENSITIVE.
RAAAA!
THERE WE GO!

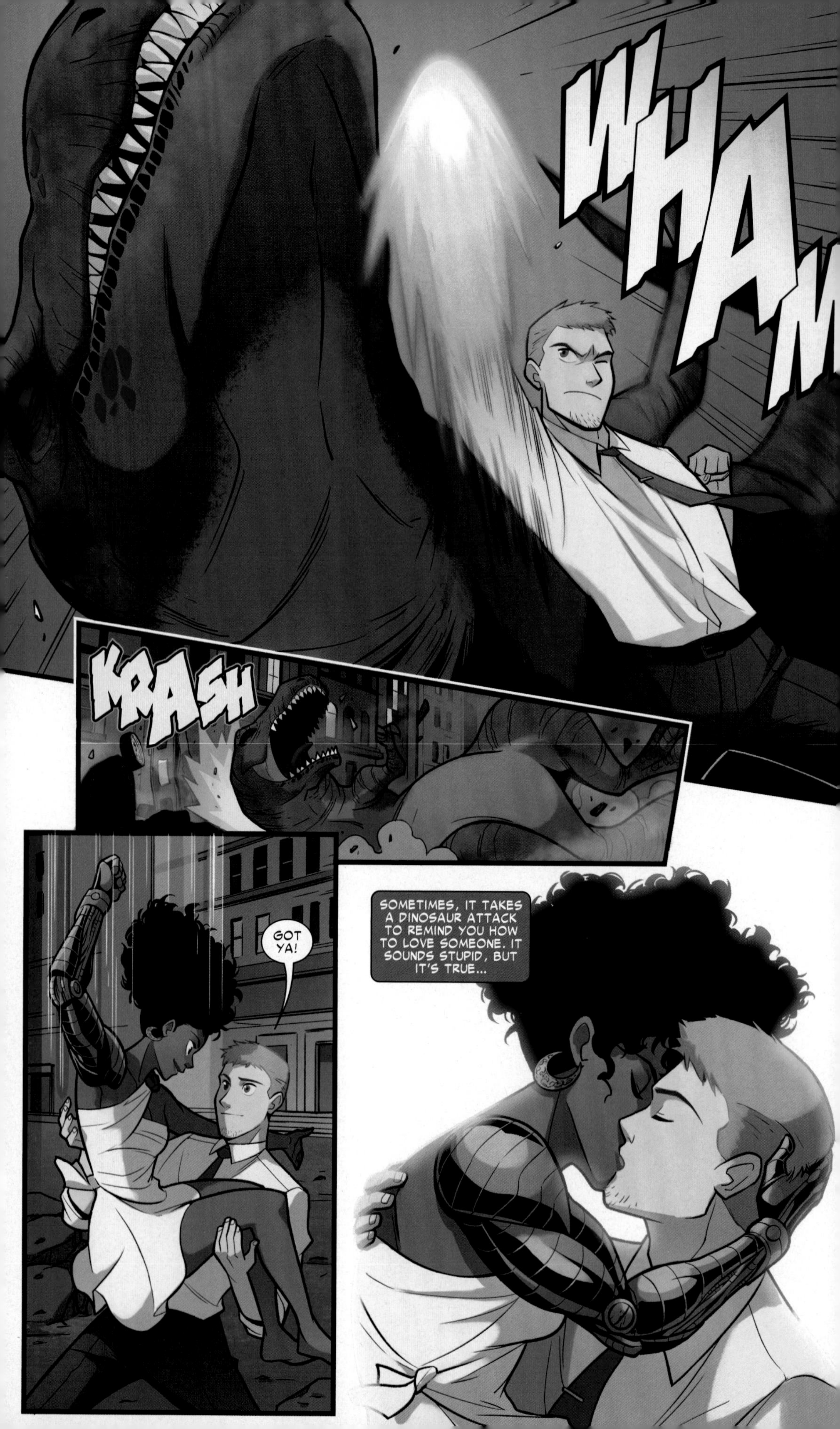
WHAM
KRASH
GOT YA!
SOMETIMES, IT TAKES A DINOSAUR ATTACK TO REMIND YOU HOW TO LOVE SOMEONE. IT SOUNDS STUPID, BUT IT'S TRUE...

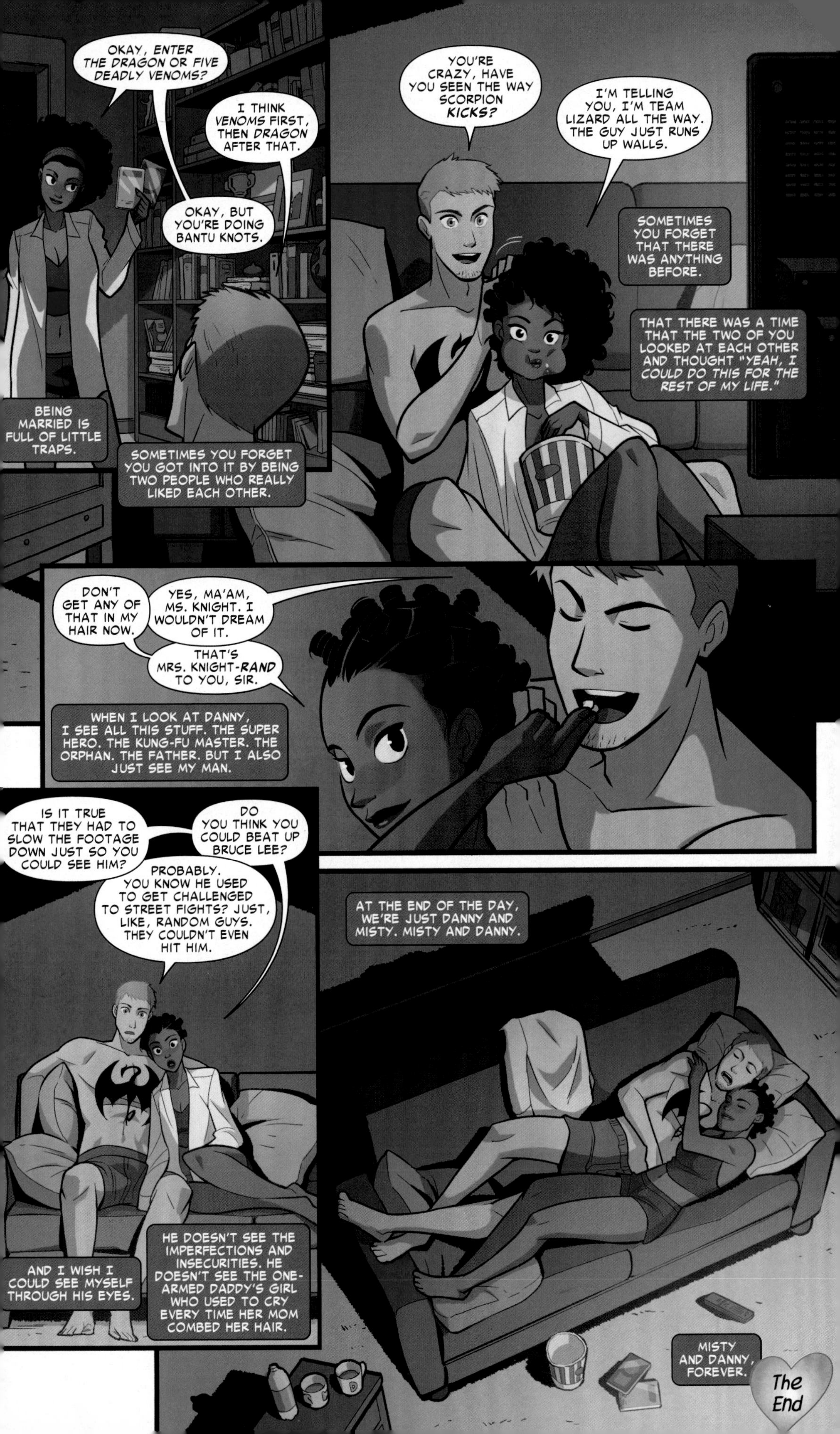

OKAY, ENTER THE DRAGON OR FIVE DEADLY VENOMS?
I THINK VENOMS FIRST, THEN DRAGON AFTER THAT.
OKAY, BUT YOU'RE DOING BANTU KNOTS.
BEING MARRIED IS FULL OF LITTLE TRAPS.
SOMETIMES YOU FORGET YOU GOT INTO IT BY BEING TWO PEOPLE WHO REALLY LIKED EACH OTHER.
YOU'RE CRAZY, HAVE YOU SEEN THE WAY SCORPION KICKS?
I'M TELLING YOU, I'M TEAM LIZARD ALL THE WAY. THE GUY JUST RUNS UP WALLS.
SOMETIMES YOU FORGET THAT THERE WAS ANYTHING BEFORE.
THAT THERE WAS A TIME THAT THE TWO OF YOU LOOKED AT EACH OTHER AND THOUGHT "YEAH, I COULD DO THIS FOR THE REST OF MY LIFE."
DON'T GET ANY OF THAT IN MY HAIR NOW.
YES, MA'AM, MS. KNIGHT. I WOULDN'T DREAM OF IT.
THAT'S MRS. KNIGHT-RAND TO YOU, SIR.
WHEN I LOOK AT DANNY, I SEE ALL THIS STUFF. THE SUPER HERO. THE KUNG-FU MASTER. THE ORPHAN. THE FATHER. BUT I ALSO JUST SEE MY MAN.
IS IT TRUE THAT THEY HAD TO SLOW THE FOOTAGE DOWN JUST SO YOU COULD SEE HIM?
DO YOU THINK YOU COULD BEAT UP BRUCE LEE?
PROBABLY. YOU KNOW HE USED TO GET CHALLENGED TO STREET FIGHTS? JUST, LIKE, RANDOM GUYS. THEY COULDN'T EVEN HIT HIM.
AND I WISH I COULD SEE MYSELF THROUGH HIS EYES.
HE DOESN'T SEE THE IMPERFECTIONS AND INSECURITIES. HE DOESN'T SEE THE ONE-ARMED DADDY'S GIRL WHO USED TO CRY EVERY TIME HER MOM COMBED HER HAIR.
AT THE END OF THE DAY, WE'RE JUST DANNY AND MISTY. MISTY AND DANNY.
MISTY AND DANNY, FOREVER.
The End

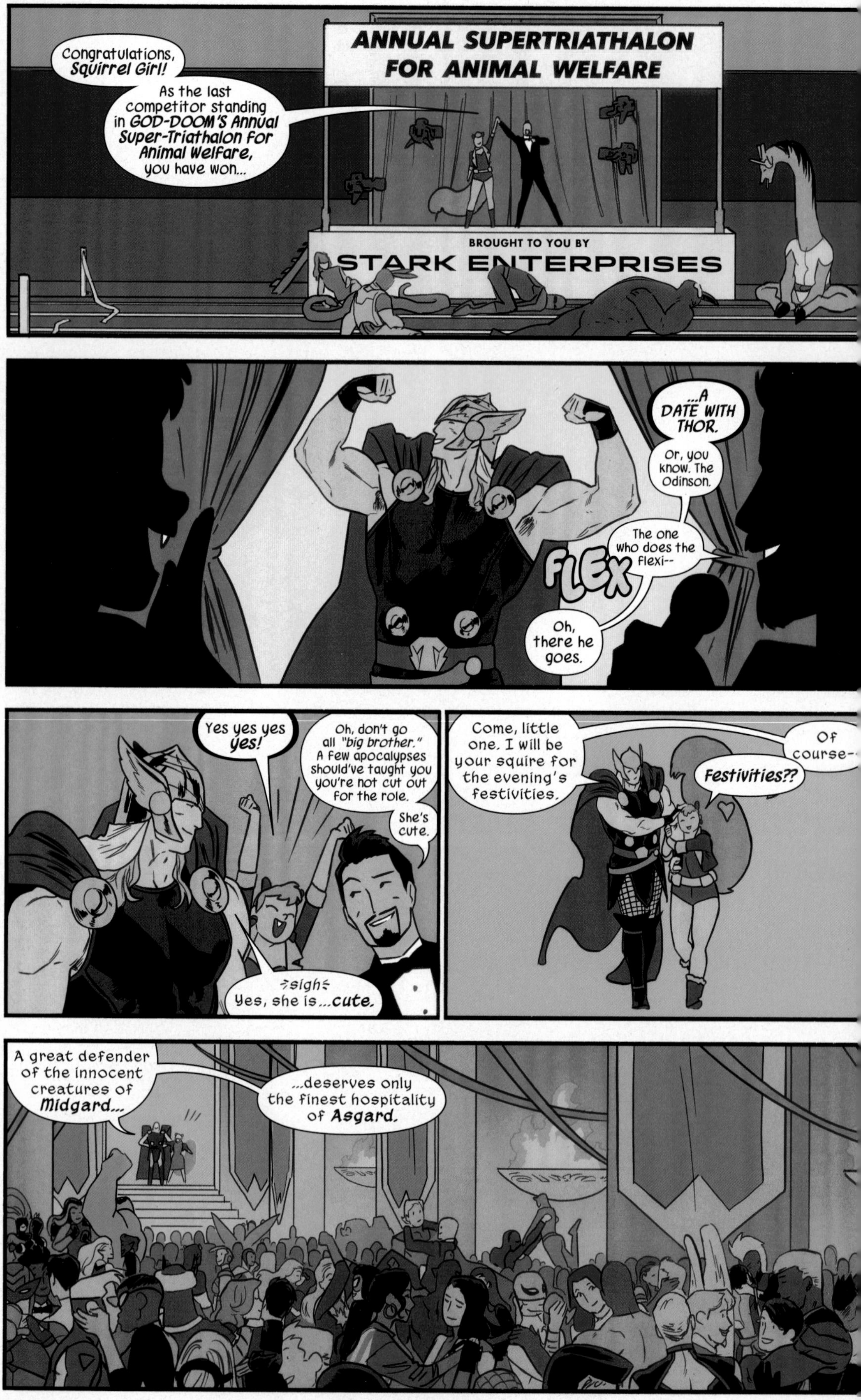

ANNUAL SUPERTRIATHALON FOR ANIMAL WELFARE
Congratulations, Squirrel Girl!
As the last competitor standing in GOD-DOOM'S Annual Super-Triathalon for Animal Welfare, you have won...
BROUGHT TO YOU BY
STARK ENTERPRISES
...A DATE WITH THOR.
Or, you know. The Odinson.
The one who does the flexi--
FLEX
Oh, there he goes.
Yes yes yes yes!
Oh, don't go all "big brother." A few apocalypses should've taught you you're not cut out for the role.
She's cute.
sigh Yes, she is...cute.
Come, little one. I will be your squire for the evening's festivities.
Of course--
Festivities??
A great defender of the innocent creatures of Midgard...
...deserves only the finest hospitality of Asgard.

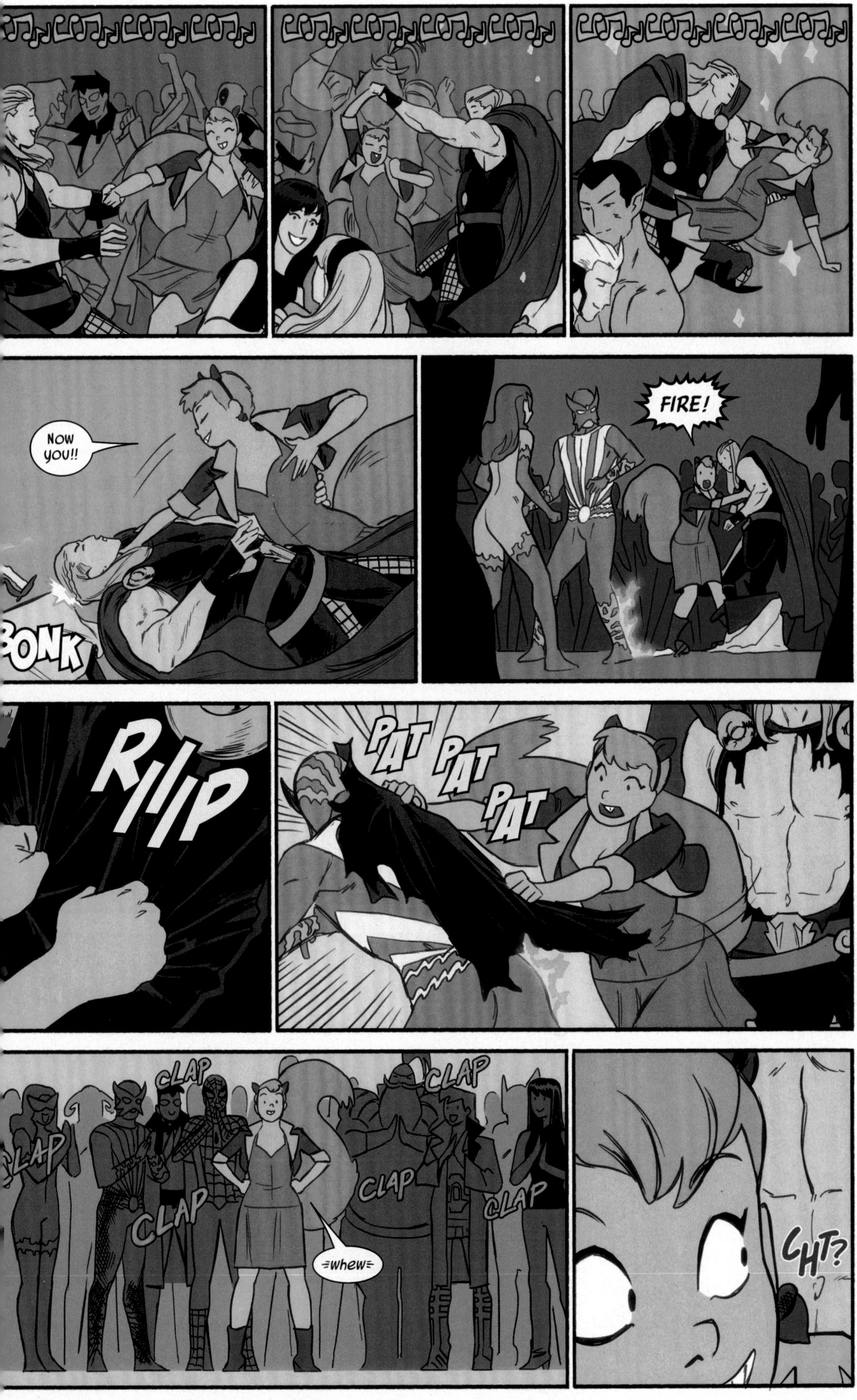

NOW YOU!!
BONK
FIRE!
RIIIP
PAT PAT PAT
CLAP
CLAP
CLAP
CLAP
CLAP
CLAP
whew
CHT?

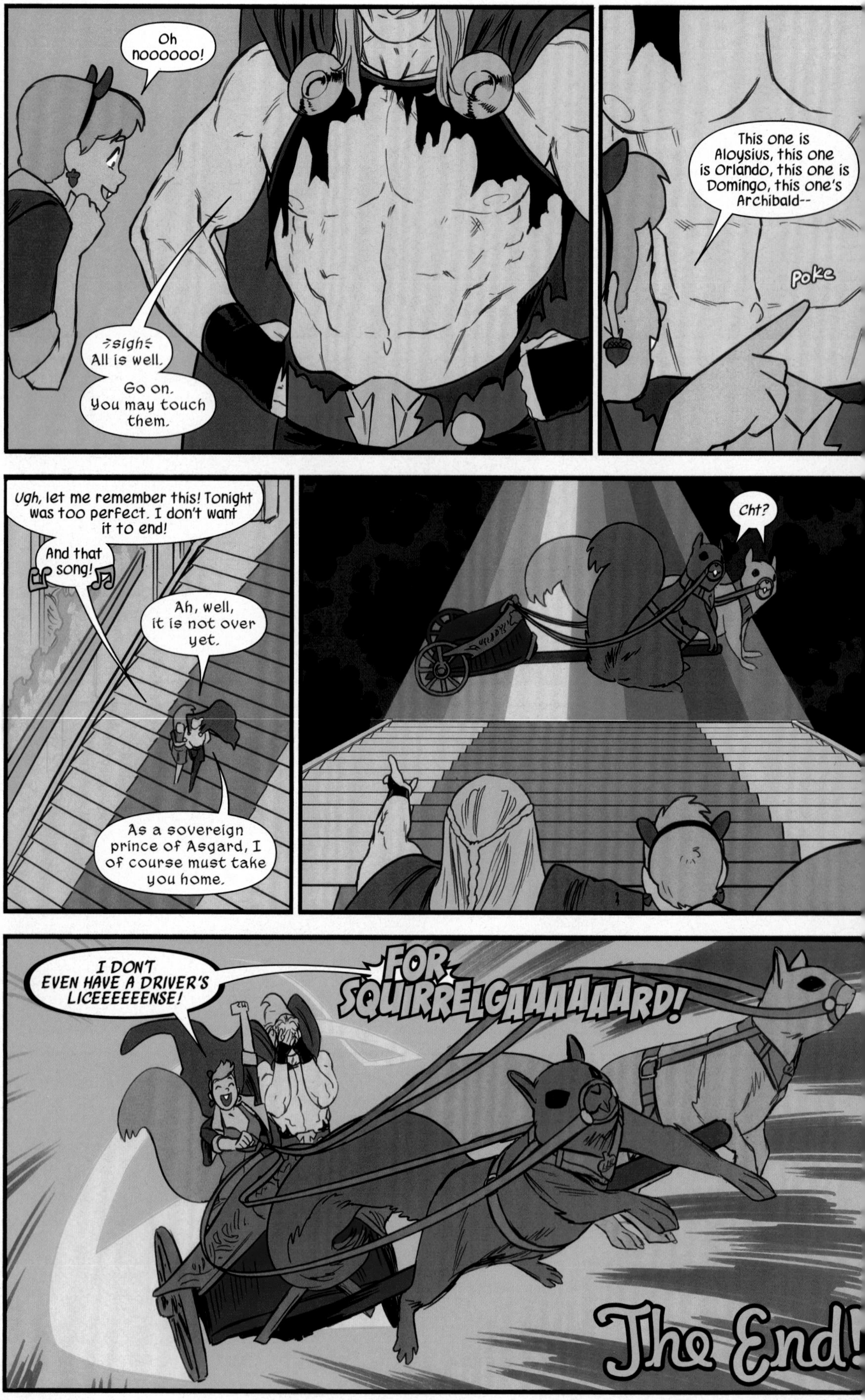
Oh nooooooo!
≷sigh≶ All is well.
Go on. You may touch them.
This one is Aloysius, this one is Orlando, this one is Domingo, this one's Archibald--
Poke
Ugh, let me remember this! Tonight was too perfect. I don't want it to end!
And that song!
Ah, well, it is not over yet.
As a sovereign prince of Asgard, I of course must take you home.
Cht?
I DON'T EVEN HAVE A DRIVER'S LICEEEEEENSE!
FOR SQUIRRELGAAAAAARD!
The End!

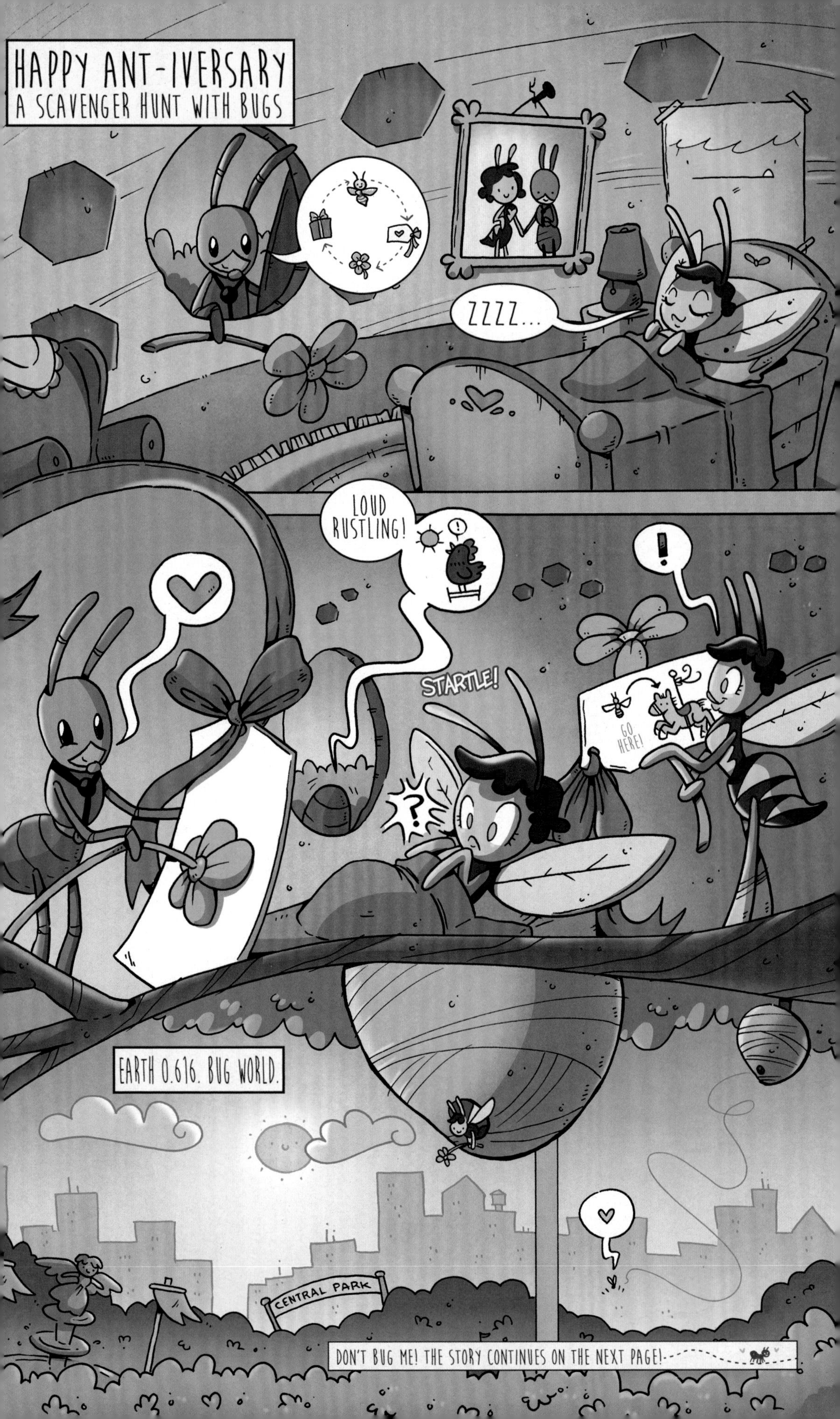

HAPPY ANT-IVERSARY
A SCAVENGER HUNT WITH BUGS
ZZZZ...
LOUD RUSTLING!
!
STARTLE!
?
GO HERE!
EARTH 0.616. BUG WORLD.
CENTRAL PARK
DON'T BUG ME! THE STORY CONTINUES ON THE NEXT PAGE!

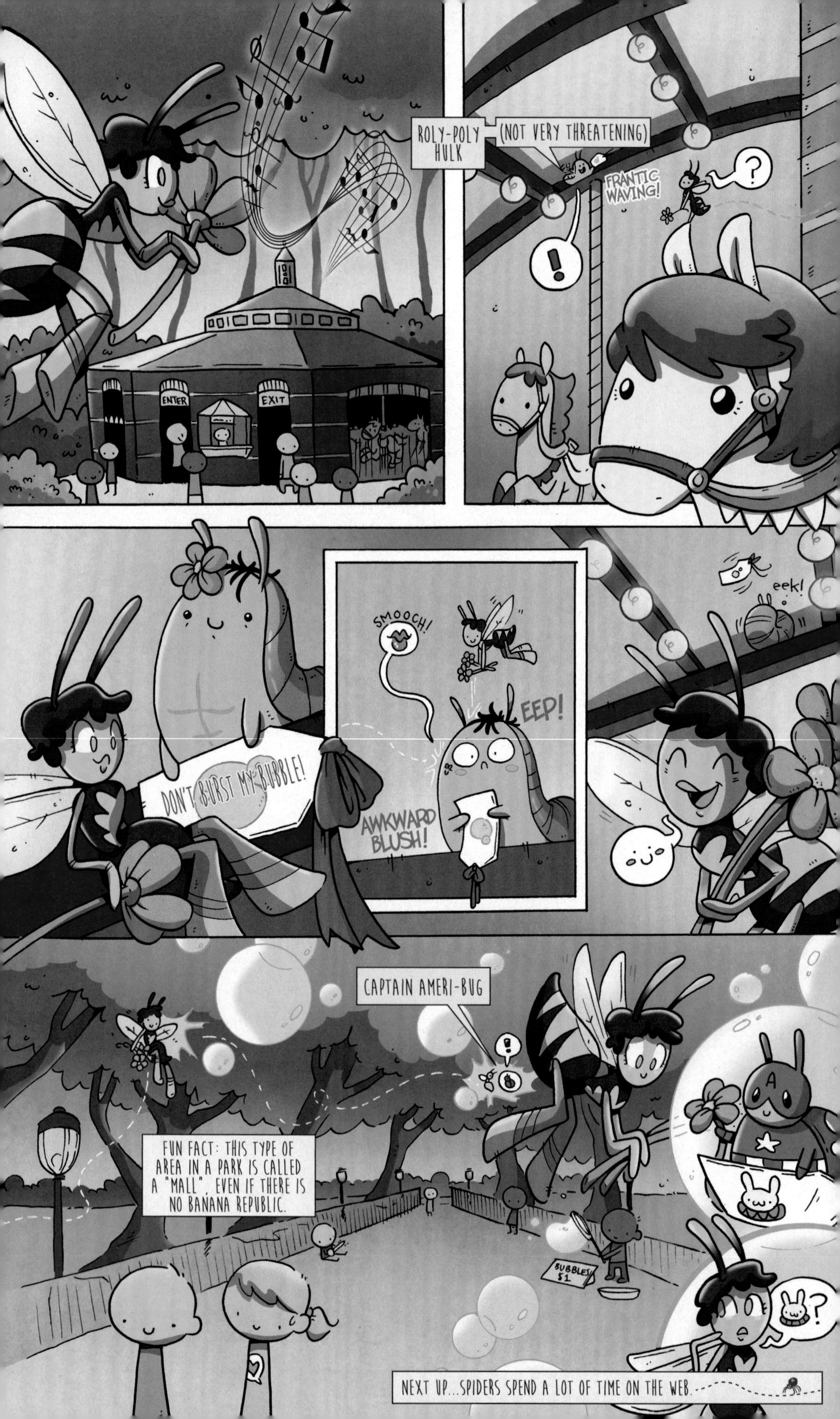
ENTER
EXIT
ROLY-POLY HULK
(NOT VERY THREATENING)
!
FRANTIC WAVING!
?
SMOOCH!
EEP!
AWKWARD BLUSH!
DON'T BURST MY BUBBLE!
eek!
CAPTAIN AMERI-BUG
FUN FACT: THIS TYPE OF AREA IN A PARK IS CALLED A "MALL", EVEN IF THERE IS NO BANANA REPUBLIC.
BUBBLES $1
?
NEXT UP...SPIDERS SPEND A LOT OF TIME ON THE WEB.

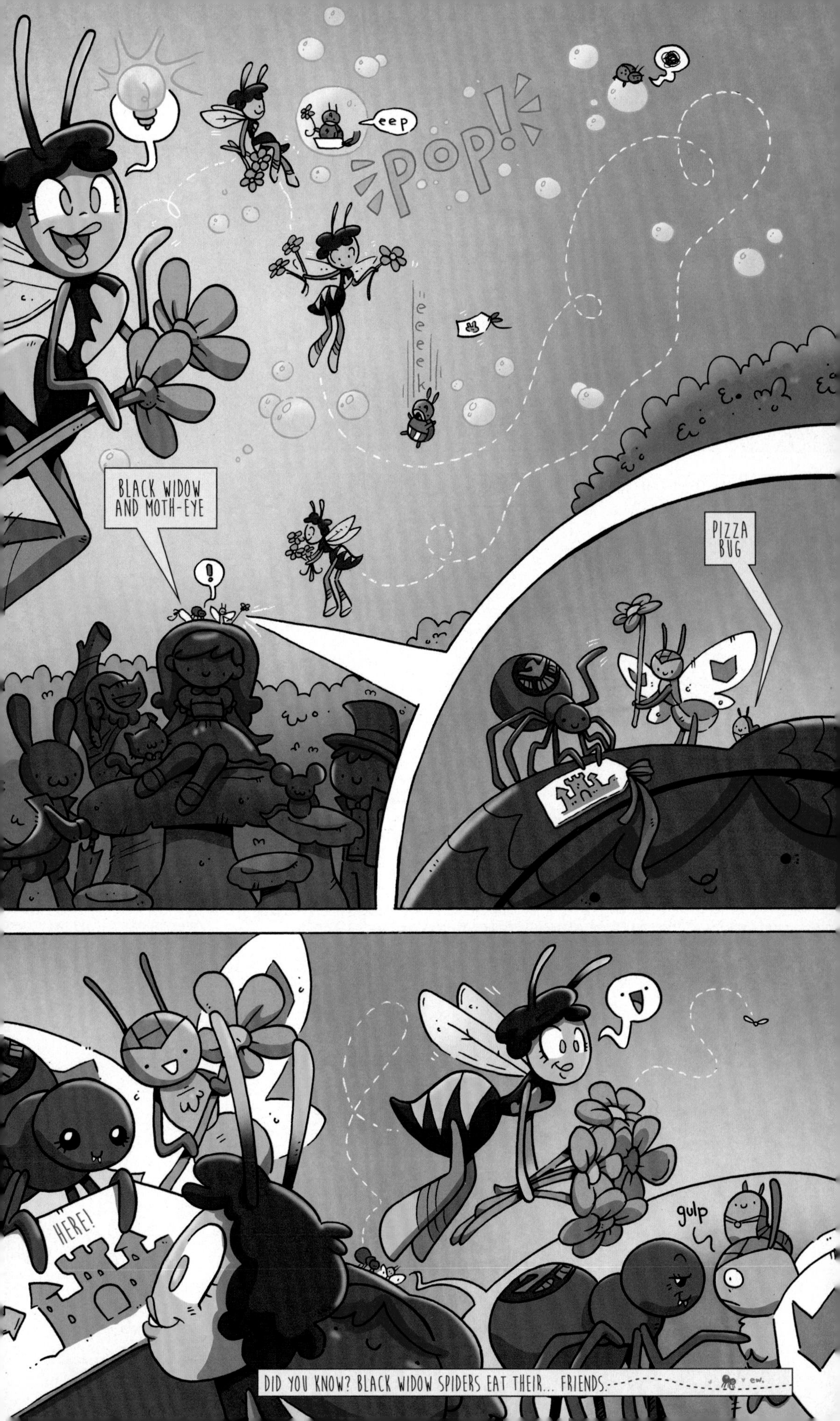
eep
POP!
eeeek
BLACK WIDOW AND MOTH-EYE
PIZZA BUG
HERE!
gulp
DID YOU KNOW? BLACK WIDOW SPIDERS EAT THEIR... FRIENDS.
ew.

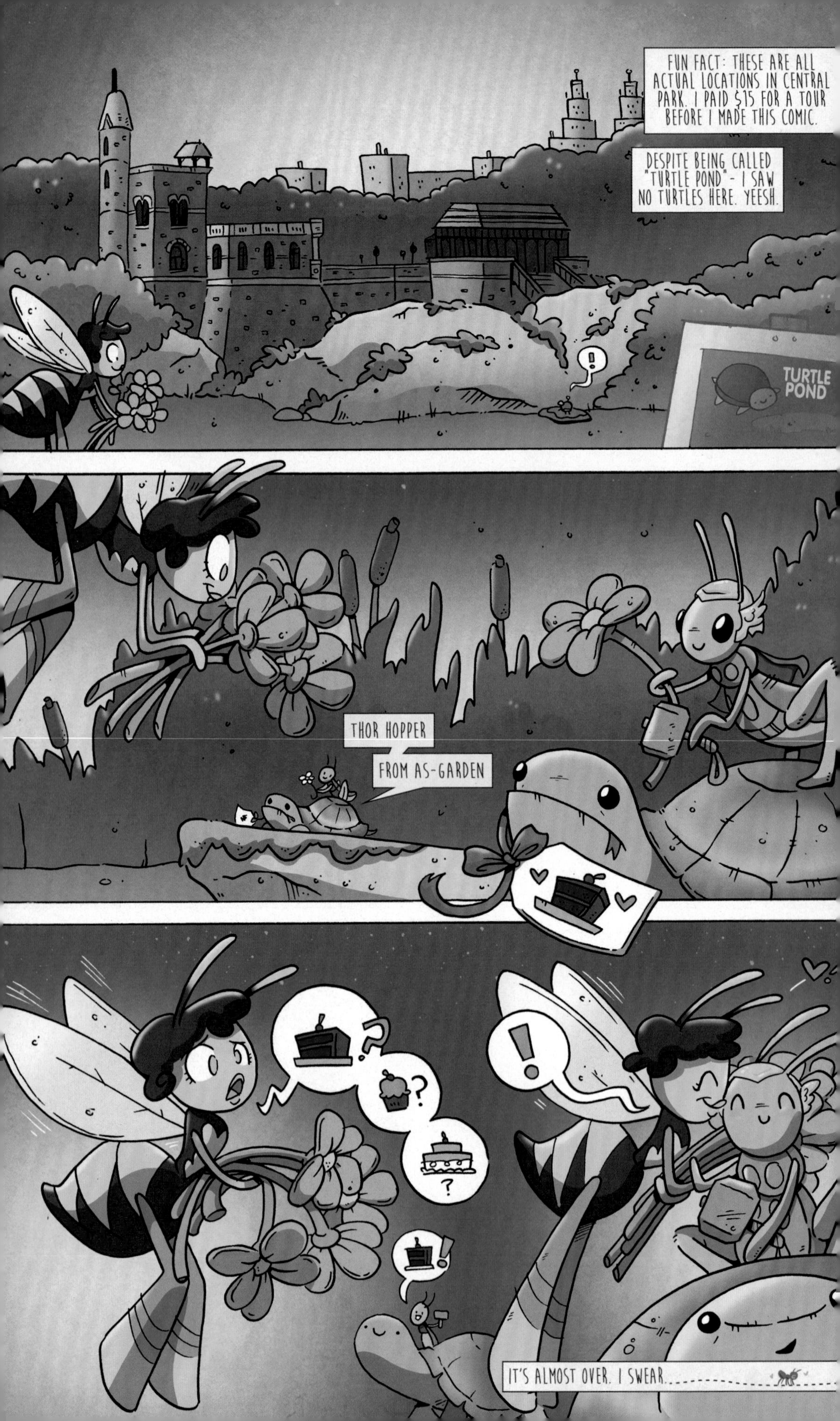
FUN FACT: THESE ARE ALL ACTUAL LOCATIONS IN CENTRAL PARK. I PAID $15 FOR A TOUR BEFORE I MADE THIS COMIC.
DESPITE BEING CALLED "TURTLE POND" - I SAW NO TURTLES HERE. YEESH.
!
TURTLE POND
THOR HOPPER
FROM AS-GARDEN
?
?
?
!
!
IT'S ALMOST OVER. I SWEAR.

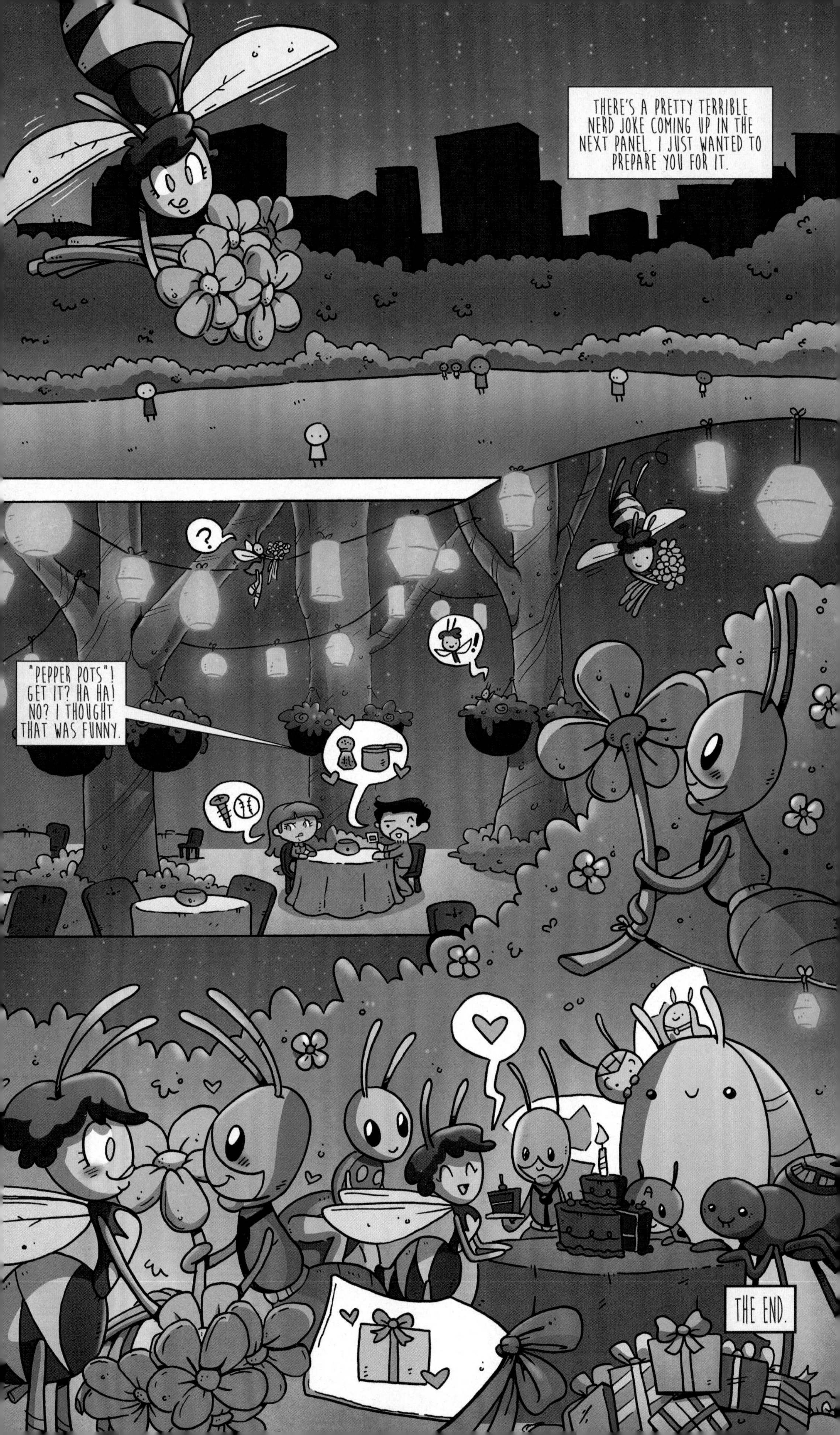
THERE'S A PRETTY TERRIBLE NERD JOKE COMING UP IN THE NEXT PANEL. I JUST WANTED TO PREPARE YOU FOR IT.
?
!
"PEPPER POTS"! GET IT? HA HA! NO? I THOUGHT THAT WAS FUNNY.
THE END.

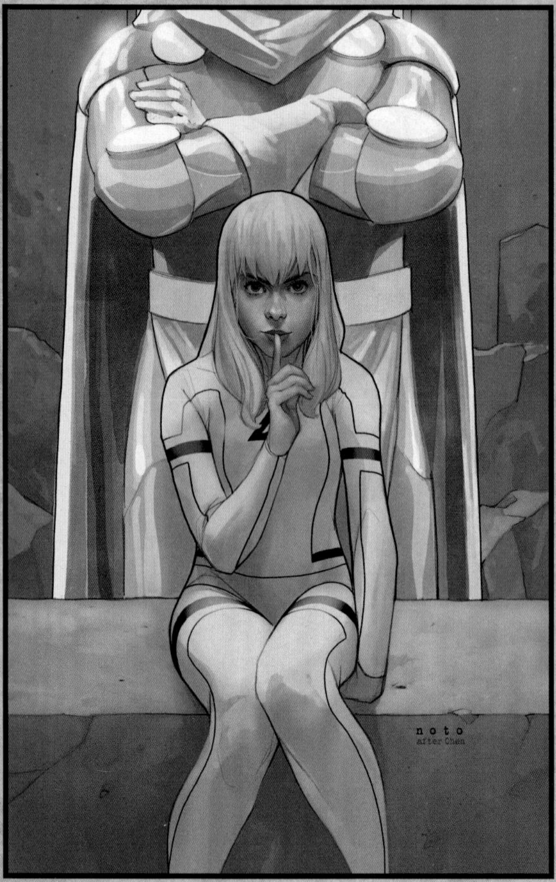
noto
after Chen

RUNAWAYS #1 Variant by Phil Noto

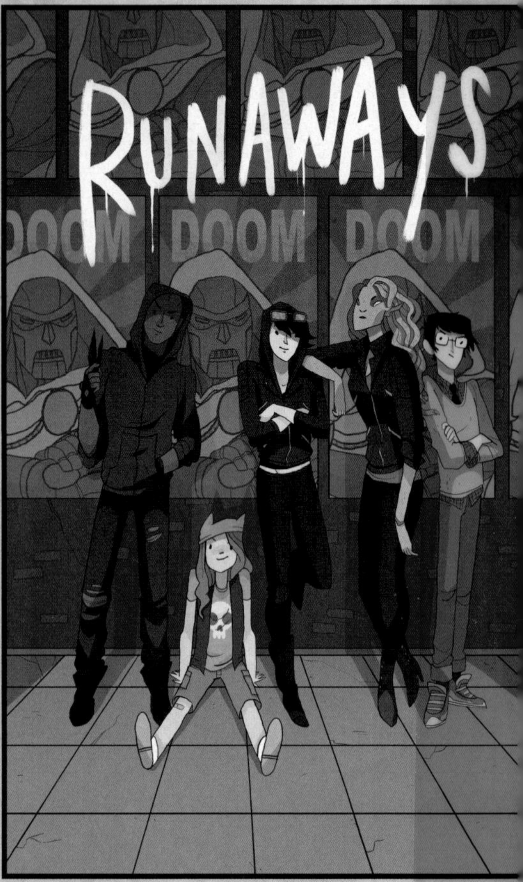
RUNAWAYS
DOOM
DOOM
DOOM

RUNAWAYS #2 Variant by Noelle Stevenson

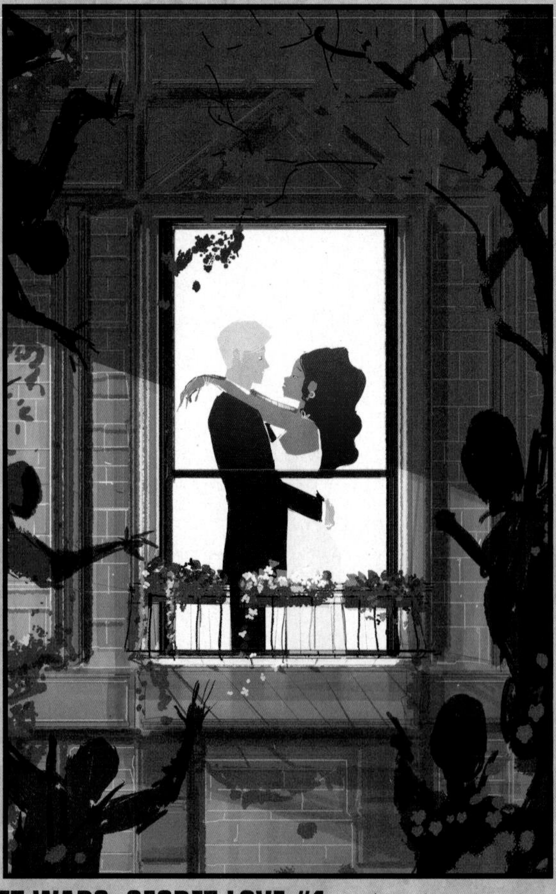

SECRET WARS: SECRET LOVE #1 Variant by Pascal Campion